THE WHEEL OF TIME

Other books by D. W. Kreger,
published by Windham Everitt Publishing:

LEWD: The Secret History of English
Dirty Words

The Tao of Yoda: Based Upon the Tao Te Ching
by Lau Tzu

The Secret Tao: Uncovering the Hidden History and
Meaning of Lao Tzu. With a revised translation of
the Tao Te Ching.

The Einstein Connection: Ancient Myths & Scientific
Theories of an Approaching Global Cataclysm

2012 & The Mayan Prophecy of Doom: The Definitive
Guide to Mythology and Science Behind
the 2012 Prophecies.

THE WHEEL OF TIME

ORIGIN OF THE HOLY DAYS

by

D. W. KREGER

Windham Everitt

First Printing 2020

Cataloging-in-Publication-Data-on-file

ISBN: 978-0-9833099-5-6

Published by
Windham Everitt Publishing
P. O. Box 1308, Littlerock, CA 93543

Ptinted in the United States of America

10 9 8 7 6 5 4 3 2 1

ACKNOWLEDGEMENTS:

I would like to dedicate this book to all the teachers and mentors that I've had over the years. And, by extension, I dedicate this book to all the teachers of the world, including my lovely wife and my neice, for all the work they do. As a child, I didn't realize how patient and giving my teachers were. They gave me the joy of learning, which made this book possible.

Manuscript Editor: Jamielly Patacsil

Cover art and interior design by: Windham Everitt Publishing

Cover photograph: Equinox Sunrise at Dolomite Loop,
by D. W. Kreger

All original illustrations, diagrams, & photographs by: D. W. Kreger

Printing and ebooks by: Kindle Direct Publishing

TABLE OF CONTENTS

PREFACE

I often like to tell people that I single-handedly discovered the ancient Wheel of Time, and in a sense I did. Years ago, I had been doing research on ancient standing stones and their possible meanings. It's clear that many of them, such as Stonehenge, marked particular days of the year such as the solstices and equinoxes. These must have been special days of the year for the people who built them. Perhaps they were holy days. It sparked my imagination, and I began drawing parallels between ancient pagan holy days and modern holidays.

I discovered connections between modern holidays and their ancient pagan meanings. I eventually came up with an over-arching concept to encompass all these holidays, both ancient and present. It was like a wheel, with all the seasons and holidays of the year on it, and other dimensions as well, such as the different seasons for agriculture, the seasons of a person's life, and even the times of the day that certain holidays are celebrated. This explained everything! I was very excited and thought I'd made a great discovery. I called it the Wheel of Time.

Unfortunately, I had independently invented an idea that had partially already existed. A similar albeit less complex concept, called the Wheel of the Year or the Wheel of Life, had been used by neo-pagans for a century. That put a damper on publishing my findings, at least for a while.

Then a few years ago, I made a discovery at an archaeological site in the California Owens Valley. It was a natural rock formation with ancient petroglyphs carved onto it. It is estimated to be about 4000 years old, and it accurately marks the equinoxes. The ancient site was known by locals, but had not been well documented before. I did time-lapse photography of the solar marker on the solstices and equinoxes, and I was astonished by what I had found.

I presented my research at an academic conference and it was very well received by the archaeological community. In talking to other archaeologists about it, I learned just how common these solar markers were among prehistoric people, and just how important they were to people all over the globe, for thousands of years. Almost every archaeologist I talked to, from all over the world, told me of a similar structure in their state or country. I found that such solar markers were a universal phenomenon, on every continent on earth, going back to the Neolithic. I realized that I was on to something. This was much bigger than I had earlier thought. It was then that I had decided to research the Wheel of Time a little more in depth and perhaps publish my findings.

That was the beginning of a long and fascinating journey into the true history and evolution of our modern holidays stretching back to the early Neolithic Age. I am excited to share with the world the amazing discoveries that I have found. I hope you are just as fascinated as I have been with these revelations. And, I don't think you will ever look at your holiday traditions the same way again.

INTRODUCTION:
A RIDDLE OF HOLIDAYS, ARCHAEOLOGY, & ANCIENT RITES

The topic of this book is broad and contains several different areas of special focus. As such, it's a hard thing to pin down. For a number of years, when people asked me about the book I was working on, I groped for words to try and condense it into a 20-second sound bite but it was no use. I would throw out a few different, seemingly unrelated topics and then say "well, you'll just have to read it," which was no help at all.

I guess the best way to describe this book is that it is an archaeological and historical study of our holidays. And, I don't just mean the holidays of America and Europe or just Christian holidays, but most, if not all, holidays of the world from all of the world's major religions.

I know that sounds overly ambitious, but it's not as ambitious as you might think. You see, I argue that all holidays from around the world stem from a few basic holidays observed by our ancestors, dating back to the late Neolithic Age, over 5,000 years ago. At that time, before there were complex cultures that existed independent of hunting and farming, people all over the world were primarily focused on nature and the seasons. They carefully observed the cycles and movements of the Sun, Moon and stars, which marked the beginning, middle, and end of each season. This formed the basis for their holy days. Basically, they celebrated the seasons as if they were holy manifestations of the Gods. And, for all they knew, they were just that.

Most people know that many of our modern Christian holidays began as pagan holidays, long before Christ. We also know that there are many ancient monolithic structures, which were used by Neolithic and Bronze Age people to track the Sun, Moon, and stars, such as Stonehenge. But, what many people do not realize is that there is a direct connection between those archaeological sites, the ancient pagan Sabbaths that they marked, and our modern Christian and other religious holidays. Also, most people do not realize that there are very similar ancient structures, such as Stonehenge, all over the world, on almost every continent, and they date back to the very beginning of the Neolithic Age, over 10,000 years ago.

By analyzing these archaeological sites around the world and the solar dates they marked, we can construct a calendar-system of all the ancient pagan holy days that they observed. You will see that this actually reveals a larger system of thought, in which the phases of the Sun and Moon, and the seasons of the year, correspond to the times of the day, and even to points along the human life cycle. They are all interconnected. All these points can be plotted on a circle or a wheel, and we call this circular times system *The Wheel of Time.*

Over the centuries, as these pagan Sabbaths were incorporated into Christianity and other religions around the world, the original meaning of these holidays were lost or changed so much that they often became unrecognizable. And yet, there are still tell-tale remnants of this ancient pagan system that are still embedded in our modern holidays. Though we have forgotten their original meaning, they are still there, like fossils of a bygone age. These last vestiges of paganism are right there in plain view in our most cherished holiday customs and traditions.

The Wheel of Time solves the mystery of why we celebrate Christmas at midnight, Easter at sunrise, and Halloween in the evening. It explains why we celebrate Pass Over on a full moon, and why the Jewish and Chinese both celebrate the New Year on a new moon, even though they are at different times of the year. It explains why our day starts at midnight, yet the Jewish day starts at sunset. It explains why we celebrate Christmas with evergreens, Easter with bunnies, and Halloween with skeletons. And, it also explains the real reason why we celebrate each of these holidays on the specific days that we do, and times of day that we do. Most importantly, it explains what it all means, or at least, what it originally meant to our prehistoric ancestors.

The Wheel of Time is not an entirely new idea. There have been versions of it floating around in neo-pagan writings and beliefs for some time. Neo-pagans are the modern day people who practice paganism as the ancients did. And, what I call the Wheel of Time is often referred to by neo-pagans as the *Wheel of the Year,* or the *Wheel of Life*. But mainstream archaeologists have often rejected the notion that this Wheel of the Year was really a part of Neolithic beliefs. They usually attribute it to modern neo-pagans, created to conjure up what they think ancient people might have believed. But, I hope to show in this book that The Wheel of Time is absolutely rooted in ancient pagan beliefs and practices. Furthermore, evidence for this can be found quite clearly in the archaeological record and in ancient writings.

Though there have been versions of the Wheel of the Year in the past, I believe that the ancient pagans actually had an even more comprehensive model for this cyclic concept of time. And, by carefully analyzing the archaeology and ethnography of ancient peoples, I hope to illuminate more subtle details of their ancient pagan beliefs. This is accomplished by first looking at a comprehensive list of archaeological sites from the late Neolithic and Bronze Age cultures.

In the first part of the book, we will examine 30 different well researched and documented sites. At each site, we will catalog what, if any, days of the year that the monuments mark. We will look primarily for solar alignments, though we will look at alignments of the Moon and stars as well.

As you will see, most sites overlap in terms of the dates of the year that they mark and celebrate, but each one adds a bit more information that we can use to create a more complete Wheel of Time, with elements that were previously missing in other versions of the Wheel.

So, as we look at each archaeological site we will gradually construct the Wheel of Time, one element at a time, based on what we find in the archaeological record. Later on, we will also look at the ethnographic evidence as well, such as ancient books and calendars, to complete our understanding of the Wheel of Time.

In the latter half of the book, we will survey religious holidays from around the world and across history, to show the depth and breadth of all these different holidays, and also to show how they are all based on the same short list of ancient pagan feast days or sabbaths. We will also show, step by step, exactly how those ancient pagan sabbaths became early Christian holidays, and then eventually how they morphed into our modern holiday traditions. We show this evolution by highlighting the ancient feast days among the Celts and early Anglo-Saxons in England, and how that evolved in England and in America over the last 2000 years.

Finally, we will conclude with a brief discussion of a relatively new and important concept, *atheist spirituality*, and how it relates to the Wheel of Time. Many millennials reject traditional religion yet yearn for a spiritual dimension to their lives. They seek contemporary and meaningful ways to celebrate the cherished holidays that they grew up with, in absence of a belief in God. Sadly, many of these same people have no knowledge of the complex and profound concepts that already exist, developed thousands of years ago by our ancestors. So, a conceptual framework, such as the Wheel of Time, seems more relevant now than ever. The Wheel of Time may be just what many people have been looking for.

The Wheel of Time celebrates the sacredness of objective reality, of life and Earth, and not gods and demons. It posits the simple idea that life itself is sacred. All life is sacred. And the phases and stages of life are worthy of celebration in their own right. It also reveals the connections between the stages of the human life cycle and the seasons, and between us and nature, as well as between humanity and our planet and the Universe. In doing so, we reaffirm our spiritual nature in a way that no theology ever could, not even neo-paganism with their gods and goddesses.

The Wheel of Time is not something unseen to believe in, on faith alone. Rather, it tells us that we should celebrate life and the world around us, here and now, as something sacred and profound. It shows us how we are all connected in a very real way, to each other and the rest of the Universe.

You might say that the Wheel of Time could be vital software for the non-religious practice of spirituality, as well as the non-religious practice of modern holiday celebrations. In a cynical world where many of us have lost faith in God, this gives us something to believe in again. And, whether you deem it sacred or not, it is based on something that is real; it is based on nature, biology, and astronomy, not someone's divine revelations or subjective beliefs.

PART I:

BUILDING THE WHEEL FROM ARCHAEOLOGICAL EVIDENCE

CHAPTER 1

UNDERSTANDING NEOLITHIC PEOPLES & THEIR PAGAN BELIEFS

To begin our investigation into ancient holidays, there are two deep and broad topics that I think everyone should be somewhat aware of in order to really understand the contents of this book. One is understanding Neolithic people, what they were really like based on archaeology, and debunking the popular caveman stereotypes. The other is a more precise understanding of what I mean when I say *pagan* beliefs. People, in general, have some fairly inaccurate ideas about both of these topics. And it's important to get up to speed on both of these first, because I refer to the *Neolithic* and *paganism* throughout the book. That is why I have thoughtfully provided for you in this chapter a brief discussion of each of these topics.

This book has two broad agendas. The first is to sneak a peek inside the mind of a Neolithic person, to understand their cosmology, their beliefs about life, death, spirituality, and the world they lived in. Then, as if that's not ambitious enough, there is another goal and that is to see the connections between those beliefs and our own religious and secular holiday traditions of today.

Unfortunately, it is almost impossible for anyone to know what ancient people were thinking, in absence of some sort of note or text explaining their thoughts. Such data is present for much of recorded history, but not pre-history, and not for much of Europe prior to the Roman conquest. Recorded history gives us quite a bit of data to study, but the really exciting part of this study is looking into the beliefs, perceptions, and conceptions of people who lived thousands of years ago, possibly as much as 10,000 years ago. That far back, there is no written text. There is, however, archaeological evidence. Such evidence indicates that they marked certain special days of the year, what we might call holy days.

Though the term, holy day, is an imprecise term for what we are studying, that is the basic idea of the cardinal points of the Wheel of Time. But to really understand what the Wheel of Time is and what it meant to the ancients, I think that you need to go on a journey of discovery, so that you the reader will learn what archaeologists and anthropologists have learned, and be able to see how the Wheel of Time was constructed based on the available evidence, and therefore what it ultimately might mean both for the ancients and for us.

NEOLITHIC PEOPLE

We start our journey by exploring what we know about Neolithic cultures. It turns out that this is one of the most exciting areas of archaeology today. Almost everything we believed about Neolithic people was wrong. Basically, we dramatically underestimated our ancient ancestors. We usually think of them as wearing bear-skins, using stone knives, and living in caves. And, all that is true, to a certain extent. But, there was a whole host of technological sophistication that we did not know about.

The reason for this is simple. Only stones and metals survived after thousands of years. Clothes, woodwork, tools, most buildings, and any paper or written texts would all be utterly destroyed by the ravages of time, after several thousand years. But there have been a few remarkable discoveries in recent years which have luckily preserved items either by being frozen, or packed in an oxygen-free environment.

One of the effects of global climate change has been the melting of glaciers, many of which are tens of thousands of years old. Beneath these glaciers, we are finding all sorts of items, perfectly preserved in cold-storage for many thousands of years.

ÖTZI: THE ICEMAN

The following is an excerpt about the body of a man preserved in ice for 5300 years, previously published in my book "The Secret Tao".

> *Late one day, a shepherd is running with a group of villagers high into the Alps, on the border between what is now Austria and Italy. It's a cold day and a storm looks like it's approach-*

ing. The shepherd is wounded. His forehead is bleeding and he's clutching his shoulder in pain. It is dangerous to be so high in the Alps this time of year, but they are frantically escaping danger. They are fleeing a warlike tribe of invaders who burned their village. The shepherds and farmers are no match for the foreign-looking warriors, but they fought valiantly as best they could. The shepherd pulls off his pack, and he huddles under his cloak for warmth. His comrades try unsuccessfully to remove the arrowhead from his shoulder. The shepherd tries to fashion a new bow and arrows from wood collected along the way. Aware that he is slowing them down, he urges his friends to continue without him. They eventually agree. He closes his eyes for just a little rest, and slowly the storm moves in, as the temperature drops.

The above scenario, or something very much like it, happened one day about five thousand, three hundred years ago. One of the best anthropological finds that we have of the Neolithic period and was discovered in 1991, when a Neolithic sheep herder was found frozen under the top of a glacier near Innsbruck Austria. And, they nick-named him Ötzi. With that discovery, modern anthropology was turned on its head.

Many of the assumptions that experts had made about these people were wrong. Judging by the ax that he carried, they assumed him to be from the Bronze Age, 2000 BCE. It turned out that carbon dating revealed him to be from the late Neolithic period, approximately 3300 BCE. This man was a contemporary of the ancient Neolithic [builders of Stonehenge]... Never before had a person been so well preserved from so far back in time, literally frozen in a block of ice for thousands of years. And, he had with him all the pieces of equipment of daily life, not just the things you find placed in burial tombs, or abandoned in rubbish heaps.

The Neolithic iceman was wearing finely made leather clothing, with a fur hat, sturdy shoes, fish net socks, and a waterproof straw shawl as a raincoat. He had well-made implements, with a flint knife, and an ax made with a finely crafted copper head. He used three feathers to stabilize the end of his arrows, a concept not improved upon in 5300 years of aerodynamics. He also had a frame pack, with extra tools and materials for mending his equipment and various medicinal items, such as dried mushrooms kept on a string, which are known by indigenous people to have antibiotic properties. There was also evidence of domesticated wheat (einkorn), berries, and other features of a diet not unlike ours today.

What does this person from the Neolithic tell us about the people of that time? More than anything else, it breaks the myth that Stone Age people were ignorant savages. It tears apart the idea that these people were somehow less complex or had a less intricate society simply because they didn't have more complex technology or live in huge cities made of stone. As cultural anthropologists know today from studying indigenous peoples around the planet, technology and stone monuments are not a fair way to judge the sophistication of a society or their belief systems. The idea that technological advancement necessarily implies cultural progress is seen as a myth, now more than ever.

The iceman from the Alps also had dozens of tattoos on his body, almost all of which were unintelligible to us today. Some of them look like a variation on the I Ching, with a series of lines clumped into groups of three parallel lines. Others we simply don't understand, such as a cross on the knees and other marks on the ankles and other parts of the body. It is assumed that these may have had a medicinal meaning. Tattoos have been used by tribal shamans as part of healing rituals. This man apparently had some arthritis in his joints (based on x-rays). The tattoos are concentrated on his joints and on his lower back. In spite of a touch of arthritis, he was in his late forties climbing to the very top of the Alps, and he also had almost all his teeth. Clearly the medicine and health management systems of the Neolithic were working for him. It appears that his downfall was most likely hypothermia, a problem that still kills hikers every year in the Alps.

Another interesting feature is the number of different types of wood he used. The iceman had many different tools and devices made of wood, including the frame for his pack. In all, he had 17 different types of wood. And it did not appear haphazard which types of wood he used for which purpose. The woods used for arrows were tough but pliable, and would not easily break in the quiver or upon entering the tough hide of a prey. The wood of the pack was tough, pliable and lightweight, not unlike the rods we use in tents and backpacks today. Hardwood was used for the ax and knife handles. The iceman clearly had knowledge of nature that approximates the refinement of modern technology, except that it was all-natural. He learned how to use the refined technology provided for him in nature.

… the iceman of the Alps … gives us some idea of the potential complexity and richness of Neolithic culture. It provides tantalizing clues as to the depth and breadth of their cultural knowledge and resources. It appears clear that, like many indigenous people today, many Neolithic people probably had well-developed systems of medicine, philosophy, and religion, as well as elegant and effective technologies, utilizing nature much more so than we do today. The biggest failing of these people, with regard to their legacy in history, is that everything they used, except for their pottery and stone tools, were biodegradable. So, other than finding a man and all his possessions frozen in ice for 5300 years, almost every trace of their culture is gone.

... the discovery of the Ice Man of the Alps helps to set the stage for understanding the religious beliefs of that time. This gives us a clue to the potential beauty, subtlety, and abstraction of their beliefs. Best of all, it gives us the actual daily-life context, in which their beliefs existed. [1]

-Excerpt from
The Secret Tao, by D. W. Kreger

NEOLITHIC CARPENTRY

Not that long ago, workers found something interesting 20 feet under the ground, at a construction site in Leipzig, Germany. Rengert Elburg, at the Saxony State Archeological office, in examining the site, found a wood-lined well, and removed it for study.[2] The sturdy wooden frame was clearly there to prevent the lower portion of the well from collapsing. That alone is not so unusual. What was remarkable about this find was its age. Carbon dating revealed the structure to be 7,000 years old! That is the oldest woodwork ever found on earth. It is believed to be so well preserved because it was packed in clay, underground, in an oxygen-free environment. What was more amazing was the sophistication of the woodwork. Expertly carved mortise-and-tenon joints made this structure not only sturdy, but almost indistinguishable from similar hand-made structures built anytime in the last century. This means that at the very beginning of the late Stone Age era in Europe, workmen already had all the tools and knowledge of 19th Century woodworking. This find is 2000 years older than the frozen man in the Alps, mentioned above, and it indicates just how sophisticated our Stone Age ancestors were.

What does all this have to do with ancient holy days, much less Neolithic belief systems? Well, it is important to keep all the above evidence in mind when we encounter other Neolithic archaeological sites, especially those sites such as Stonehenge. After all, we have to make some basic assumptions when we interpret these enigmatic upright stones at Stonehenge. If we imagine the builders were bare-foot, wearing bear-skins, carrying stone knives, and living in caves, we might make certain assumptions about the purpose of Stonehenge. But, if we suppose the builders were living in a complex and relatively advanced culture, then we might make significantly different assumptions about the buildings and their purposes. The difference could be significant, indeed.

So, before we begin to examine various ancient archaeological sites, marking various holy days of the year, it is wise to have some notion of just how sophisticated these people were. For instance, if there is an alignment of certain stones with the Sun at sunrise on a certain day of the year, we can now be fairly certain that that is not just a coincidence. These people may have been many things, but they were not stupid and, as we shall continue to see, they had a scientific sophistication that continues to surprise us to this day.

PAGANISM

It will often be mentioned throughout this book that our pre-historic ancestors were, for the most part, pagans. What does that mean? What is a pagan? We get the word pagan from the Latin *paganus*, meaning villager or civilian.[3] This was likely a name developed by the Roman army to describe locals in various foreign countries where they were deployed. The term came to be specifically applied to the local rural people's beliefs, as opposed to the more complex Roman or Christian religions. So the term really means something like *country-folk religion.*

Amazingly, the pagan beliefs encountered by the Roman soldiers were very consistent across the Mediterranean and Europe. It turns out that this so-called folk religion was in fact a singular belief system that had existed all over the world, for thousands of years. It was a religion steeped in the practice of agriculture, hunting, foraging, and living close to the land. The rural people depended on Mother Earth for survival, and so they came to worship and revere her and all her subtle changes and nuances. They worshiped and celebrated each change in the seasons and every aspect of the ever-changing annual cycle of nature and life.

Some people might think of paganism as simply non-Christian, or even devil worship. Actually, it is quite independent of any other religion. By observing contemporary pagan tribes, we know that being pagan actually means that you believe that Nature itself is sacred, and so you celebrate it by celebrating each milestone of the year, as seen in the seasons. Planting season, growing season, harvest season, they are all seen as sacred manifestations of nature, created for our well-being. So, paganism is really a form of spiritual worship centered on the Earth, and on the practice of agriculture, where nature takes on a metaphysical importance and significance.

This too is an important thing to keep in mind when examining Neolithic archaeological sites. We will see throughout this book that there is a great deal of consistency between the archaeological finds at various Neolithic sites around the world and the pagan beliefs observed by Julius Caesar, Pliny the Elder, the Venerable Bede, and even that of modern Neo-pagans. Why so consistent? Because when you construct a spiritual belief based upon nature, agriculture, and the seasons then it is predictable that, no matter where you live or in what period of history, you will likely end up with certain common features.

After all, given the same general latitude, winter is winter no matter where you live, and it must necessarily involve very similar meanings on every continent and in each and every millennium of history. Spring is a time of new life, summer a time of growth, and the fall is a time of maturity, harvest, and death. So, this is a useful lens through which to view archaeological sites commemorating such dates in the annual calendar.

SUMMARY

Neolithic people were clearly far more sophisticated than we might have thought. They were basically not unlike us, but they utilized nature much more for what we might call *technology*, and likewise worshipped Nature as a manifestation of what we might call *God*. These were a smart and complex people who, in absence of anything else, placed nature at the center of their lives.

Now that we have the proper mind-set, we are prepared to examine the archaeological record to see what, if anything, we can infer about their specific beliefs. These inferences must be perceived through the lens of the parameters outlined above. We know two things for sure. First, they were just as smart as we are, and had just as complex a culture in their own way as we do, so it is naïve to underestimate their intellect or the complexity of their culture. Secondly, an understanding and preoccupation with nature was at the very center of their lives, beliefs, and culture. Throughout the year, they planned their lives around the various seasons. Literally, every aspect of their lives was tied to the agricultural and logistical tasks necessitated by each season. This was not entirely by choice, as such slavish devotion to every nuance of nature was required for their very survival.

In the chapters that follow, we will examine first the archaeological record. As we do this, we will construct our model of ancient cosmology, the *Wheel of Time*. We will construct this one element at a time, based on what we find at each archaeological site we examine.

Then we will examine the ancient texts, which fill in gaps in the archaeological record. Looking at historical records also helps us to understand how these ancient traditions persisted and/or changed over the last two thousand years.

In the end, this line of research may be more helpful in understanding our future than our past. A quick look at the evening news will clearly show that, after thousands of years of civilization and continual progress, we still do not have all the answers. Perhaps we have lost something over the millennia. Perhaps by looking at our past we can better chart our course for the future.

As we will see, our ancestors had an organizing philosophy for understanding nature, life, and time itself. But what exactly is it, and how does it work? That is the mystery of the Wheel of Time.

CHAPTER 2

ARCHAEOLOGICAL EVIDENCE OF THE BRITISH ISLES

We begin our construction of the Wheel of Time with the most widely known and enduring monuments to this concept, the ancient standing stones of Great Britain and Europe. We now know that most of these standing stones, or *Menhirs*, were ancient solar observatories constructed of standing stones, producing shadows that align with specific markers at certain times of the year such as the sunrise of the spring equinox, or the sunset of the winter solstice. But, it has long been a puzzle to understand why these monuments were built, and what role these monuments played in the life of the ancient Neolithic people who built them.

The most famous of these is probably Stonehenge, on the Salisbury plain in Wiltshire, England. But it is by no means the largest or the oldest of its kind. As we shall see, there were thousands of such markers throughout Europe and around the world, and almost all of them are quite ancient. There have been standing stones found in France, Switzerland, Portugal, Scandinavia, Armenia, the Czech Republic, and even in Africa, India, Iran, Serbia, and the Americas.

Not all of these ancient structures were made of stone. We now know that there were similar structures made of wood, and some structures were removed at some point, leaving just holes in the ground where they stood. Some, such as Warren Field, were nothing more than a series of pits. They all had two things in common, however. They were all quite ancient, and they all formed astronomical alignments for marking the passage of either the moon or sun or both. They were essential time-keeping tools for our Neolithic ancestors to be able to accurately know the exact day of each solstice, equinox, and track the 18.6 year lunar nodal cycle. But, why was that so important to them? What did it mean to them?

Some say it was just a practical necessity to know when to plant certain crops, and to predict the changing seasons, hence the change of the weather. But, many believe it was a lot more than that. Most researchers believe it was in some way related to their religion, their philosophy, and cosmology. But, what exactly were those beliefs? From each of these ancient sites, we gain clues as to their beliefs, and the role that these sites played in their culture.

We will now go one by one and document key features of over 30 such sites from around the world. Each one tells us something unique about its purpose and meaning. And, as a group, they reveal patterns of similarities, across both time and continents. We begin with the British Isles. Thanks to recent excavations, here in Britain we can find all the clues we need to decipher the cosmological framework of these people, why they needed to build these monuments, and what meaning it held for them.

As we examine each site, we will take information

found at that site and use it to begin to build our Wheel of Time. As we go along, we will add new holy days that the sites mark, and add new dimensions to the Wheel as we begin to learn what these sites and these holy days meant to the ancients who built them. By the end of the first section we will have constructed The Wheel of Time, a complete and concise model of all the special days of the year observed by our ancestors and what they might have meant for them. We start with one of the oldest sites in Britain, Warren Field.

WARREN FIELD

Site: Warren Field

Location: Aberdeenshire, Scotland

Date: 8,000 BCE

Site Description:
Twelve pits, each shaped to represent a different phase of the lunar cycle, and a fixed point that is aligned with the sunrise on the Winter solstice.

Point on the Wheel of Time:
Winter Solstice

The oldest of the British calendar monuments was discovered in 2004 in Warren Field, in Aberdeenshire, Scotland.[1] The site is not very impressive to look at, but what makes it so important is how old it is. It has been dated to approximately 8000 BCE. That's over 10,000 years old, and it means that it was constructed during the Mesolithic era, at the very beginning of the Holocene Age. That is many thousands of years before Stonehenge or any recorded history, and over 5000 years before the first of the Mesopotamian calendars.

How did they find the exact day of the Solstice?

We normally think of the solstice as relating to the length of the day, with the winter solstice being the shortest day of the year, and the summer solstice being the longest day of the year. This is true but it would be very hard for Neolithic people to measure the length of the day without an accurate clock, although I'm sure they sensed the days getting shorter. And, a sundial would be far too crude of a measurement to indicate the exact day of the solstice, and it's useless when it is cloudy or raining. No, the way they could identify the solstice and the other phases of the solar year is by looking at the location of the sunrise against a fixed marker on the horizon, from a fixed position

In the northern hemisphere, starting at midsummer, each day the sun rises on the horizon a little further to the south than the day before. Finally, at the winter solstice it stops its movement, and after about 3 days it begins moving back, rising a little northward on the horizon each day. If you have a fixed point to cast a shadow from the rising Sun, then you can accurately chart the solar year. And, this is exactly what we find at these Neolithic solar observatories. [2]

What makes this site a solar observatory is that it contains a fixed topographic alighnment that is aligned in such a way that it marks the sunrise on the day of the mid-winter solstice. As the seasons change, the Sun appears to rise in a different place on the horizon each day. At this site, there is an alignment that points to the exact place where the Sun rises on the winter solstice.

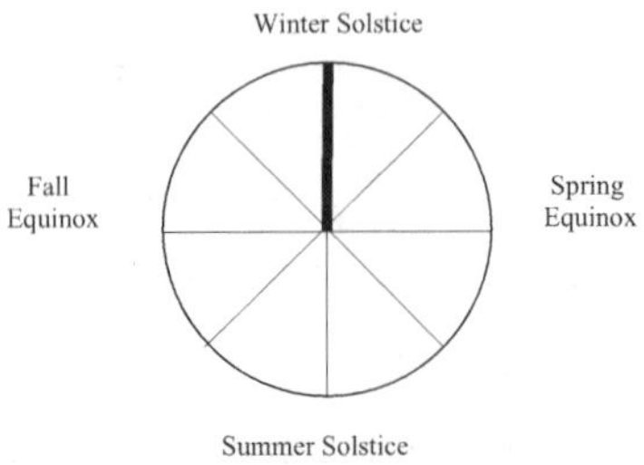

So, here we can begin to construct our Wheel of Time. You will see above a rudimentary wheel, representing the annual phases of the Sun as a circle. The top of the circle is the winter solstice, midwinter. The bottom is the summer solstice, and the mid-points to the left and right are the equinoxes. We will darken the top vertical line of our wheel to indicate that this site marks the winter solstice. As we go on, we will add this data to information from other sites to create a more elaborate cumulative Wheel of Time, based on multiple sites.

This site also contains 12 pits, each shaped to represent a different phase of the Moon. This feature indicates that they had what we call a lunisolar calendar. In other words, they tracked the phases of the moon and the number of moons that make up a solar year. But it would still be essential for them to create a solar marker as well, in order for their lunisolar calendar to be accurate. They could easily count days, and see the passage of weeks and months by the moon. But because there are 12.368 moons in the year, and approximately 365.25 days in the year, it was very hard to accurately predict the solstices or equinoxes by counting days or moons alone. Within a few years their calendar would be seriously out of sync with the seasons. So, they had to have a solar marker of some sort to recalibrate their lunisolar calendar each year. And, this archaeological site, with its fixed point to mark the solstice and 12 pits for the moon, is exactly what would be needed to do that.

We know many such sites in this part of the world

marked the midwinter solstice. As such, this site is not so unusual. The most mysterious aspect to this site is the question of who created it, and why? It is believed that this was constructed by hunter-gatherer peoples. This would be unique, as it was generally believed that only sedentary farmers needed accurate calendars for planting and harvesting.

Of course, such an annual marker might have helped the hunter-gatherer peoples as well. They may have found it useful to recalibrate their lunisolar calendar to know when certain migrating animals or birds would be coming through, and when to look for certain seasonal wild grains, vegetables, roots and other foods. But, there is another reason for them to create this marker.

If these people carefully observed the sun, the moon, and the passage of the seasons, then they might well have celebrated the passage of the midwinter sun, just as we do today with Christmas. Why? Well, it must have been terrifying to see the days getting shorter and shorter, and the nights longer and longer. With the waning Sun, most all of the plants died, wildlife became scarce, and less food meant more hunger. To make matters worse, it became increasingly colder.

Finally, on the day of the winter solstice, the midwinter Sun stopped its slow march to the South, paused for a few days and then on about December 25th began coming back northward again. This meant that it would soon be spring again, and then summer. Warm days, wildflowers, berries, grains, and perhaps honey, would soon return for their people. This would make the day of the winter solstice a very important day, what we might call a Holy Day, or *holiday* as we say now.

The shape of the various pits in the form of the phases of the moon, confirms that they had reverence for the phases of the moon, but it tells us something else as well. It tells us that their interest in the phases of the Moon went beyond any practical advantage it might offer. After all, why would it be important for them to mark whether the moon is waxing, waning, crescent, or gibbous? There is no advantage there for planting crops, and it's clearly visible when the moon is full or close to full, to provide light for night hunts.

So, why is it important to mark each particular phase of the moon? It's not, unless there is some symbolic meaning to these celestial events. Perhaps there was some spiritual or superstitious connection being made with the phases of the moon. For instance, there is an old pagan tradition that it is bad luck to get married on a waning moon.

From this we can clearly see that marking the phases of the moon indicates the beginnings of a pagan belief system. It is likely that this would be true for the marking of the winter solstice as well, especially for hunter-gatherer peoples. This was not a pragmatic device used for hunting or gathering. It was more likely an early pagan monument to mark important days of the year that were meaningful to them and their pagan beliefs.

Stonehenge

STONEHENGE

Site: Stonehenge

Location: Wiltshire, England

Date: 3,000 BCE

Site Description: A vast complex of ditches, berms, and burial mounds, centered around a ring of giant standing stones. Later, another ring of wood posts were discovered nearby.

Points on the Wheel: Summer solstice, Winter solstice and 13 other alignments

The ancient standing stones on the Salisbury plain of Southern England is perhaps the most famous of all such monuments. This is in part due to its size and grandure, and in part due to being in a well-traveled area not that far from London. But, Stonehenge is turning out to be as important archaeologically as it is famous.[3] Two different research projects have yielded invaluable information about the purpose and meaning of this and other similar monuments. The Riverside Project, headed by Mike Parker Pearson at Sheffield University, which ran from 2003 to 2009, investigated the relationship of Stonehenge to various other features of the nearby landscape, including the Durrington Walls, Woodhenge, the Avenue, the Cursus, and the River Avon.[4] Then starting in 2010, a group of researchers lead by Wolfgang Neubauer from the Ludwig Boltzman Institute and Vincent Gaffney from the Univeristy of Birmingham created the Hidden Landscapes Project, which used magnetometer measurements and ground penetrating radar to complete a virtual excavation of the entire 15 square mile area around Stonehenge.[5]

First, here are some basic facts about Stonehenge. It is a prehistoric group of standing stones that is over 5000 years old. We know the surrounding ditch dates to 3100 BCE, the standing bluestones (the smaller stones) were added perhaps 100 years after that. Then nearly a thousand years later, between 2200 and 2400 BCE, the largest sarsen stones were added, with lintel stones resting on top of the standing stones to frame the now familiar structure. The largest of the stones are 13 ft. high, nearly 7 ft. across, and are arranged in a circle 108 ft. across. Then there is another horseshoe shaped ring of sarsen stones in the center pointing to the entrance. Each of these large stones weigh as much as 25 tons. And, the large stones were quarried from at least 25 miles away. Many of the stones are now missing, but it is believed that the original monument contained over 75 of the large stones.

Though the stones are now various shades of grey and black, we know that they were originally cut and polished to reveal the bright white sarsen stone inside. And, of course, most people know that there is an alignment of the stones that points to the rising sun, on the summer solstice.

In fact, it is the horseshoe shaped ring of sarsen stones in the center and the processional entrance to the circle that points toward the rising sun on the summer solstice. There is another alignment that points to the setting sun on the summer solstice. And, as we shall see, there are other alignments in the area that also point to the rising and setting sun at the winter solstice as well. All in all there are 15 different astronomical alignments that have been identified, but the most prominent and obvious is the summer and winter solstice alignments, as shown on the wheel below.

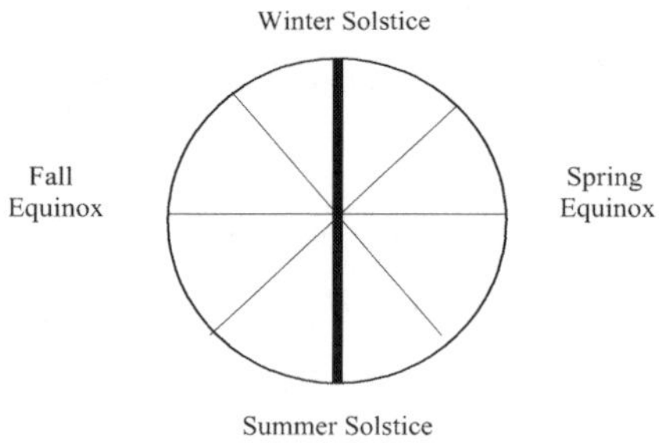

Last but not least, a large deposit of cremated remains have been found buried in and around Stonehenge. In fact, it is the oldest known cremation cemetery in Britain. That's the basics, and that would be enough, but what we've learned in the last 10 years about this monument and the people who made it is the really interesting part.

THE RIVERSIDE PROJECT

There are many features to the landscape surrounding Stonehenge and the other ancient archaeological sites in the area. The goal of the Riverside project, headed up by Dr. Pearson at Sheffield University, was to do focused excavations aimed at looking for connections between these different sites, hopefully telling us more about the people who built them, and what they were up to.[6] Dr. Pearson's research was influenced by a fortunate accident.

Dr. Pearson had previously studied archaeological sites in Madagascar, which one might think would have absolutely nothing to do with Stonehenge. But, one of his colleagues there pointed out to him that all the monuments to the dead and burial chambers on Madagascar were built of stone, because they thought of it as a dead material. All of the homes and shops used by the living were made of wood, because that is a living material. The connection is clear enough, and when a colleague from Madagascar came to Stonehenge and learned that it was a cremation cemetery, he pointed out the connection. Of course, Stonehenge must be a cemetery, his colleague said, because it is made of stone. And that prompted Pearson to ask, could the ancient builders of Stonehenge have had similar beliefs about building materials? And, if this is a monument to the dead, is there a monument to the living? And, in fact, there was!

In the 1960s they had already discovered post-holes of a timber circle in the area of the Durrington Walls, just two miles up the River Avon from Stonehenge. It is nearly identical in size to Stonehenge. And both sites contain what appears to be a processional path from the monument to the River Avon. Pearson concluded that this might well be the companion to the Stonehenge monument to the dead. Woodhenge, as it's called, may have been a monument to the living. His excavations there confirmed his hypothesis. While Stonehenge contained cremated remains, Woodhenge was surrounded by other structures also made of wood, with articles of daily use, reflecting a living and thriving population with many homes and other buildings surrounding it. So, Stonehenge was most likely a cemetery and funerary temple, just outside of a large village of Neolithic people residing in and around a temple of life.

They found several interesting features at both sites. Both sites have a large well-defined processional walkway called an avenue that serves as an entrance to and from the circles. Both avenues lead to the River Avon. Both avenues were marked by large bonfires where they intersect with the river. This indicates that there may well have been a procession from one monument to the other, via the River Avon.

When we examine the solar alignments of both sites, however, Stonehenge and Woodhenge become even more interesting. And, it has to do with the alignment of each site to the winter and summer solstices. Because while the avenue leading from the river to Stonehenge is aligned with the summer solstice sunrise, the avenue leading to Woodhenge is aligned with the winter solstice sunrise. But, that's not all.

One can also say that Stonehenge is aligned with the winter solstice sunset and Woodhenge is aligned with the summer solstice sunset, depending on which direction you are looking. The paths are reflexive, as shown below. So, there are alignments to both sunrise and sunset, at both solstices, and at each site. It just depends which way you are looking, toward the circle from the path, or toward the path, from the center of the circle.

WOODHENGE

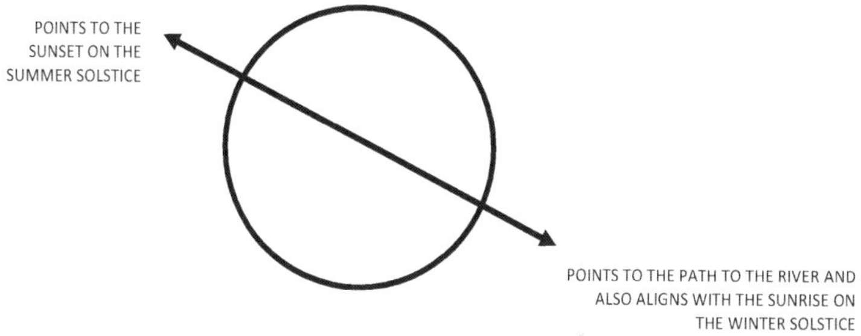

STONEHENGE

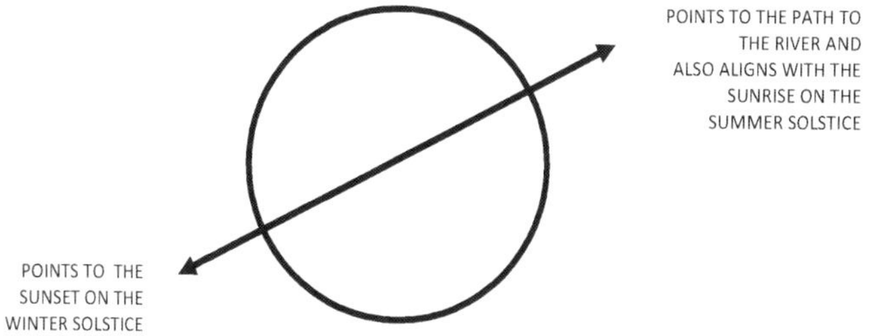

CIRCLE OF TIME

It turns out that the same alignment which points to the summer solstice sunrise also points to the winter solstice sunset from the opposite direction. Likewise, the same path that aligns with the winter solstice sunrise also points to the summer solstice sunset.[7] And, all of this conveys a sense of circular motion. If you consider that sunrise is the beginning of a day and sunset is the end, then perhaps the same is true for a processional march down the avenues. In that case each sunrise alignment marks the beginning of a march, and each sunset alignment marks the end, with the River Avon being a medium connecting the two avenues.

This symbolism of a river is also important in many cultures' concept of the journey from this world to the after-life. In many ancient myths, there is a ferryman who conveys spirits from this world to the next. And, coins were given to the dead to pay the ferryman for the trip. So, it makes sense that a journey by boat, on the river Avon, might have been one leg of a processional march.

If they walked from Woodhenge down the avenue at sunrise on the winter solstice, facing the sun, then they would complete their journey walking directly into the sunset of the winter solstice, straight down the avenue to Stonehenge. Likewise, if they began a procession from Stonehenge walking down the avenue straight toward the rising sun on the summer solstice, they would conclude their journey at Woodhenge, walking up the avenue toward the setting sun of the summer solstice, always walking in the direction of the sun.

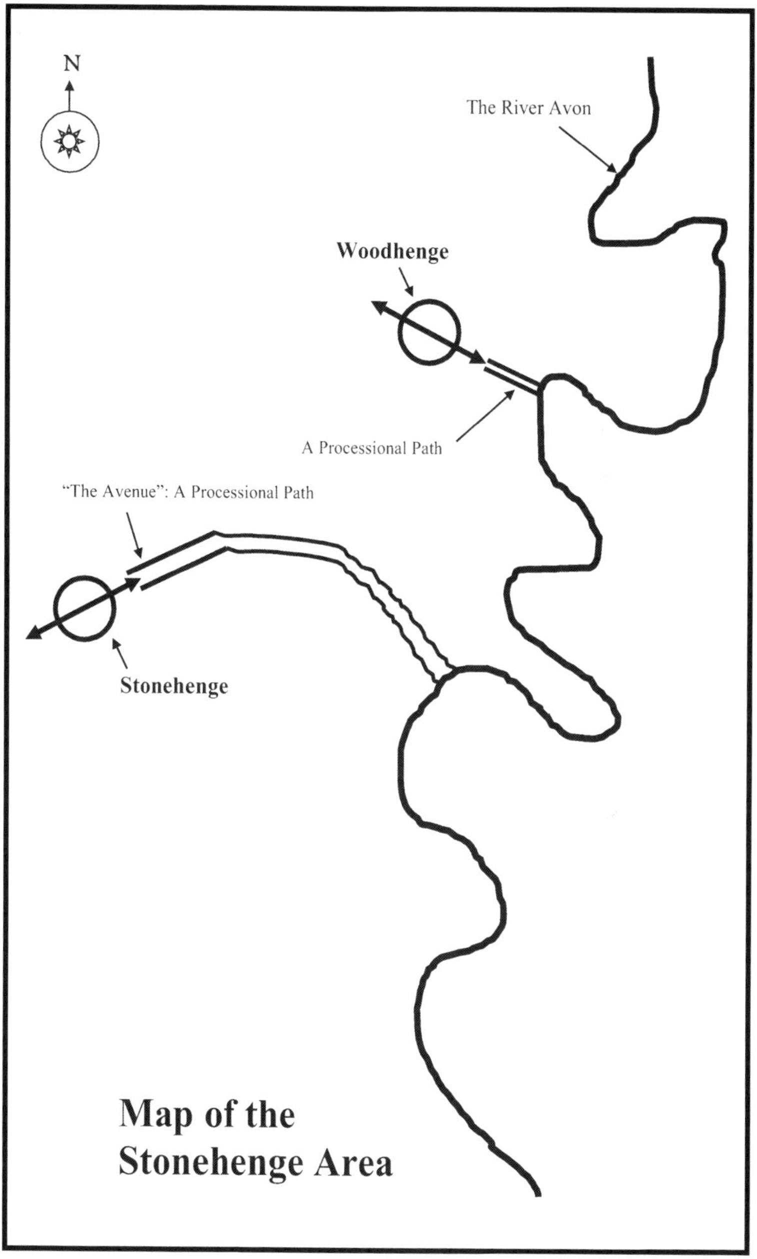
N
The River Avon
Woodhenge
A Processional Path
"The Avenue": A Processional Path
Stonehenge
Map of the
Stonehenge Area

This is not just mere conjecture. There are many archaeological details that suggest that this was indeed a procession from one temple to the other.[8] This would indicate that they had a procession from Woodhenge to Stonehenge at midwinter and another from Stonehenge to Woodhenge at midsummer. Each procession went down the avenue that led to the river, and then from one avenue to the other by river, concluding at the other monument at sunset. But why? What does it all mean?

The motion of the sun from the cold, dead, middle of winter to the warm summer, and then back again, is cyclical. It repeats over and over, like a circle, from summer to winter and back to summer again. And, this mirrors the circle of life, from life to death and back to life again. So, the two processions mark the very real movement of the sun and seasons, from life to death and then from death to life. So, why does it go from the temple of life to the temple of death in winter? And why does it go from death to life in summer?

In each case, the procession mirrors the movement that the sun has completed. So in midwinter the sun has traveled from the season of life and arrived at the apex of the season of death. In midsummer, the sun has completed the opposite journey, from the middle of the season of death to the apex of life. In each case, at the end of the day, there is evidence of bon fires and feasts at each location. So, the feast of midwinter would have been held at Stonehenge, the temple of death. And, on the evening of midsummer they would have arrived at Woodhenge, at a feast at the temple of life.

Mike Parker Pearson neatly summarizes all these finds by saying, "It's about life and death."[9]

THE WHEEL OF TIME

When you analyze this processional path and its significance for understanding the metaphysical beliefs of its builders, the results are astounding. What we find is nothing less than solid evidence of what we call the Wheel of Time, and it is the oldest evidence of this concept ever discovered. What is The Wheel of Time? This is the concept that life and death are cyclical, and this cycle reverberates through every dimension of life on earth and the human experience. Also, this is a philosophical foundation through which one can understand the nature of all things, especially all living things and possibly much more.

According to Julius Caesar, the ancient Celtic people believed in reincarnation, that just as there are cyclical seasons for plants, which appear to die in the fall only to be reborn in the spring, there are seasons of life and death for the immortal human soul.[10] So, it is logical to assume that their ancestors, the builders of Stonehenge, also saw the seasons of the human soul mirrored in the seasons of the Earth.

Here we see several different dimensions to this Wheel of Time; there is day and night, marked by sunrise and sunset, and by the two poles of midnight and midday. Then, there are the seasons of the year, marked by spring and fall, and the two poles or solstices, midwinter and midsummer. And then there are the seasons of humanity, marked by birthing and dying, and the two poles, life and death. And, just as the days and the years repeat their alternating cycles, so too does the human soul. This gives us a rudimentary concept of a wheel with three concentric circles (see Figure 1). Each phase of the day correlates with the phases of the year, and the phases of life.

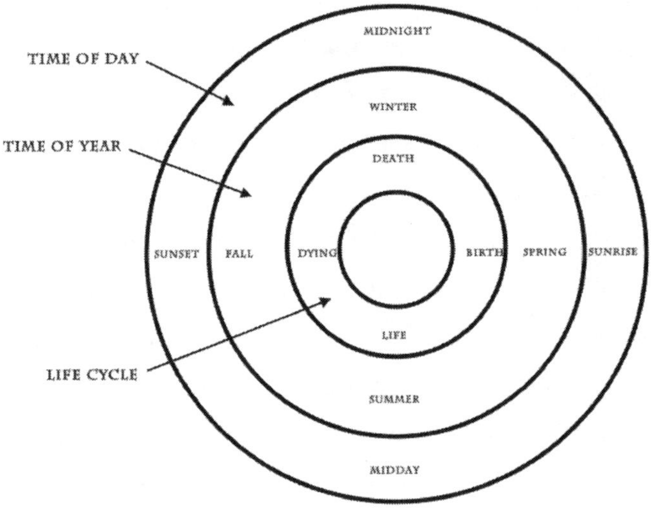

Figure 1

As you can see in the figure above, this gives us a way of understanding time as inherently cyclical. Perhaps more importantly, it can be a template for thinking about the cyclical nature of all living things. Just as was written by the Chinese Philosopher, Lao Tzu, in the Tao Te Ching (circa 500 BCE), *"Ten thousand things arise and fall. I observe their cycle. Things mature, multiply, multiply, and return to their root. Returning to the root is tranquility. (It) Is called the cycle of destiny."*[11] This seems like it would accurately characterize the beliefs of the builders of Stonehenge & Woodhenge as well.

Interestingly, there is more to this passage by Lao Tzu that may also explain why these monuments and the processional avenues were so important. It was not just important to know this concept of life and death, but to celebrate it and ritualize it as a part of their life. Lao Tzu goes on to write "The cycle of destiny is our eternal nature. To know our eternal nature is enlightenment. To not know our eternal nature is disastrous." And finally he concludes, "Death of the body is not extinction."[12]

This seems to summarize all aspects of the belief system of the builders of Stonehenge. Clearly this cycle of day and night, summer and winter, and life and death was sacred, and understanding this principle must have been something like what we call *enlightenment* to them. Most important is the reaffirmation in the belief of immortal life and reincarnation, that death is not the end, but is only one reoccurring season of the eternal life cycle.

THE HIDDEN LANDSCAPES PROJECT

The Hidden Landscapes Project, led by Wolfgang Neubauer from the Ludwig Boltzman Institute and Vincent Gaffney from the University of Birmingham, now in its fifth year, has added even more data to our study of Stonehenge and the surrounding area.[13] Though it may be less relevant to our investigation into the Wheel of Time, it has filled in gaps in our understanding of the site and the ancients who lived here. By surveying the entire area with ground penetrating radar, they uncovered what would normally have taken over a century of slow, painstaking, ground-digging excavations to uncover. They found a vast Neolithic village around Woodhenge, much bigger than previously thought, with well over 1000 buildings, and many other circular henge-type structures, perhaps used as other types of temples, family shrines, or alters to specific gods or goddesses. They also found evidence of other previously unknown processional paths and solar alignments.

One of the interesting finds of this research project is the Durrington Walls Superhenge, a giant ritual center, most likely the largest in the world, that has a circumference of nearly a mile (1.5 kilometers). Furthermore, the findings document activity and structures in the area dating back more than 11 thousand years, much earlier than anyone had previously thought. We also know that "The Avenue" that leads to Stonehenge existed long before there were people here. The Avenue was originally a petrified riverbed, perfectly aligned with and pointing to the setting sun on the winter solstice. Perhaps that is why Stonehenge was originally built in that location in the first place.

We also know that the Cursus, built 400 years before Stonehenge, which is a two-mile long, straight path with henge-like ditches and berms on either side, running east-west just north of Stonehenge, had openings in the berms for processional paths and also contained two pits at either end of the Cursus. These large pits, about 5 ft. deep and 16 feet across, probably contained bonfires and were perfectly aligned with Stonehenge so as to point to the midsummer sunrise to the east and midsummer sunset to the west. And there is a much smaller cursus to the west of that called the Lesser Cursus. There also appears to be another path that runs perpendicular to the avenue of Stonehenge, and leads to burial mounds near the Cursus, due north of Stonehenge.

The survey has revealed new information about hundreds of burial mounds, and detailed evidence of Neolithic, Bronze Age, Iron Age, and Roman settlements. The wealth of data uncovered will likely take years to fully analyze. Ultimately, excavations will have to be completed with a shovel and trowel to understand these sites better, but now we know where to dig. We now see that the Salisbury Plain, where Stonehenge sits, was once something like the New York City of the Neolithic Age.

And, thanks to the Hidden Landscapes Project we have one massive digital map that shows every single post-hole, rock, and burial in an area, covering many square miles. Perhaps when all these sites have been excavated and the artifacts analyzed we may have an even deeper understanding of the beliefs of the builders of Stonehenge and of their Wheel of Time.

NEWGRANGE & THE MOUND OF THE HOSTAGES

Site: Newgrange & The Mound of Hostages

Location: County Meath, Ireland

Date: 3,200 BCE

Site Description: These are two separate sites about 10 miles apart, both from the same period. Both are burial mounds.

Points on the Wheel: Winter solstice, Samhain, & Imbolc.

There are many interesting sites such as Stonehenge throughout the British Isles, and Ireland is no exception. In Ireland, there are some spectacular burial mounds. One of the largest is Newgrange which is 249 ft. across and 39 ft. high, covering over 1.1 acres. It is beautifully decorated with rock carvings of spiral designs, perhaps representing the cyclical nature of time. And it is over 5000 years old, dating to 3200 BCE.

Like other burial mounds, it has an alignment with the winter solstice sun as well. It contains a window that illuminates a 63 ft. long passage and fills the chamber at the end with light at dawn on midwinter day. Actually, this phenomenon occurs each morning, beginning on December 19th, grows brighter each day and peaks on about the 21st, the solstice, disappearing by the 23rd. Archaeologists say this is more than just a burial mound; it is a Neolithic cathedral. There are two other similar mounds nearby, the Knowth Mound and the Dowth Mound, though they are not as spectacular. But, for our purposes, the most interesting of these ancient Irish mounds is the nearby Mound of the Hostages.

Less than 10 miles away, is the Mound of Hostages (*Dumha na nGiall* in Irish), on the Hill of Tara, and it also dates to the same period. It is a burial mound approximately 69 ft. in diameter and over 11 ft. high, covering a passage tomb over 13 ft. long. Inside they found the cremated remains of approximately 250 to 500 bodies.[14] There were also funerary goods buried with them, such as stone beads, urns, bone pins, and various pieces of pottery. It appears that the site was built about 5200 years ago and was used throughout the Bronze Age, until there was no more room left. But what is really interesting about this site is its unusual alignments with the sun.

There is an east facing alignment with the winter sun as you might expect, being a burial mound, but it is not aligned with the winter solstice. Instead, it aligns with the winter sun on two specific times, the beginning of November, and the beginning of February. The lighting phenomenon begins to illuminate the passage chamber about a week before, and then peaks at about November 1st or 2nd and then begins to fade over the next week.[15] Then, it does the same thing three months later, peaking in the first days of February. And, this is very interesting because we know that these two times of the year correspond with two well-known holidays in Celtic paganism; Imbolc, which is celebrated around the first of February, and Samhain, which is celebrated around the first of November. I say that it's *around the first* because, just like the solstices and equinoxes, it's not actually on the same day each year, but often moves a day or two, due to leap year.

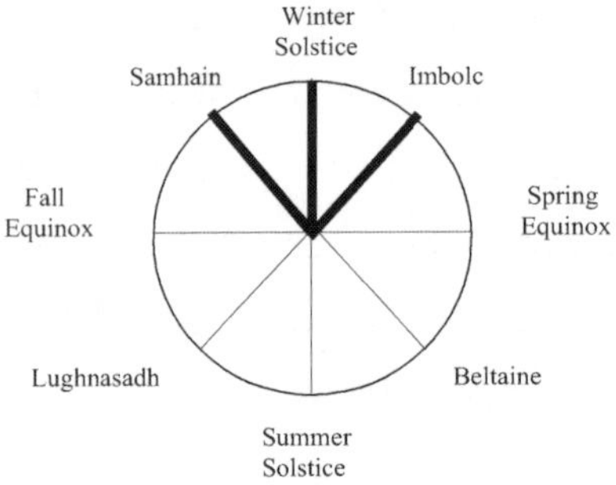

Here we see in the above wheel diagram of the year that these two burial mounds are clearly related to winter; together they mark the start of winter (Samhain), the middle (Solstice), and the end of winter (Imbolc). So, what is Imbolc and Samhain? And, why are these seemingly random days so important? Well, remember that the four main days that mark the seasons are the two solstices and the two equinoxes. In addition to these 4 main holidays, the Celts also celebrated what we call cross-quarter days. These consist of the midpoints between each of the four cardinal points on the calendar. So Samhain (pronounced Sah-win) is the midpoint between the fall equinox and the winter solstice. Likewise Imbolc (pronounced i-molk) is the midpoint between the winter solstice and the spring equinox.

What is so interesting about this is that many scholars believe that the observation of the cross-quarter days were only recently added by neo-pagans of the 19th Century. Many scholars assert that there is no proof that the Neolithic builders of monuments such as Carnac, Stonehenge, or Newgrange, actually celebrated or even knew of these cross-quarter days. This site, just 10 miles from Newgrange and dated to the same period, offers very clear evidence that the Neolithic people did, in fact, both know of and mark the cross-quarter days. The solar alignment of the Mound of the Hostages is exactly what we would expect to see if its ancient builders were observing the cross-quarter days. But what does this mean for our model of the Wheel of Time? What was the possible meaning of these days for the ancient people who built it?

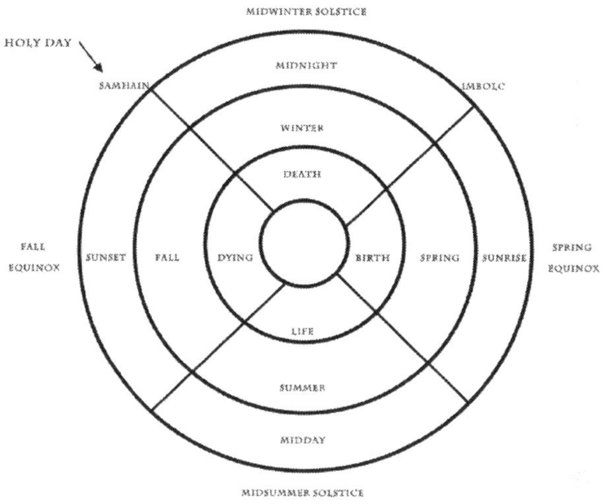

Figure 2

This peculiar solar alignment of the Mound of Hostages doesn't just reaffirm The Wheel of Time concept but adds new clues. To analyze the meaning of these days we have to remember that if the winter solstice is the peak of the season of death, literally mid-winter, then Imbolc and Samhain are the beginning and end of winter, the season of death. We can now plot these two points on our model of the Wheel of Time (see Figure 2 above). But, these are only points on the annual calendar. How do these correspond to the other dimensions of the Wheel, the times of the day, or seasons of the human life cycle? Well, looking at the Wheel diagram in Figure 2, if midwinter is midnight and the spring equinox is sunrise, then Imbolc would be around 3 am. Likewise, if the fall equinox is sunset on the diagram, then Samhain is around 9 pm. This seems like two arbitrary times of the day, but when we examine the phases of life on the diagram, it does not seem so arbitrary.

Remember that Caesar had documented the Celts' belief in reincarnation. Well, if winter represents death in the human life cycle of reincarnation, then it's quite clear that the beginning of winter, Samhain, represents the beginning of our death, the act of dying. Likewise if midwinter represents the peak of the afterlife, and the spring equinox represents birth of new life, then Imbolc would represent conception.

And this is not just logical speculation; you can actually see both these events in nature. It is approximately at the beginning of November that leaves, already displaying brilliant fall colors, die and fall to the ground. Likewise, it is around the beginning of February that buds begin to form on those same trees. Buds that will not begin to unfurl for another three to six weeks, already have clearly-formed pods, pregnant with new life, ready to burst open after the first full week of warm spring weather.

Clearly this speaks volumes about the meaning of the Mound of Hostages and its solar alignments. Unlike Newgrange or even Stonehenge, there were arguably as many or more bodies cremated and buried in this mound than any other. Stonehenge had many cremated and buried remains, and so did Newgrange, but they were surrounded by other burial mounds. This, on the other hand, was one of the most concentrated deposits of human remains of any burial mounds we've found. So, it seems very fitting that this mound is not only aligned with the midwinter sun, but it is very specifically marked by the beginning and end of winter, and hence represents the space between the beginning and end of death. You might say that, for the builders of this monument, this mound represented the *domain of death.*

So, we now have a fairly complete wheel of life. But, at this point we clearly need to add another dimension to our model. I identified how the buds that we see in early February are the necessary precursors to new vegetation in spring, and this brings up another important point. At some point the builders of these monuments began living a sedentary life-style, tending to crops and livestock. As such, they had another very important reason for keeping track and celebrating the seasons, as this directly related to when they plan, till, plant, prune, weed, and harvest crops. Probably their solar calendars also kept them on track for breeding, milking, shearing, and slaughtering livestock as well. So the next addition to our model of the Wheel of Time needs to be the agricultural dimension (see Figure 3).

Our Wheel is not complete yet, but already we see a system that coordinates each and every aspect of the movements and events both on Earth and in the heavens. For the people of that time, it would have clearly shown the relationship of the movement of the sun and moon to the growing of crops, tending of livestock, and even to the phases of human life: birth and youth, reproduction, old age, and death. Most importantly, it would have demonstrated clearly and concretely that reincarnation is a normal, rational part of the universe, and therefore the human soul must also be immortal, enduring eternal cycles of life and death.

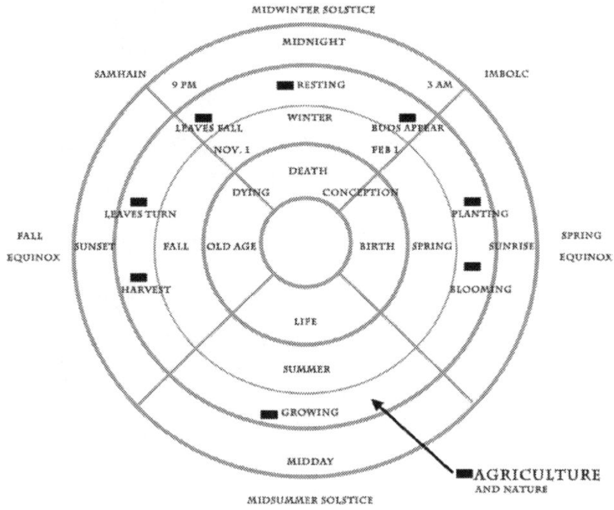

Figure 3

There are two other important sites that we need to explore to complete our wheel of time. One is near Stonehenge, and the other is also in Ireland. First, let's stay in Ireland and explore a very interesting circle of standing stones with a unique solar alignment, named Beltany.

BELTANY STONE CIRCLE

Site: Beltany Stone Circle
Location: County Donegal, Ireland
Date: 1,400 BCE
Site Description: There are 64 standing stones, but just one stone has carvings on it, and that one stone is aligned with the rising sun on the cross-quarter day, Beltaine, pronounced *Beltany.*
Points on the Wheel: Beltaine

In County Donegal, Ireland, and dated to 3400 years old, the 64 standing stones here are not the largest or most elaborate of stone circles but there is something odd about this one. The first thing you may notice if you are familiar with pagan holidays is the name Beltany. This is a clear reference to the pagan holiday Beltaine, which is an anglicized name for the Gaelic May Day festival, pronounced *Beltany.*

May Day is another one of those ancient, cross-quarter holidays that stem from ancient times and corresponding pagan celebrations. This is the midpoint between the spring equinox and the summer solstice. This occurs on or about May 1st, hence the English name May Day. According to tradition and ancient Roman chroniclers, the ancient Celts would have a huge fire festival where they lit bonfires.

Beltaine, or May Day, is a fertility celebration, that corresponds to the fertilization of crops and fruits, necessary for production of food, and the reproduction of plant-life. Likewise, the tradition would hold that young men and women would have sex in the fields around the bonfires to fertilize human life and to impart this fertility to the growing crops. According to legend, if a girl had sex this night she would be sure to get pregnant.

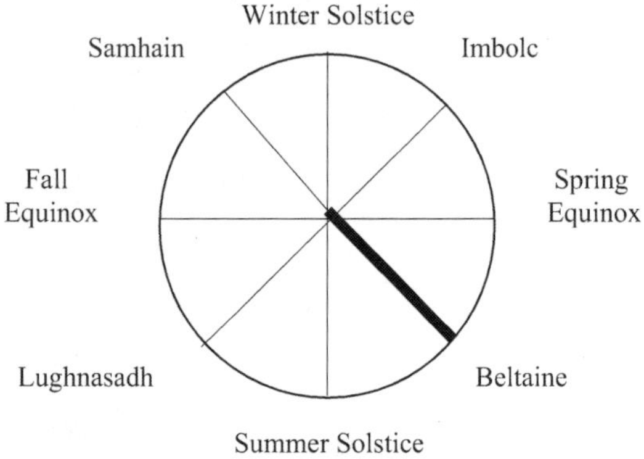

There is also a Beltaine tradition in some areas to pick two young people to become the May King and May Queen. They would live like a married couple and have sexual relations before the May King was either symbolically or actually killed, and his blood spilled in the fields to give the crops added fertility. Well, that is all very interesting but is there anything about this site other than the name that would indicate that it is a monument marking May 1st?

It turns out that there is something interesting about this site. Of all the stones, only one has any markings on it. It is covered with small gouges, that look like cups, that have been apparently ground out of the rock. This type of petroglyph has been associated with fertility, and coming of age ceremonies, in some cultures, such as Native Americans of the Southwest. We see this at Morteros Village, a Native American boys' puberty initiation site in Southern California. In that ancient village, there is a large rock covered with these cup shaped impressions called *morteros* in Spanish (or mortars in English), which are ground into the rock each year at the boys' puberty ceremony. And, there are similar traditions elsewhere, but this alone is not conclusive evidence. The question remains, is there a solar alignment to May first? It turns out there is.

Beltaine, which is usually celebrated on May 1st, is actually on a different date every year, since it is the midpoint between the spring equinox and the summer solstice. And, at Beltany Stone Circle, precisely on the sunrise of Beltaine, at the very point atop the stone, the only stone with petroglyphs carved into it, there is an alignment with the rising sun.

This is really rare because, while we know ancient people here celebrated this holiday, we rarely have any stone monuments marking this day, or aligning with the Beltaine sun. But, here it is, a unique alignment with the only stone that has any markings on it at all. This clearly explains why it was given the name Beltany, which is phonetically closer to the original Gaelic pronunciation of the holiday name, Beltaine, and which we call May Day.

So this gives us another segment of The Wheel of Time, which we can now fill in. In Figure 4 below, you will see the addition of Beltaine, and with it all of the corresponding points within the wheel. So, for the time-of-day it corresponds to the midpoint between sunrise and noon, or about

9am. Regarding agriculture it represents the time when the crops and fruits are fertilized by the birds and the bees. So, naturally it corresponds to the time when humans begin mating and having children of their own, what we call puberty. Hence the ancient Beltaine tradition of mating in the fields.

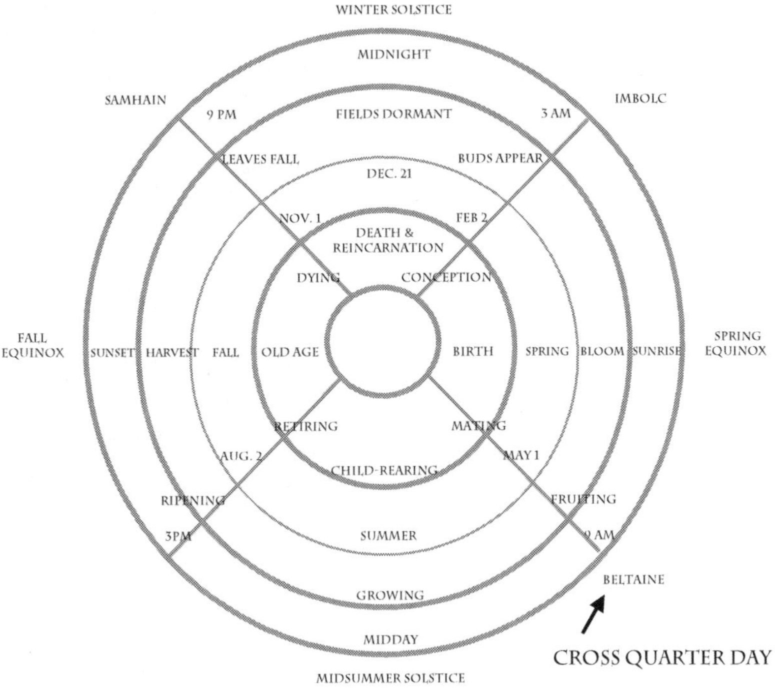

Figure 4

This leaves us with one more quadrant yet to be filled, in our diagram, but for that we must return to the area of Stonehenge, where we have gained so much information already.

SILBURY HILL

Site: Silbury Hill

Location: Wiltshire, England

Date: 2,400 BCE

Site Description: Larger than any other burial mound, it is a human made hill, nearly 550 ft. wide, and 131 ft. tall. In ancient times it was associated with the feast of Lughnasadh, a cross-quarter day between Summer solstice and the fall equinox.

Points on the Wheel: Lughnasadh

In the county of Wiltshire, near Stonehenge, lies Silbury Hill, part of the Stonehenge, Avebury, and Associated Sites, a UNESCO World Heritage Site. There we find many burial mounds, but one mound is different than the rest. Silbury Hill is one of the largest mounds of its kind. It stands over 100 ft. high and covers 5 acres. It is the tallest man-made prehistoric mound in Europe and one of the tallest in the world. It is made of chalk and clay, taken from the nearby chalk downs. Its origin and purpose is still debated, but one man has studied this site extensively and he thinks he's solved the mystery.

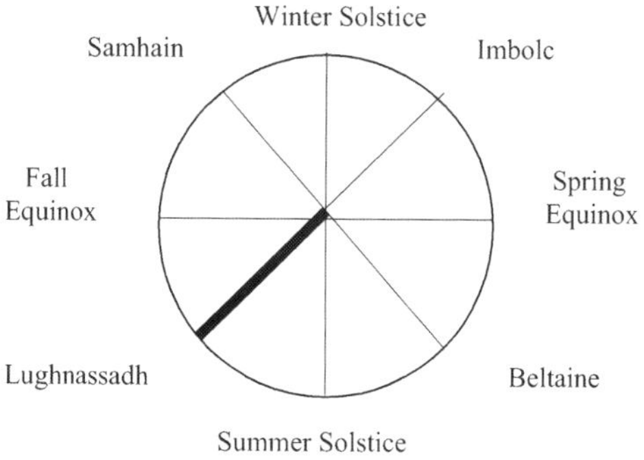

Author and historian, Michael Dames, believes that the hill is an effigy of an ancient Mother Goddess, associated with fertility rituals practiced at various times of the year. And, he has found evidence that this site was associated with the ancient harvest goddess rituals of Lughnasadh, which is celebrated on the midpoint between the summer solstice and the autumn equinox, which usually falls on or around the beginning of August.

Dames has written two books on this topic, *Silbury Treasure: The Great Goddess Rediscovered,* and *Silbury: Resolving the Enigma*.[16] In his latest book, *Silbury: Resolving the Enigma*, he argues convincingly that not only was the site known in antiquity to be associated with Lughnasadh, but we have archaeological evidence from a recently excavated Roman town nearby to support this idea. The local Romans evidently had merged their own worship of the Roman goddess Ceres with the Gaelic harvest goddess, celebrated on Lughnasadh.

Ceres was the Roman goddess of grain and agriculture. And, in addition to evidence of Ceres worship in the Roman village near Silbury Hill, we know that it was a tradition for the local people to make straw effigies of the grain goddess or Earth Mother, as part of their harvest rituals. These goddess figures are known variously as corn maidens, corn mothers, or corn dollies, and they were created and used in harvest rituals all over Britain and Europe. In fact, they continue to be used as part of the celebration of Lughnasadh, or Lammas, as it is also known among Neo-pagans even today.

Dames also suggested that the position of the Hill,

relative to other sites in Avebury, and Kennet Long Barrow nearby, further suggest this site was mainly used as a ritual site at the first of August, to celebrate the first grain harvest of the year *as delivering an annual First Fruits birth.* The hill, he believes, is meant to reflect the pregnant belly of the Mother Earth goddess. This gives us our last segment of a now complete and symmetrical Wheel of Time, seen in Figure 5.

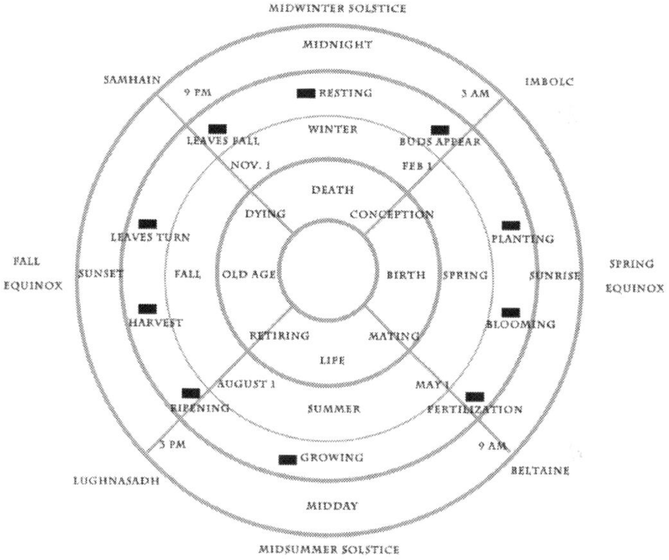

Figure 5

This, the final segment of the radiating points of the wheel, has corresponding points in each concentric circle within the wheel. The time of day corresponds to the midpoint between noon and sunset, or about 3 pm. This corresponds to first harvest, or a ripening of crops and fruits on the agricultural calendar.

On the human life cycle, this is the start of the golden

years in the human life cycle. This time of year corresponds to the phase of human life when we get older, become grandparents, slow down and eventually retire. It is at this point in the year when we begin to reap what crops what we have sown in the fields. And, it corresponds the time in life when we begin to reap what we have sown in our life as well.

THE WHITE HORSE OF UFFINGTON

Site: The White Horse

Location: Uffington, England

Date: 550- 1,380 BCE

Site Description: A giant horse, 350 ft long, carved into the white chalk of the hillside, marks the Winter Solstice, with an image of a horse galloping from east to west toward the setting sun.

Points on the Wheel: Winter Solstice

There is one more site in England that is worth mentioning because it is completely different than the other sites we've seen thus far. In the hills of southern England is a large geoglyph, which is unique for that area. A geoglyph is a giant image carved into the earth. The most famous geoglyphs are the Nazca lines, in Peru. Many can only be clearly seen from airplanes.

Carved into the white chalk of a hillside of Uffington, England is a 360-foot-long image of a running horse. For many years, this giant horse was a mystery. We know that it is from the Bronze Age, 550-1380 BCE, but what did it mean? Was it meant to mark a territory or what? Finally, a University of Southampton archaeologist, Joshua Pollard, thinks he has solved the riddle.[17] He discovered that it can only be clearly observed from another hilltop. From that vantage point, on the winter solstice, the sun rises behind the horse and, over the course of the day, the sun seems to gain on the horse and finally passes it. The horse seems to be galloping toward the sunset on the shortest day of the year.

Dr. Pollard came up with this explanation in part because of the ethnography of the area. He cites a popular belief among people of that time, that the sun either rode a horse across the sky or was carried on a chariot, pulled by a horse. "*The White Horse is depicted as a horse in motion*" Pollard says, *"I think this explanation –that it is tied to the sun- makes sense."*

This rare English geoglyph again underscores the importance of the winter solstice as a time of great reverence and ceremony for the people who made it. And, like the last site we looked at, Silbury Hill, this site also incorporates imagery of their mythology into the monument.

SUMMARY

Now the basic foundation of The Wheel of Time is complete. We will continue to embellish it in the next few chapters but this is the core of the Wheel. And, already it explains so much about our holidays.

In the Introduction I promised that The Wheel of Time would solve many mysteries of our holidays, such as why we celebrate Christmas at midnight, Easter at sunrise, and Halloween in the evening. Well, now you can see what I meant. There is a direct, one to one correspondence between the life and death of the year and the life and death of a day. The Wheel also explains why we celebrate Christmas with evergreens, Easter with bunnies, and Halloween with skeletons. This is because there is a one-to-one correspondence to the human life cycle as well. Easter represents fertility and birth, Halloween represents death, and Christmas represents eternal life through the promise of reincarnation.

Furthermore, the Wheel of Time explains the real reason why we celebrate each of these holidays on the specific days that we do, because these days mark the phases of the Sun, in the life of the year. Most important, it explains what it all means, or at least, what it originally meant to our prehistoric ancestors. The times of the day and phases of the Sun are microcosms of the human life cycle, which are echoed in all of Nature. They were worshipping life, nature, and the interconnections between all the elements of the Universe.

Now you know the rest of the story. What we have found from the latest archaeological discoveries only validates what we have always known about the local pagan people from eye-witness accounts going back 2000 years, from the earliest Roman soldiers and Christian monks.[17] The people here celebrated the seasons of the year as important milestones of nature, as seen in the daily cycle and in the phases of human life. They marked the solstices and equinoxes, but more importantly they marked and celebrated the four cross-quarter days, which are the midpoints of each of the segments of the solar year, creating an eight pointed Wheel of Time.

This last point is an important one because there are still prominent scholars who maintain that the eight pointed Wheel of the Year is a fairly modern invention. The last time I checked the Wikipedia entry for the *Wheel of the Year* I saw a line that read: *Many historical pagan traditions celebrated various equinoxes, solstices, and cross-quarter days. But, none were known to have held all eight days above all other annual sacred times.* But, this statement is not only factually incorrect, it is simply obtuse.

First, what other *sacred times* are there? As we will show later, almost all holy days can be linked to these eight points on the Wheel. Secondly, all four cross-quarter days are listed as the start of the four seasons in The Ulster Cycle, set in the 1st Century, and recorded from oral tradition between the 8th and 9th Centuries.[18] And, these cross-quarter days could only be determined by monitoring the solstices and equinoxes. There is no other way. That means that they regularly identified and marked all eight points of the solar year.

Later, when we explore the historical and ethnographic evidence for the Wheel of Time we will show that all of the cross-quarter days, and the corresponding fire festivals among the early Britons, were documented by Roman historians. And, the Roman scholar Varro himself conceptualized the year in eight parts, defined for the most part by the solstices, equinoxes, and the four midpoints between them.[19]

By the way, I would be remiss if I did not mention a minor mathematical discrepancy in the traditional dates of the cross-quarter days. They are supposed to be the midpoints between the equinoxes and the solstices. But, if the spring equinox is on March 21st and the summer solstice is on June 21st, then Beltaine, the midpoint, should be on May 5th, not May 1st. This is true for all 4 cross-quarter days. Most should be between the 5th and the 7th of the month. They are all off by up to a week. This isn't astrophysics; anybody with a calendar who can count should be able to figure this out.

So why do we celebrate the cross-quarter days on the 1st or 2nd of the month? Even Giulio Magli, an expert in archaeoastronomy, rightly identifies that Beltaine should be on May 5th. But, the ancient solar observatories, such as Beltany Stone Circle, appears to mark the *traditional* cross-quarter days, not the actual midpoints. Eventhough some are only acurate to within a week, this remains a bit of a mystery.

So far, we have seen evidence for all eight points of The Wheel of Time completed just through looking at ancient monuments in England, Scotland and Ireland. Based on this, many mainstream archaeologists might think that this concept of the Wheel of Time only applies to cultures within the British Isles. But, this is not the case. In fact, as you will see in the next chapter, it is in mainland Europe that we find even more compelling evidence.

Not only do we see many more henge-like structures and standing stones with identical solar alignments in Europe, but we find something there that is nothing short of an archaeological miracle. You might say it's like striking gold.

CHAPTER 3

STRIKING GOLD IN PREHISTORY EUROPE

So far we have only looked at monuments in Scotland, England, and Ireland, but there are some interesting archaeological finds from inland Europe, to be sure. Though our 8 pointed wheel is now complete, the sites on continental Europe definitely add scope and dimension to what we've already learned.

There are three such finds that I think are especially interesting, each for various reasons. They are the Carnac Stones of Northern France, the Goseck Circle and the Golden Hats, both from Germany.

THE CARNAC STONES

Site: Carnac Stones

Location: Carnac France

Date: 6,850 BCE

Site Description: A large concentration of over 3000 standing stones, set in rows with many solar and lunar alignments including the 18.6 year-long lunar nodal cycle.

Points on the Wheel: Primarily the Winter and Summer Solstices.

The next oldest solar calendar that we will explore is by far the largest. The Carnac stones in northern France contains over 3,000 prehistoric standing stones. It is comprised of three major groups of stones called alignments, one of which (the Kermario alignment) is over three quarters of a mile in length. Many of the stones are aligned in long parallel lines, several stones across, like the formation of an advancing army.

The Carnc Stones, Carnac France

But there are other features here as well; there are stone circles, rectangles, tumuli (burial mound), and domens (tombs constructed of giant stones). And the site appears to be quite ancient. It is believed that the bulk of the stones were placed here between 5300 and 6500 years ago. There have been several phases of construction and the very first stones were placed here as far back as 8,850 years ago, predating Stonehenge by several thousand years. [1]

The most impressive part of this monument is simply its size and complexity. For instance, the Ménec alignment consists of eleven rows of stones, in a formation that is approximately 3800 ft. by over 300 ft. One of the smaller groups, the Kerlescan alignment is a mere 2600 ft. in length, and contains 13 rows of stones. Additionally the burial mounds or Tumuli, are just as impressive. The Saint Michel tumulus is over 400 ft. across, and nearly 40 feet high. It is composed of over 45,000 cubic yards of earth. Its function was likely a tomb for important persons. When it was excavated in the early 20th Century, it was found to contain 15 stone chests, jewelry, and pottery.

Of course what we are most concerned with is its function as a solar calendar and, to be sure, there are a few interesting alignments here. For instance, both the Gavrinis and Kercado mounds have passages with entrances facing the winter solstice sun. One section of the Kermario group of stones is in line with the sunset on the winter solstice, and also aligns with sunrise on the summer solstice. This may not seem like much considering its immense size and scale, but there may be something even more interesting about the Carnac alignments.

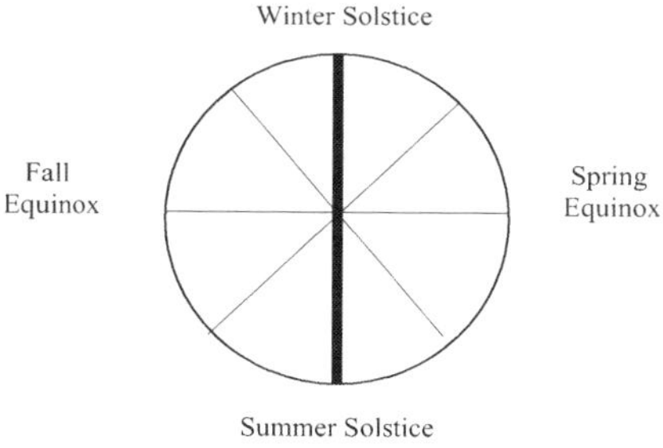

Some researchers such as Alexander Thom suggest that Carnac was originally a lunar observatory.[2] Apparently, the Grand Menhir base, when used as a back-site for other markers, could track the movement of the 18.6 year lunar nodal cycle. According to Thom, the site was converted from a lunar observatory to primarily a solar observatory about 5000 years ago. This is certainly consistent with findings from Warren Field, and it also fills-in the history of these sites a bit more. By the time of the construction of Stonehenge, these types of sites were built primarily for tracking the sun's annual phases, though they may still have contained lunar or lunisolar alignments as well.

Carnac is significant for the study of ancient pagan beliefs because it provides not just evidence of the use of lunar calendars, but also a progression from lunar calendars to lunisolar calendars, and eventually to predominately solar calendars. This gives us some idea of which celestial bodies were most important to them.

GOSECK CIRCLE

Site: Goseck Circle

Location: Near Leipzig, Germany

Date: 5,000 BCE

Site Description: A round wooden enclosure with several concentric circles around it, and with three openings, which are aligned with the north-star, Polaris, and both sunrise and sunset on the Winter Solstice.

Points on the Wheel: Winter and Summer Solstices.

Goseck Circle consists of a large ditch, about 220 ft. across, with concentric circles within it, lined by two palisades, made of wood, a mound and three openings or paths leading to the center of the circle. One opening is due north, and the other two align with the rising and setting sun on the winter solstice, as viewed from the center.[3] It also has an alignment with the summer solstice.

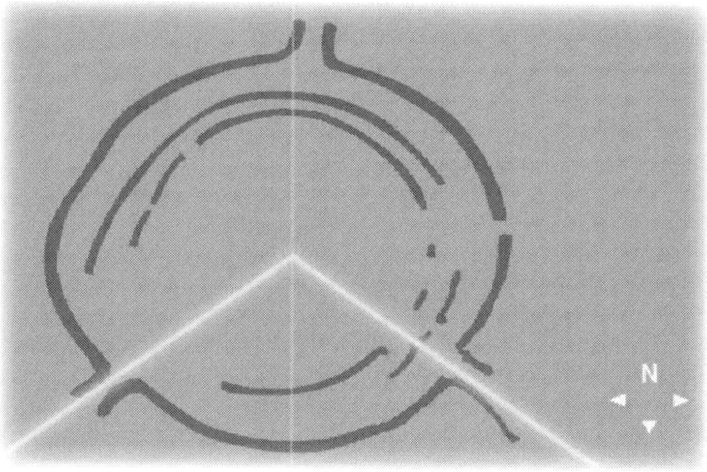

Diagram of Goseck Circle

Compared to the other impressive sites that we just explored, Goseck Circle might seem like a meager morsel for archaeological study. And, it is not unique; Goseck is only one of approximately 150 circular enclosures like it throughout Central Europe, all with similar features, many are in the area of modern day Germany, Austria, and the Czeck Republic. But there are a few interesting things about this site.

First, it predates Stonehenge and several other sites we've looked at. It is believed to be about 7,000 years old, overlapping construction activity at Carnac. Secondly, it is approximately the same latitude as Stonehenge. It is only 1 minute of latitude off, which is approximately a mile difference from the latitude at Stonehenge.[4] This means that, just like at Stonehenge and Woodhenge, when viewed from the opposite direction, the alignments mark the sunrise and sunset of both the winter and summer solstices.

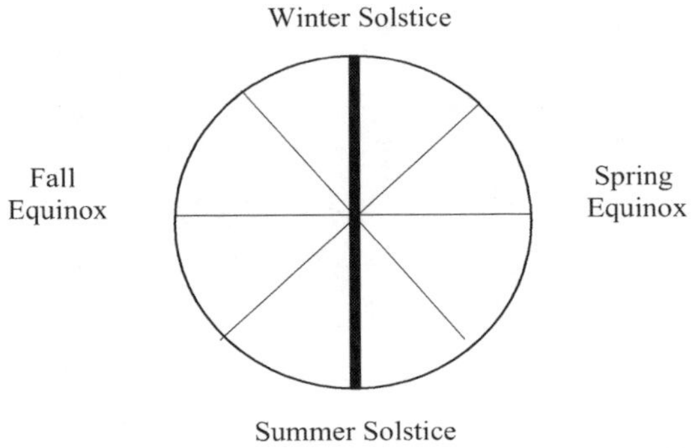

So, once again we have this inverse relationship of summer and winter with the same solar alignments. This is important because it shows that the sites in the British Isles that we explored were not just isolated cultures or solar cults, but were part of a larger group of cultures that spanned Europe throughout the Neolithic and shared a common preoccupation with certain dates.

And, both in the British Isles and on mainland Europe they erected monuments to mark and celebrate these dates, and the monuments shared specific features. Again, we see parallel dimensions in the Wheel of Time, corresponding to the extremes of the cycle of time; they mark both sunset and sunrise, on both midwinter and midsummer. But, this is not the only interesting find in Germany.

GOLDEN HATS

> **Site:** Golden Hats
>
> **Location:** Found in Germany, France and Swizerland
>
> **Date:** 6,850 BCE
>
> **Site Description:** A tall cone shaped object, possibly used as a hat, made of stamped gold. The images on the hat are actually a lunisolar calendar, corresponding to the 19 year-long, lunisolar Metonic Cycle.
>
> **Points on the Wheel:** All points on the Wheel.

There may have been books and wooden tablets with writing, and even written parchments created in prehistory, but none of it survived the ages. If they existed, they have long since rotted and turned to dust. But, what if we could find a prehistoric shaman's notebook, stamped in metal? That is exactly what we find in Germany, and it validates and reaffirms everything we have discovered so far in Britain and Europe.

The puzzling artifacts known as the Golden Hats are one of the great mysteries of Ancient Europe. Found in four different locations, in Germany, France, and Switzerland, and dating to between 3400 years ago and 2800 years ago, the hats are very complex, detailed, and accurate lunisolar calendars, made of stamped gold.[5] They may or may not have actually been used as hats. They are cone shaped and the size of the opening is about the size of a human head. They are oval like a human head rather than round, but they are unusually large, close to 3 ft in height.

Whether used as hats or not, there is no doubt that they are very accurate lunisolar calendars. The symbols on the hat form a logarithmic table, which predicts the movements of the sun and the moon. The 1,739 symbols on the Berlin hat, for instance, corresponds precisely to the Metonic Cycle, discovered by the Greek astronomer Meton, almost a thousand years later in 432 BCE.

One of the Golden Hats

Who made these? Why, and how were they used? Were they worn at certain rituals? Perhaps they were worn at the sunrise and sunset ceremonies at the two solstices. We just don't know.

In fact, there is much about these hats that we don't know. But they do provide us with some valuable insights into the ancients who built the ancient solar observatories. As Thom noted in his study of Carnac, and as was observed at Warren Field, the ancients not only tracked the sun but also the phases of the moon, and likely observed a lunisolar calendar. But Thom believed that there was a progression in the phases of construction at Carnac, from lunar observations to mostly solar observations over time.

What makes these hats so interesting is that it shows that they were still using a lunisolar calendar thousands of years after the construction of monuments such as the Goseck Circle and Carnac. If it appeared that they featured predominantly solar observations at their monuments, such as at Goseck, perhaps that is because it is much harder to calibrate the year accurately without solar observations. Hence, monuments like Goseck were necessary to create an accurate lunisolar calendar.

As mentioned before, there are 12.368 lunar cycles to one year. So, each year it would have been necessary to recalibrate their lunisolar calendar. This adjustment simply could not have easily been done without a solar marker of at least one of the three cardinal points of the sun's movement, either marking one of the solstices or having an equinox marker (both spring and fall are the same). And this is apparently why solar observatories were so widespread. What these hats show, however, is that they never stopped using a lunisolar calendar.

We have seen evidence of very early lunisolar observatories at Warren Field and Carnac, now these hats from the Bronze age show a detailed knowledge and observation of a lunisolar calendar was still in practice as late as 2800 years ago. Then, nearly a thousand years later, as early Romans noted, the Celts were still using a lunisolar calendar at that time. And, as we will see later in the book, the practice was still in use in England hundreds of years later, according to the historian Bede, who supported the idea of preserving Easter as a lunisolar holiday, which it still is to this very day.[6] Historically, Easter was celebrated on the first full moon after the spring equinox. And that's what we still do to this day. That is why Easter falls on a different day each year.

So, why have a lunisolar calendar? Well, without one you could not predict when a lunisolar holiday would fall. Let's say we wanted to know what day Easter will fall on next year. Because it is a lunisolar holiday, there is no way of knowing, off the top of your head, what day it will fall on. It could be anywhere from March 21 to April 21st. How about Chinese New Year? Yes, that's another lunisolar holiday. The Chinese New Year is celebrated at the second new moon after the winter solstice, and it could be anywhere from about January 21st to February 21st, roughly the same time as Imbolc on the Celtic Wheel of Time. In fact, there is no way of knowing in advance what day the Chinese New Year will fall without an accurate lunisolar calendar tracking both solar and lunar movements.

In fact, it is because of the Golden Hats that we know that the Neolithic monuments, marking the passage of the sun, were probably used specifically for the marking and celebration of holidays. If it were not to predict lunisolar holidays to the day, then they would have little need of such a specific and accurate calendar. Knowing the general points of the sun's movement would be sufficient for agricultural needs and preparing for changes in the weather. No, this type of calendar is exactly what you'd expect to find if their makers were concerned with the planning of ritual lunisolar holidays.

STRIKING GOLD

All this makes sense, but it leaves one important question. Why did they want to celebrate these holidays on a specific lunisolar day in the first place? Why not celebrate their holidays on the solstice or equinox, or a cross-quarter day, regardless of the phase of the moon? What was so important about the phase of the moon? Answering this question gives us the most important information of all. It helps to explain what the ancients were thinking when they built their monuments, and it explains the importance of the Wheel of Time as a foundational concept in prehistory thinking. The answer is that if they did not include the moon in planning their holidays, it would not include all aspects of heaven and earth in a cyclic unity. The lunisolar calendar created a kind of unified theory of nature. In short, without including the phases of the moon, it would not fit with a comprehensive Wheel of Time, which reveals a concordance between solar and lunar cycles.

As we have seen in the previous chapter, there is a deeper level of meaning to be found here. Example: we all know that in the early fall we have a Harvest Moon. But, perhaps a Harvest Moon is just a full moon that occurs at the time of harvest, with no deeper meaning to it than that. It might be, but how would you explain the Mourning Moon? This is the first full moon after Samhain, the midpoint between the fall equinox and the winter solstice, and this has been celebrated by the Celts for at least 2000 years. What is it about that time of the year that makes people think of the death of loved ones and our mourning for them?

Well, on the Wheel of Time, we know that fall is the death of the year, when plants appear to die, when grass dies and the leaves on trees dry up and fall off. So, for ancient people, this time of year represented death for all life, including people. But what does that have to do with the moon? Obviously, the 12 different moons of the year each had a specific meaning that was the very same meaning as that of the sun and the season. This is the very definition of the Wheel of Time, a concordance between the life and death of the day, month, year, and all living beings.

This is important because it reveals that the Wheel of Time is not just a modern invention, rather it must have been the foundation of an ancient cosmological belief system. Why else choose the moon that occurs when the grasses and trees appear to die, to mourn our loved ones who have died? And, what possible reason could they have for celebrating the new year on a new moon? Clearly this can only come from seeing a symbolic alignment of a new moon, new life, and a new year, which is exactly what the Wheel of Time represents.

The Golden Hats prove that prehistory people were obsessed with finding a concordance between solar and lunar phases on one lunisolar calendar. This confirms the validity of the Wheel of Time as a basis for Neolithic cosmology. For an archaeo-psychologist like myself, who seeks to understand what the people of prehistory thought and believed, this is truly like striking gold.

Thus, we add a new dimension to the wheel of time, the Lunar dimension (see figure 6). In this new dimension of the wheel, a new moon is much like a new day or a new year, so we will put it at the top of the wheel. The Full moon marks the apex of the Month, much like summer is to the year, or noon is to the day, so it goes in the bottom of the wheel. And, of course, the half moon marks the mid points between a new moon and a full moon, not unlike the sunrise and sunset is to the day, so it goes on either side. The moon is waxing to the right then waning to the left, in a clockwise movement.

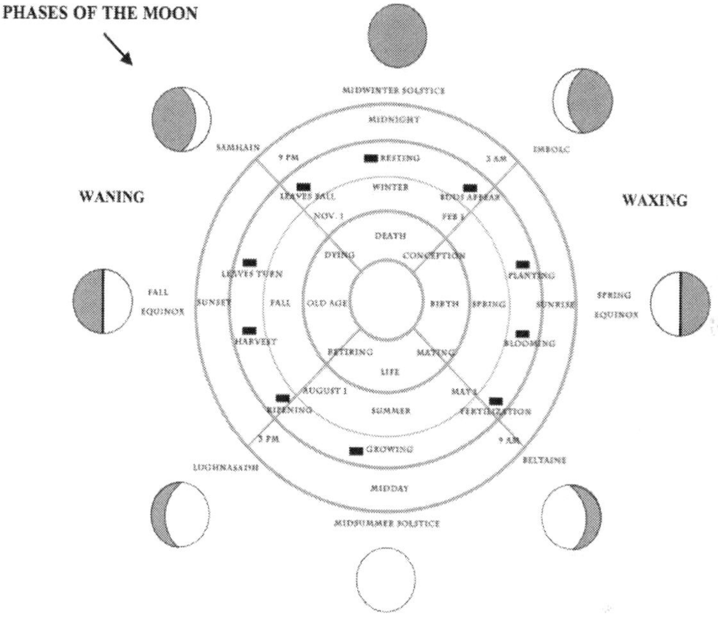

Figure 6

WHEN IS THE NEW YEAR ON A LUNISOLAR CALENDAR?

You may notice a discrepancy. I earlier mentioned in passing that the Chinese aligned the new year with the new moon closest to Imbolc, on the Wheel of Time. But, as shown in the above Figure 6, the new moon is not aligned with Imbolc but rather with the winter solstice. So, which is it, Imbolc or the winter solstice? It turns out that the new year is a somewhat arbitrary point on the Wheel of Time. Since it is a wheel, there is no beginning and no end. You can set the beginning of the year to wherever you want. So, while a new year is almost always celebrated on a new moon, you can set the new year on a lunisolar calendar to whichever season you choose.

Let's say that you want to start the new year to coincide with Imbolc, on the solar calendar (around early February). You would rotate the wheel of moon phases to align the new moon (start of the new month) with Imbolc. This is exactly what the Chinese did, by celebrating the second new moon after the solstice, which is the new moon closest to Imbolc. And this makes sense as you can see on the Wheel of Time, since it symbolizes the beginning of new life. In fact, it symbolizes the very conception of new life at the completion of the season of death. In this Chinese wheel, the very last phase of the moon corresponds with the very last phase of death, just before new life is conceived.

Each culture has a different idea of when the wheel starts, but I choose to align the new moon with the winter solstice, as shown in Figure 6, because of its correspondence with the phases of the sun. On the solar calendar, it is on the winter solstice that the days start getting longer. Though spring is still not near, nevertheless we know that spring will come again and there will be new life again.

If there is such a point in the phases of the moon, I think it is the point when the moon begins waxing again, which is the new moon. This promises that there will eventually be another full moon. Regarding our life cycle, the idea is that at some point after death you stop moving away from life and begin moving back toward it again, eventually to be born again. This is the concept of reincarnation, which Caesar documented as a core belief of the ancient Celts. This was the original meaning of the winter solstice, the celebration of eternal life through reincarnation.

SUMMARY

There are many other sites in the British Isles and Europe. As mentioned above, there are well over a hundred henge-like enclosures such as Goseck Circle, in central Europe alone. In Europe, there are many other spectacular sites such as Arkaim in Russia.[7] Arkaim has been called the Stonehenge of Russia, and reportedly over 18 astronomical phenomena have been discovered there.

Unfortunately, artifacts such as the Golden Hats are all too rare. This does not mean that they did not have more of these calendars. Other hats with similar markings, though not nearly as elaborate, have been found as far away as the western Iberian Peninsula, in Spain. All this evidence suggests that the concepts represented in the Wheel of Time (Figure 6) were most likely a wide-spread phenomenon, observed and celebrated throughout the Neolithic, Bronze Age, and beyond.

Because of the vastness of time, the only artifacts left for us to study are those made of stone, metal, or monuments built in the earth. We have lost all other records of calendars that may have been made of wood, parchment, or other biodegradable materials, which would have likely been the bulk of the materials they used for calendars.

Next we will explore the width and breadth of these archeological monuments throughout the world. There are similar amazing sites throughout the Mediterranean, in Africa, India, China, the Pacific Islands, and throughout the Americas. In fact, as I will show, there is hardly a place on earth that does not have some kind of archaeological site, which marks the movements of the sun, moon, stars, or all three, and almost all of them are for predicting lunisolar holidays.

The concordance between the archaeological sites in the British Isles & Europe and that of the rest of the world is astounding. This documents that our ancestors from the Neolithic and Bronze Ages really did have a basic foundation of ideas and beliefs based on the common observations of the sun, moon, and seasons, which somehow managed to extend to cultures around the world.

CHAPTER 4

ANCIENT MONUMENTS FROM AROUND THE WORLD

We already have a complete Wheel of Time, as seen in the last chapter. But there are many such sites around the world. The ancient monuments contained in the Mediterranean and Egypt are some of the most famous and spectacular in the world. So, at this point, we are just adding to the list of cultures that used solar markers as a part of their traditions. By finding similar stone monuments in other lands, we hope to show that Europe and the British Isles were by no means unique in this type of celestial-based belief system.

This is a somewhat debatable issue. We can prove that a particular culture in some other part of the world was marking the equinox and solstice thousands of years ago, but it is a bit more difficult to say that they were therefore seeing a connection between the phases of the moon, the phases of the annual solar cycle, and the phases of the life cycle. If we have evidence that a particular culture, say the ancient Egyptians, did mark the solstices and equinoxs, that is only part of the evidence we need. Later, we will also look at the holidays that were observed in each culture, when they were celebrated, and what the meaning of those holidays were.

If we find that a culture celebrated a particular holiday at a particular time of the year, such as new life in the spring or the promise of reincarnation at the winter solstice, then that adds the additional evidence needed. Then we have some validation of why they were marking these phases of the sun, and what it meant to them. If there is a concordance with the Wheel of Time, and this occurs with multiple holidays, then we can say that the evidence is beyond coincidence. In fact, even if there is only evidence of the use of a lunisolar calendar, that alone is evidence of the use of a Wheel of Time, because why else would they need such a calendar if not to find a concordance between solar and lunar phases?

First we will list monuments that we found from around the world that mark the phases of the solar year. And, as you will see, this is a universal phenomenon, found in cultures all over the globe and throughout prehistory. We will start with those cultures that are the next closest to Europe, the cultures around the Mediterranean.

THE MNAJDRA TEMPLE

There are many ancient temples on the island of Malta. One of the largest and best known is Ħagar Qim.[1] It is a vast complex with incredibly large heavy stones, weighing up to 57 tons. And, just as we've seen at Stonehenge and other

Site: Mnajdra Temple

Location: Malta

Date: 3,100 - 3600 BCE

Site Description: Part of a very large temple complex, there is an altar and two monoliths on either side. They are alighne with the door to indicate the Solstices and Equinoxes

Points on the Wheel: Both Solstices and both Equinoxes.

stone monuments, it is quite old, dated to over 5000 years ago, but the stonework here is far more advanced than at other sites. These are not just standing stones. These are elaborately built temples with many chambers and altars within them.

About 500 meters away from the main temple complex at Ħagar Qim is another temple, the Mnajdra.[2] It is dated to about the same time period, perhaps as much as 5600 years old. It is similar in many features but what makes it unique is that it appears to be a solar observatory. It is a wide room, with a short and narrow hallway at the entrance. In the back of the room is an altar perfectly aligned with the entrance. The altar is flanked by large monoliths on either side.

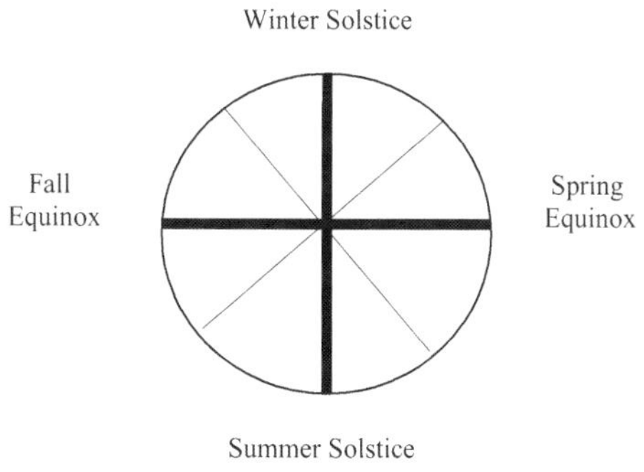

On the equinox, the sun is perfectly aligned so that the rays of the sun go straight through the entrance and illuminate the altar. Then as the sun arrives at the winter solstice, the rays of the sun only illuminate the megalith to the right of the altar. On the summer solstice, the rays only illuminate the left megalith. This is one of the most beautiful and elegant of the monuments we've examined so far. Interestingly, the megaliths, also known as *orthostats,* at either side of the alter are decorated with small shallow holes or mortars, similar to the cupping or morteros that we've seen at other monuments, such as the Beltany Stone in Ireland.

KOKINO OBSERVATORY

Site: Kokino Observatory

Location: Macedonia

Date: 2,000 BCE

Site Description: There are two rows of monoliths, two on top and four on the bottom, which creates multiple alignments.

Points on the Wheel: Winter and Summer Solstices and both Equinoxes.

The Kokino is a megalithic observatory in modern day Greece.[3] It dates to about 4000 years ago, and it too marks all four of the sun's cardinal points of the annual solar cycle, the equinoxes and both solstices. This arrangement of stones is actually similar conceptually to the Mnajdra. The only difference is that the condition of the Kokino monument is so decrepit you would not even know it was human made unless someone told you.

On the very top of a mountain, there are two rows of stones, an upper level and a lower level. In front of that is a stone platform where people stand. There is a gap in the middle of the upper stones that allows the sun's rays to pass.

Below it are 4 stones, mistakenly called thrones. When you are standing below the stones on the platform, at the winter solstice, the sun illuminates the very end of the stones to the far left. At the equinoxes the rays are directed straight in the middle of the 4 stones. And, at summer solstice, the sun's rays reach the far right of the stones. So, as we've seen at Mnajdra, the movement of the sun's rays over the course of a year are contained within the span of these four stones, as shown in the figure below. And, as we'll see later, this is one of the most common types of solar observatories worldwide.

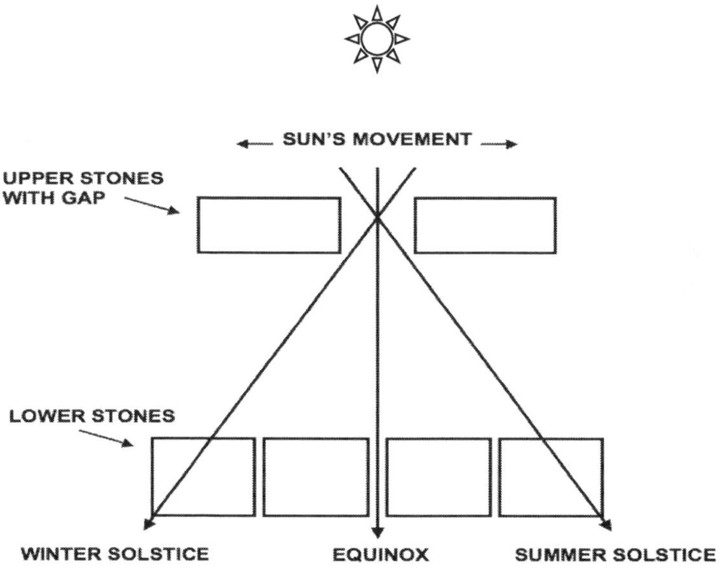

Kokino Observatory

CARAHUNGE OBSERVATORY

Site: Carahunge Observatory

Location: Armenia

Date: 2,000-5,500 BCE

Site Description: 223 standing stones, 80 of which contain small holes. The holes were used for alignments, like a surveyor's transit.

Points on the Wheel: Winter and Summer Solstices and both Equinoxes.

Near the town of Sisian, in the Syunik Province of Armenia, is another primitive stone monolith, known locally as Zorats Karer in Armenian, but better known as Carahunge (also spelled Karahunj, or Qarahunj), the Armenian Stonehenge.[4] This is an interesting site, because it not only is a solar observatory that marks the equinox and the two solstices, but it also marks the phases of the moon as well.

This site is similar to countless other ancient sites of standing stones around Europe. The age of this site is unknown but, like many similar sites, it is believed to be a middle Bronze Age site, approximately 4000 years old, but it has been suggested that it may be as much as 7,500 years old. It is large, with 223 menhirs, or standing stones, some weighing as much as 10 tons. And, there are some interesting features of this site that make it unique.

About 80 of the menhirs contain a small circular hole. In about 37 of these stones that remain standing, it appears that the holes were used for astronomical alignments. Like a transit, a device used by surveyors, it makes precise alignments possible. It appears that 17 of the stones are aligned with the sunrise or sunset of the winter solstice, summer solstice, and equinoxes, and there are also 14 stones that are aligned with the lunar extremes. This is important because it indicates that this was not just a solar observatory, but one that was used for mapping a lunisolar calendar.

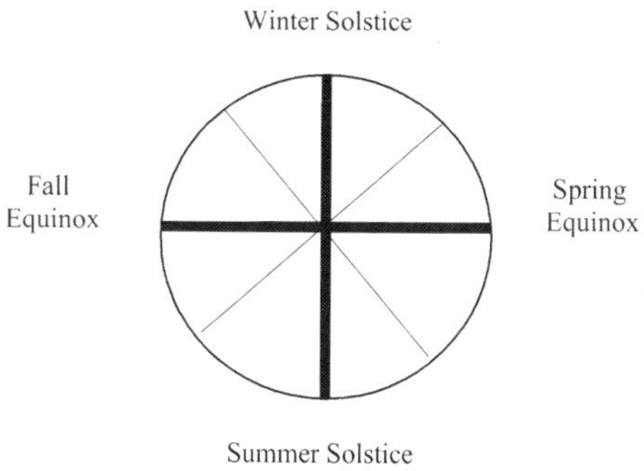

There are two other interesting features of this site. First the name Carahunge means "speaking stones" in Armenian. It is believed that this is because of the many holes in the stones, which whistle when the wind blows. Also there are very elaborate and strange carvings on many of the stones. One of these carvings depicts two small figures, frail like a child, but with a large head and a very small chin. It has large almond-shaped eyes. They look like what we would clearly recognize today as a typical grey alien. This has, of course, fueled speculation by ancient astronaut theorists, such as Erich von Däniken.[5] But, that is for another book.

The Great Pyramid of Giza, and the Sphinx

THE GREAT PYRAMID OF GIZA

Site: The Great Pyramid

Location: Giza, Egypt

Date: 2,560 BCE

Site Description: The Largest pyramid on Earth. Each side is subtly concave, casting a half shadow on the North and South faces on the Equinoxes.

Points on the Wheel: Both Equinoxes.

At last, we come to the great grand-daddy of all ancient monuments, the Great Pyramid of Giza.[6] This is one of the most extraordinary of all ancient monuments. For that matter, it is extraordinary for any modern standards in the world today.

The pyramid is thought to have around 2.3 million blocks, that weigh anywhere from 2 tons to as much as 70 tons each, yet the pyramid appears to make no indentation in the sand, as if weightless. The base is over a half million square feet in size. The temperature inside the pyramid is constant, and just happens to be the mean temperature of the planet Earth, at 68°F. The outside of the pyramid was covered in 144,000 limestone casing stones, polished to 1/100th of an inch, each weighing about 15 tons.

There are many, many more amazing features of the Great Pyramid, such as the mathematical relationship between Pi and Phi is expressed in the basic proportions of the pyramid. The curvature (unseen to the naked eye) designed into the faces of the pyramid perfectly matches the radius of the Earth. The descending passage was aligned with the North Star, over 4,000 years ago, when built.

There are alignments with stars in the constellation Orion, and so on. But, for our study, there is one feature that is more important than any other. The structure is aligned with true north, and is one of the most accurately aligned structures on Earth. It is only .05 of one degree off of true north.

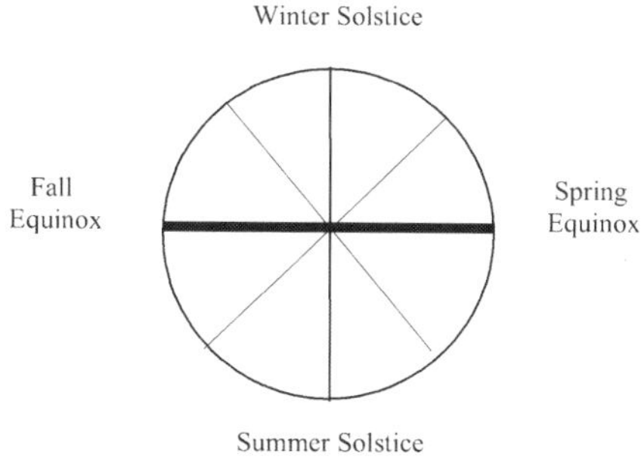

It is actually because of its alignment that it is able to mark the spring and autumn equinox. You see the Great Pyramid is different than the other pyramids because it is actually an 8 sided pyramid. Each face of the apparently 4-sided pyramid is actually concave, with two sides and a dividing line going right up the center of each face. At both the sunrise and sunset of each equinox, one half of the pyramid's face appears to be in shadow while the other half is illuminated (see diagram below). This occurs on both the North and South Faces, but only on the equinox.

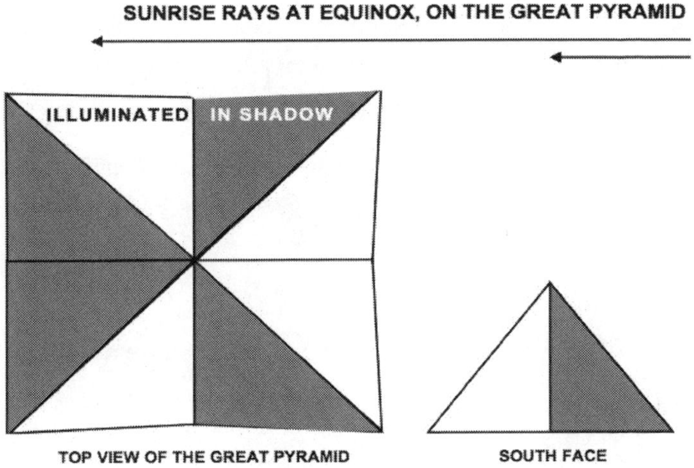

Ironically this effect is so subtle that it can only be seen clearly at a great distance, such as from space, or from an aerial view. This concave 8-sided shape went unnoticed for centuries until the age of aviation. It was in 1940 when a British pilot was flying over the Great Pyramid, that it was first discovered. But, in truth it could be seen from Cairo, if you looked at it on the sunrise of the equinox. Because of its height, the top of the pyramid could probably be seen from as far away as Israel.

Abu Simbel Monument

ABU SIMBEL

Site: Abu Simbel

Location: Egypt

Date: 1,300 BCE

Site Description: Similar to the Mound of Hostages in Ireland, this giant temple has an opening which allows the Sun's rays to enter, illuminating sculptures on exactly two lunar months before and after the Winter Solstice.

Points on the Wheel: Exactly two months before and after Winter Solstice.

There is another monument in Egypt that is quite interesting, and that is the temple of Abu Simbel.[7] It consists of two massive rock temples, located in southern Egypt near the Sudan border. The temples were carved out of the mountainside during the reign of Pharaoh Ramesses II, about 3,300 years ago. The entire temple was taken apart and moved in 1968, when they flooded the valley by the Aswan Dam, to create Lake Nasser. Prior to its relocation, however, there was an interesting alignment noted here.

It is interesting because it is one of the few monuments outside of the British Isles that appears to mark cross-quarter days on a lunisolar calendar. Well, sort of. It is unique in that it marks two days that are clearly on the wheel of time, if not exactly the same days acknowledged by the ancient Britons. On exactly 60 days (2 lunar cycles) before and 60 days after the winter solstice, the Sun's rays penetrate the dark depths of the temple and illuminate the back wall, and the sculptures positioned there.

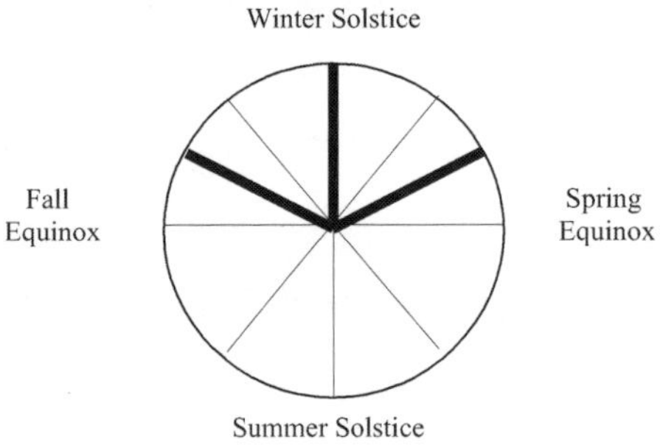

Remember that this is very similar to burial mounds found in Ireland that mark Samhain and Imbolc, approximately November 1st, and February 1st. The difference is that this monument marks October 21st, and February 21st.

This does not appear to be a random coincidence. These dates are allegedly the king's birthday and coronation day. October 21st was also the helical rising of the star Sirius (Sothis) and the period of October through February marks the beginning and end of the annual agricultural season of planting, growing, and harvesting crops in the Nile Valley, due to the seasonal flooding of the Nile. Another feature that does not appear to be random is that the only sculpture that is never illuminated by the Sun in the temple is that of Ptah, the god of the Underworld, which is perpetually in darkness.

Such a unique, non-random, lighting event, which does not occur on a solstice or equinox, is further evidence of some rudimentary understanding and observance of the Wheel of Time. It is, in fact, almost exactly what we observe in burial mounds in Ireland. The only difference is that for them it was the growing season in the Nile Valley. But, why did they choose to mark these points of the year, which are exactly 60 days before and after the winter Solstice? Why not the midpoint between the equinox and solstice? It could be that it fit more precisely with the growing season. We may never know for sure, but it suggests that they were taking into account the lunar cycle. They may have preferred to include 2 whole lunar cycles before the solstice, as opposed to one and a half lunar cycles, which may have seemed more arbitrary to them.

NABTA PLAYA

Site: Nabta Playa

Location: Western Egypt

Date: 4,500-6,100 BCE

Site Description: A giant ring of standing stones, with concentric rings, which align with the Summer Solstice sunrise, and other star alignments.

Points on the Wheel: Summer Solstice

Dubbed the Egyptian Stonehenge, Nabta Playa is located about a little over 60 miles west of Abu Simbel. It is far more primitive than the other monuments in Egypt we've examined, but that is because it is far older. It's believed to be about 6,500 years old, and possibly as much as 8,100 years old. The site was once on the beach of large lake that began filling 11,000 years ago, and finally dried up about 5,000 years ago, due to changing weather patterns and the encroaching sands of the Sahara. The people who built it are likely the same people who settled in the Nile valley about 5,000 years ago.

The site consists of a group of standing stones or menhirs. It is about .8 miles wide and 1.8 miles long. It has 10 slabs, 9 feet high, 30 rock-lined ovals, nine burial sites for cows, each covered in 50 rocks of about 200 to 300 pounds each, and a "calendar circle" of large standing stones. There are three alignments. One clear alignment is with the summer solstice sunrise, as we might expect. But another interesting alignment is with Orion, or rather where Orion was 7,000 years ago, as well as the stars Sirius, and Dubhe. That's important because it again shows another alignment with the stars, not unlike how the Great Pyramid of Giza and Abu Sibel marked alignments with either Sirius or the constellation Orion respectively. And there are connections between Sirius and Orion in Egyptian mythology as well.

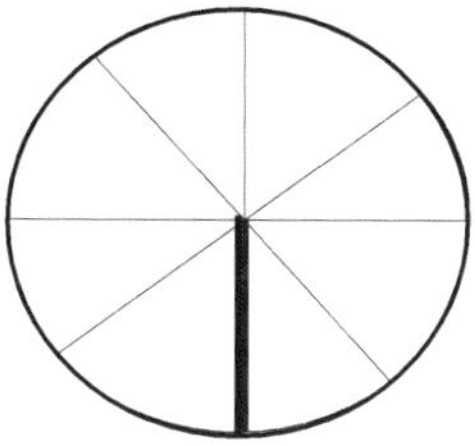

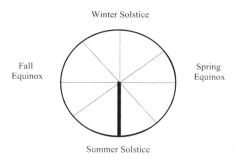

This shows that while using a basic concept of a Wheel of Time, each culture had their own seasons of nature that were important to them on the wheel, and they had specific observations in the night sky that were important to them as well. So the Wheel of Time is more of a general framework, rather than a fixed set of specific days of the year that were observed.

NAMORATUNGA

Site: Namoratunga

Location: Kenya

Date: 2,400 BCE

Site Description: Similar to Nabta Playa, it is a ring of standing stones, with alignments to all Solstices and Equinoxes, and other stellar alignments.

Points on the Wheel: Summer and Winter Solstice and both Equinoxes.

In modern day northwestern Kenya, there is a collection of 19 basalt pillars, or menhirs, which appear to be arranged in a non-random pattern, aligning with certain stars and constellations. [8] The site marks the annual solar arc, from winter solstice to summer solstice and points in between. Recent carbon dating reveals this site to be 4,400 years old. This shows the prevalence of prehistoric observatories, even in Sub-Saharan Africa.

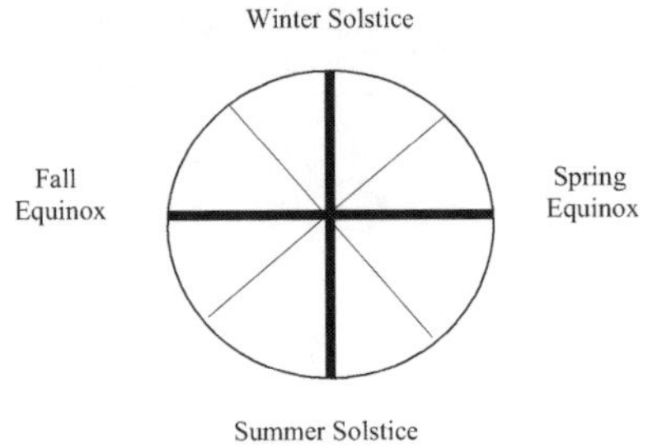

Interestingly the modern-day, local Cushitic people still use the same stars to calculate an accurate calendar. So, it is likely that this practice has been in use since the time that these standing stones were erected. This is important because it is the only evidence of such detailed astronomical knowledge and accurate calendar keeping in this part of the world, from so far back.

EASTER ISLAND

Site: Easter Island

Location: South Pacific

Date: 1,250 CE

Site Description: Stone figures with large heads stand all around the island facing inward. The only figures that face the sea, face the setting sun at the Equinox.

Points on the Wheel: Both Equinoxes.

On this remote island in the South Pacific Ocean, about 2300 miles from Chile, there stands over 880 megaliths, called Moai, carved into figures with large heads, standing in a row around the island, with their backs to the sea.[9] They range in size, the larger ones being over 30 feet tall, and weighing up to 150 tons.

Although most of the Moai are located at the beach, there are 7 Moai at Ahu Akivi and they face the setting Sun on the Equinox. Interestingly, these are the only Moai that face the sea. There is also a solstice alignment with the Moai at Tongariki. Further, we know from ethnographic research that they did have accurate knowledge of the stars and celestial cycles.

They tracked Vega, Canopus, Antares and many other stars, but they were especially interested in the stars they called Matariki (Pleiades) and, like the Egyptians, Tautoru (Orion's belt) as well as Sirius. We know that they observed the heliacal rising of these stars. The heliacal rising of a star occurs annually when it first becomes visible above the eastern horizon for a brief moment just before sunrise. And, we know that the heliacal rising of Matariki, followed by Tautoru marked the beginning of the year, while it's disappearance from the sky in April, marked the end of the fishing season.[10]

We really know very little about their ancient culture and the meaning of the seasons for them. There are hieroglyphic writings that explain these monuments and their meaning, but they have never been able to translate them. All we can say for certain is that they too carefully tracked the movements of the sun, moon, and stars, all of which helped them to predict and observe the times of the year that were important for them, on their own Wheel of Time.

WURDU YOUANG

Site: Wurdu Youang

Location: Mount Rothwell, Victoria, Australia

Date: Approx. 9,000 BCE

Site Description: Over 100 stones, arranged in a tear-drop shape, aligns with the setting sun on the Solstices and Equinoxes.

Points on the Wheel: Summer and Winter Solstice and both Equinoxes.

Not to be left out, Australia has one of the more interesting solar observatories in that part of the world. At Mount Rothwell, in the vicinity of Little River, Victoria, there is a stone monument constructed by the Australian Aboriginal people, that is estimated that it was constructed in around 9000 BCE, making it about 11,000 years old, and one of the oldest solar observatories in the world.

The monument is a collection of over 100 basalt stones ranging anywhere from 8 inches to 3 feet high. The purpose may be ceremonial, but clearly the site marks all three points in the annual solar cycle. It marks the winter solstice, the summer solstice and the equinoxes. The site accomplishes this feat with an extreme simplicity and economy of design.

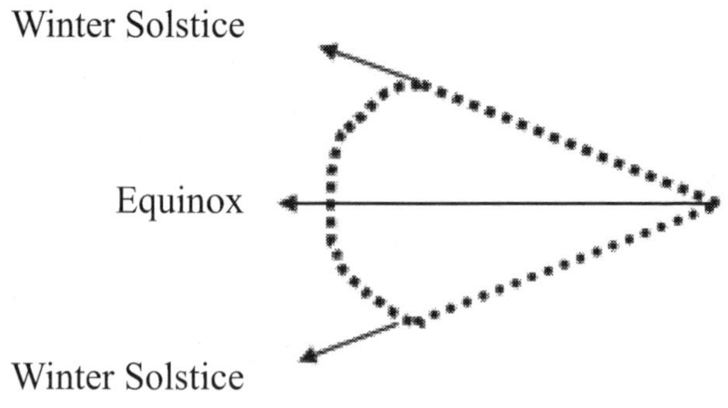

They simply laid out two rows of stones diverging from a single point. One line of stones points to the sunset on the winter solstice. The other line of stones points to the sunset on the summer solstice. Then there is an arc, which connects the two divergent lines of stones with each other. The midpoint of that arc points to the equinoxes.

TAOSI OBSERVATORY

Site: Taosi Observatory

Location: Shanxi, China

Date: Approx. 2,100 BCE

Site Description: A platform where 13 monoliths, each 13 ft. high, once stood. From the center you can see the sun rising through the 12 gaps between the stones.

Points on the Wheel: All points on the wheel.

As we already discussed in the last chapter, we know that the Chinese have long used a lunisolar calendar, called the Han Calendar, and that is how they determine the Chinese New Year. So, it should not be surprising that there are some ancient solar observatories in China. One of the most famous of these is the Taosi Observatory in the Shanxi province of China.[11] Perhaps not coincidentally, it is also dated to about 4,100 years old, a very similar date as many of the observatories we've studied so far from around the world (See the Appendix for more about this interesting phenomenon).

This puts the date of the observatory to the very beginning of the first dynasty of China. Taosi was a walled city, one of the largest in prehistoric China. But, it was not until 2003 that they excavated the observatory, found within the walled city. According to ancient documents, we know that the Chinese leader King Yao had an official astronomer as early as 4,100 years ago, but it's exciting to actually unearth an observatory from that time period. This is quite possibly the observatory of King Yao himself.[12]

The observatory consists of a large platform where a semi-circle of 13 standing stones, measuring about 13 feet tall, once stood. From a fixed point in the center of the platform, one can see the rising sun on the horizon through 12 gaps in the 13 stones. This is very much like similar sites found in prehistoric Scotland and elsewhere. The numbers 12 and 13 are not coincidental. Because they had a lunisolar calendar, they were simultaneously tracking the moon and sun. And, there are between 12 and 13 lunar phases each year. By dividing the year into 12 moons or months, they were able to see which full moon or new moon was closest to the desired phase of the sun, as we have shown in previous chapters.

These 12 gaps do indeed correspond to specific times of the year such as the winter solstice, summer solstice known as the Duanwu Festival, the autumn equinox,

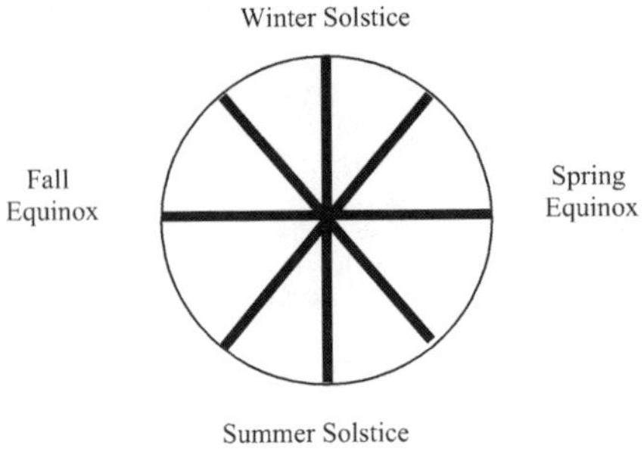

the vernal equinox, and Imbolc or the Chinese New Year.[13]

What is most important here for our study is that this site clearly supports our thesis that the Wheel of Time was being used by the ancient Chinese. This is because, as we've already shown, the ancient Chinese celebrated holidays such as the New Year on days that marked a concordance of the lunar and solar phases, as well as phases of life reflected in nature and agriculture.

Their new year was on a new moon, closest to the midpoint between the midwinter solstice (death) and the vernal equinox (birth), around February 1st, which is also at a time when new, as yet un-open, buds start to form on the vines and trees. They saw this as the conception, or very beginning of the new year. Seeing a concordance between the cycles of the Sun, Moon, and Earth is the very definition of the Wheel of Time (as shown below).

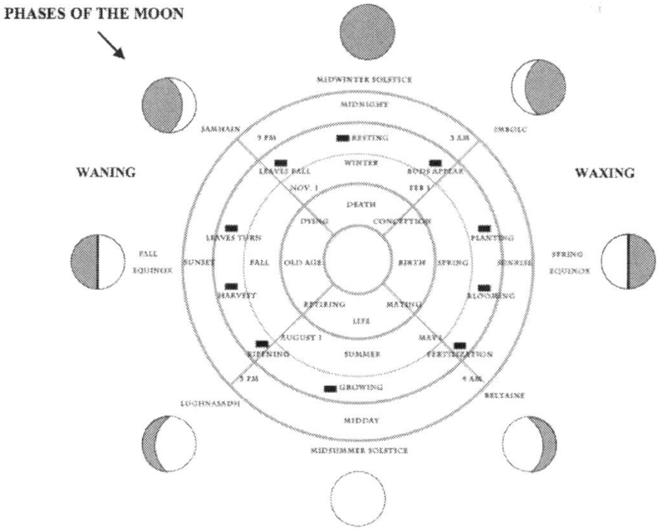

Figure 6

DHOLAVIRA OBSERVATORY

Site: Dholavira Observatory

Location: Bhachau, India

Date: 2,650 BCE

Site Description: This is a builting within a large ancient city, containing two separate observatories, used to track the Sun, Moon, and stars.

Points on the Wheel: All points on the wheel.

The Harappan civilization of the Indus Valley, on the border of India and Pakistan, has long been known as one of the oldest civilizations in the world.[14] The Harappan civilization had very advanced ancient cities such as Mohenjo Daro, with indoor plumbing, sewers, and what appears to be modern urban planning, some 4,500 years ago. Further, we have found over 1500 separate archaeological sites belonging to the Harappan civilization. So it should not be surprising that they also had a solar observatory, but until recently one had not been discovered. Finally, in 2012 archaeologists excavated the first Harrapan observatory ever discovered, at the ancient city of Dholavira, in Bhachau, in the district of Gujarat, India. [15]

The site is part of a larger building, with two circular rooms being used for celestial observations. This is not a remarkable site by itself, and it is consistent with other sites we've seen around the world, but it is the first we've found from that date in India. This site is also important because the oldest writing in India, the Vedic Scriptures, more than 3500 years old, contain astronomical tables, with precise observations and predictions of celestial phenomena. So, we knew that they observed the Sun, Moon, and stars, but until now we simply had no archaeological evidence of observatories. Later in the book, we will explore the Vedic Scriptures more in depth, revealing a very advanced science of astronomy, not rivaled until the 18th Century, in Europe.

So far, we have found similar monuments and observatories on almost every part of the world: Europe, Africa, Asia, the South Pacific, and even India. But, by far one of the greatest concentrations of solar observatories outside of Europe and the British Isles is in the Americas. So, we've saved that continent for last.

MACHU PICCHU

Site: Machu Picchu

Location: Near Cusco, Peru

Date: Unknown

Site Description: There are two solar alignments within the ancient mountain-top city. One is a tower marking the Summer Solstice, and one is a cave, marking the Winter Solstice.

Points on the Wheel: Summer and Winter Solstice

Machu Picchu is probably one of the most famous archaeological sites in the world, next to Stonehenge and the Pyramids of Egypt. So, it should be no surprise that we find ancient observatories there as well.[16]

At Machu Picchu we find the Torreón, which was originally thought to be a sentry tower, but we now know that it was a solar observatory which marks the passage of the sun throughout the summer months, from May 1st through August 1st, and specifically marks the summer solstice.[17] That alone is very interesting because it suggests that the Incas may have been observing the cross-quarter days of Beltaine (May 1st) and Lugnasad (August 1st). What is more interesting is the discovery of a new site, Intimachay, the companion site to the Torreón. Remember that at Stonehenge we found there was a temple of life and a temple of death, celebrated respectively on the winter and summer solstices, Machu Picchu appears to have a similar arrangement.

The Torreón is clearly a structure that served as part of the living community, along with residential and sacred buildings. And, it marks the sun during the summer months, and specifically the summer solstice, which is the peak of life on the Wheel of Time. Intimachay, on the other hand, is a cave, high above the city, not near the village residences, and may have been used as a burial chamber. Not coincidentally, it marks the winter solstice, the peak of the season of death on the Wheel of Time. The narrow opening to the cave only admits the sun's rays deep into the cave for a very brief period time before, during, and after the winter solstice.

This is uncanny, as it precisely echoes themes and structures found at Stonehenge, literally on the other side of the world. This is a clear indication that the ancient Incas not only tracked the sun in order to mark the solstices or other holy days, but that they had a schematic concept of the seasons and their meanings, that is precisely what we see in the British Isles and elsewhere. It appears that they too were using the Wheel of Time.

There is one inconsistency here, and that is the

age of the monument. We don't really know how old it is. Machu Picchu is made of stone, and the date that the stones were laid cannot be radio-carbon dated. We can only date organic matter found there, and that dates to the Inca civilization, about 550 years ago. But does that mean that it was built 550 years ago, or just that it was last inhabited 550 years ago? It could have been inhabited off and on for thousands of years, and finally abandoned 550 years ago. We just don't know.

Many researchers reject the idea that it was built 550 years ago because of the strange stone-working techniques that were used there. It seems far more advanced than the Incan culture that existed at that time. Suffice it to say that the stonework at Machu Picchu is one of the most interesting archaeological finds in the world.

The age of the site is not so important, except that it is not only inconsistent with the date of other observatories we've seen, but it's even inconsistent with the rest of Mesoamerican and South American archaeology and archaeo-astronomy. For instance, the famed Mayan calendar was so advanced that it measured the calendar year to 365.245 days long, and enabled them to predict lunar and solar eclipses, and transits of Venus, to the day, thousands of years in the future. But the Mayan calendar wasn't really created by the Mayans, whose culture began to reach its peak about 1700 years ago. It was created by the Olmec culture that preceded them. And, we know that the Olmec culture began somewhere between 3,200 and 4,500 years ago. This is much more consistent with the dates of other similar sites that we've explored from around the world.

When we combine the above inconsistencies with the architecture of Machu Piccu, which employed stone-working techniques that were far more advanced than anything we have today, it suggests that perhaps these amazing stone structures were built some other time, by some other civilization. But, exactly when and by whom we may never know.

CHANKILLO, PERU

Site: Chankillo

Location: Ancash, Peru

Date: 300 BCE

Site Description: A row of 13 towers, spread out over 1000 ft. There are two observation points, to the east and west, to observe the rising and setting sun between the gaps.

Points on the Wheel: All Points.

There is another site in Peru that is of some interest because we know that it is significantly more than 500 years old. Chankillo is an ancient observatory in the Peruvian desert, and it dates to approximately 2,300 years ago.[18] The site is about 500 miles from Machu Picchu, and only about 60 miles from Chavín de Huantár, which is known to be more than 2,200 years old. The site is similar to what we saw at Taosi in China. It contains 13 towers in a long row, about 1000 feet in length, running from north to south. Each tower is about 1000 square feet in size.

They have found two different vantage points, one

to the east and one to the west, each about 750 feet from the towers. From these points they would have seen both the sunset and sunrise between the 12 gaps in the towers. The observations precisely span the entire solar arc, from winter solstice to summer solstice, and everything in between.

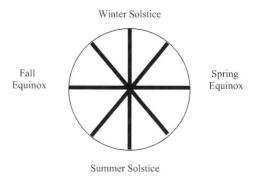

Again, just as in Neolithic Scotland and China, the builders chose to place exactly 13 towers with 12 gaps, to correspond to the 12+ moons of the year. And, we can only assume that it was for precisely the same reason, to construct a lunisolar calendar, and observe certain lunisolar days that were significant for them. Just looking at this archaeological site, we cannot say what dates were most meaningful to them or what the meaning of a given day was. We can only say that it is consistent with other cultures that kept a lunisolar calendar. But, based upon what we have already seen at Machu Picchu, just a few hundred miles away, it is reasonable to conclude that they were observing their own version of the Wheel of Time, as a cosmological model for understanding the cycles of the Sun, Moon, the seasons and the lifecycle.

CHICHEN ITZA

Site: Chichen Itza

Location: Yucatan, Mexico

Date: 600 CE

Site Description: The ancient city contains a large step pyramid and an observatory. The observatory contained 28 sight lines to track the cycles of the Sun, planets and stars.

Points on the Wheel: All Solstices and Equinoxes.

If you followed news stories back in 2012 about the Mayan Prophecy of Doom, allegedly predicting the end of the world on December 21st 2012, then you might have heard of the temple of Kukulkan. This is a rather large and beautiful pyramid in the ancient Mayan city of Chichen Itza. The reason why it was famous in connection to 2012 is that, in certain interpretations of ancient texts, it was predicted that the god Kukulkan would return to Earth to Chichen Itza, and to the temple that bears his name, on the last day on Earth (12/21/2012).

Many people took this prophecy quite seriously. In the years leading up to 2012, I actually wrote a book on the 2012 Mayan prophecies and, as I explained in my book, the prophecies were misunderstood and we were in no real danger.[19]

As luck would have it, I was right. The date simply marked the end of the 4th Age and the beginning of the 5th Age, in Mayan cosmology. But, in doing research for that book, I was amazed by the brilliance and advanced knowledge of the Mayan culture.

Most of the thousands of books that they had created were destroyed, burned by misguided missionaries, thinking that the writings were the work of the devil. Only a handful of books survived, known as the Mayan Codecies. From what we can tell from those few books, theirs was a highly advanced society. Their greatest accomplishments were in the fields of mathematics, science, and astronomy. In those areas, they were far more advanced than the Europeans at that time, hundreds of years more advanced. So, it is no surprise that they too had observatories.

There are two different structures in Chichen Itza that acted as markers for the phases of the Sun. One such very flamboyant marker was the temple of Kukulkan, also known as El Castillo.[20] This was a step pyramid, designed and built like many other step pyramids in the Mayan civilization. But it had one interesting feature. Every equinox, the setting sun would cast a rather unique shadow on the side wall of the central staircase on the pyramid.

The stepped pyramid would cast a zig-zag shadow, that appeared to look like a serpent crawling on the pyamid as the sun set. At the foot of the wall, which displayed the moving serpent image, was a giant stone carved into the shape of a serpent's head, which completed the illusion. Of course, this only happened on the equinox. They had many observatories, but Kukulkan was a most unusual and striking solar equinox marker. It is all the more meaningful, as Kukulkan was a serpent god.

Chichen Itza was also home to one of the most

elaborate Mayan observatories. The observatory called El Caracol is one of the more remarkable structures in Chichen Itza. [21] Unfortunately, the building is now in ruins, but from what we can tell it was quite amazing. It appears to have been a round observatory and, from what we can tell, it looked very much like modern observatories. But, there was no telescope inside, as far as we know. Instead, the Mayan building had openings all around the building creating unique sight lines, when viewed from the center of the building.

We have found 20 such sight lines for astronomical events, and given their texts we believe that when the building was intact there were another 8 such alignments. The astronomical events marked by the observatory include the solar equinoxes and solstices, as you might expect, but also other unusual observations.

For instance, they marked the cycles of Venus, and they knew that 5 Venus cycles would equal 8 solar cycles, and they marked the northern most point of the Venus cycle, and the southern-most point in the Venus cycle. Because of this they could accurately predict the solar transits of Venus, which occurs in a pattern that repeats only once every 243 years. They predicted the transit of Venus that occurred in 2012, which lasted over 6 hours. And, they predicted each and every transit for the next 3,000 years. They also tracked Mercury and the other planets as well as certain stars, such as Sirius and Orion's belt.

THE MAYAN E-GROUP

Sites: Tikal, Uaxactun, Cerros, Caracol, and many others.

Location: Mexico, Guatemala, and Belize

Date: 1000 BCE-900 CE

Site Description: The E-Group is a style of architecture that is found in many ancient Maya cities throughout Mesoamerica. Each city contains buildings with built-in alignments to the Sun.

Points on the Wheel: All Solstices and Equinoxes.

Perhaps more incredible than the Observatory at Chichen Itza, is that each and every city of a certain size, in the Mayan civilization, had a solar observatory to mark the solar arc, both the solstices and the equinoxes. The buildings are called E-Groups, and we've found them all over the Mayan empire.[22] These date all the way back to the Preclassic period, approximately 3000 years ago.[23]

Some of the more well-known of these cities are Tikal, Uaxactun, Caracol, and Cerros, but there are many more. In fact, there are 60 such cities discovered so far.

In an E-Group, there are four buildings: one observation platform on a pyramid, and three buildings in a row on top of a rectangular platform. They sit opposite each other in the town square (see diagram below). From the observation platform you can see that the winter solstice sun rises over the peak of the building to the south. Then, at the equinox the sun rises over the peak of the middle building. And on the summer solstice, the sun rises over the building to the north.

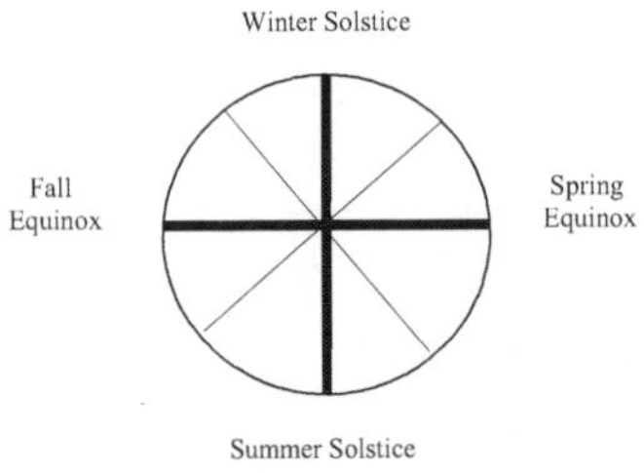

In this way a solar observatory was built into every Mayan city's town square, though perhaps the most learned astronomers worked at the great star observatories in the larger cities, such as the one in Chichen Itza.

But, this gives us some idea of how important these special days of the year were to the Mayan people. If it were a minor astronomical observation, it would have been confined to observatories, not a major feature of every town square. Important public rituals were probably performed on these days, in the town square where all could see.

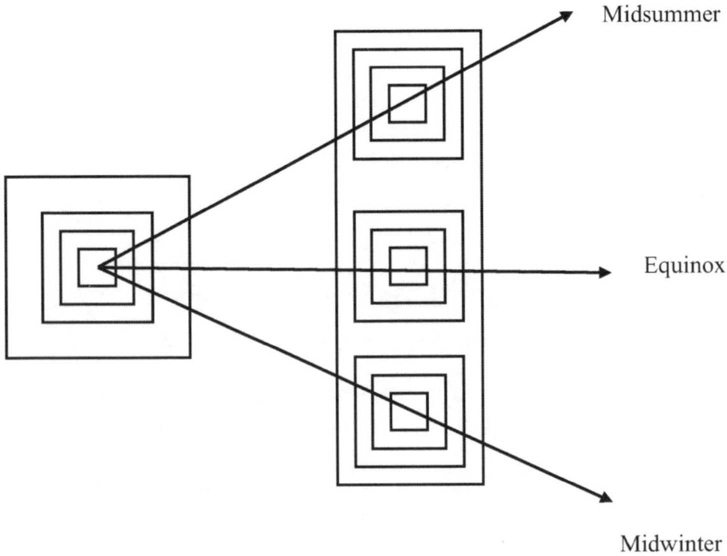

SUMMARY

There are many other interesting sites from around the world, too many to mention all of them. We have only just highlighted the most impressive, or most famous among them. Many are even more spectacular but they just have not been studied well enough, or the archaeo-astronomy research has not been conducted to see if the sites are indeed ancient observatories or solar markers.

One such site is Túcume, along the northern coast of Peru. It is a truly amazing site with 26 major pyramids and burial mounds, and another 250 smaller pyramids, made of brick. This is clearly the site of a very large city in the distant past. It's not clear how old it is but it could be as much as 1,200 years old or more. And, it is rumored to contain solar alignments similar to the Mayan pyramid E-Groups to the north. Unfortunately, there has been no solid research done on the solar alignments at Túcume as yet. And this is only one of many fascinating sites from around the world, awaiting further research to unlock their mysteries.

There are many sites that are exclusively lunar markers, marking the lunar standstill, every 18.6 years, such as the well of Santa Cristina on the island of Sardinia, which is over 3000 years old. Other sites, appear to primarily mark the rising or setting of certain stars or constellations. And there are still other sites that simply have not yet been studied enough. For instance, preliminary study of

Göbekli Tepe, in Turkey, estimated to be 11,600 years old, indicates that it may have been used for the celebration of the spring equinox, though more research is required.[24]

In this chapter, we've seen many variations on the type of phenomenon seen at Stonehenge and the British Isles. Using stones with precise alignments, solar and lunar alignments were created to mark the solstices, the equinoxes, and the phases of the moon. Additionally, they also sometimes marked the cross-quarter days, or some other point in the annual calendar that was special to them. Most, if not all, of these cultures were apparently keeping a lunisolar calendar, revealing a perceived interconnection between the phases of the Sun and Moon.

What is really amazing is that these structures were built all over the world, in Europe, the Mediterranean, the Middle East, Sub-Saharan Africa, China, the South-Pacific, and South America. Amazingly, we see the exact same design of 13 towers or standing stones, with 12 openings to mark the solstices and equinoxes and the 12 moons of the year in Scotland, Africa, China, and South America. And, what is even more astounding is that, for the most part, they all date to around the same period in history, the late Neolithic and early Bronze Age. Some, such as Wurdi Youang in Australia, date all the way back to the dawn of the Neolithic Age.

As impressive as this data base of archaeological evidence may be, we are still not done yet. The last continent is North America, which we will explore in the next chapter. As we shall see, the United States contains as many or more solar markers than any other place on Earth. And, they are as varied and interesting as any that we've looked at so far.

CHAPTER 5

EXCAVATING ANCIENT OBSERVATORIES OF NORTH AMERICA

We now come to North America, the final continent we will study. And, one might say we saved the best for last. The ancient solar observatories built by Native Americans are among the oldest and most elegant in all the world. Ironically, they are the least well known. And, for whatever reason, mainstream archaeologists have been late in recognizing and validating the existence and purpose of these sites. In fact, more solar observatories are being excavated all the time, but it has been a struggle to gain acceptance among American archaeologists.

In 1996, the renowned archaeologist David S. Whitley expressed his skepticism: "Some researchers believe rock art sites were solstice observatories,… Popularity aside, the support for this interpretation is at best equivocal." He goes on to say that "the enthusiasm of rock art researchers to relate the few instances of seemingly nonrandom lighting events to the solstice overwhelms their scientific objectivity. The effort of reaching a remote site before dawn in the middle of winter to watch the sunrise can lead people to interpret meaning into their observations when none exists."[1]

Whitley then cites ethnographic evidence for both solar observatories and The Wheel of Time apparently without even realizing it. He writes that "the winter solstice was an important ritual period for them and they knew when to expect it by tracking the sun. …For example, one of their most important and most elaborate religious rituals – the Mourning Ceremony – was conducted during the (winter) solstice; but its purpose was to commemorate the dead, not to observe the solstice."

I think Dr. Whitley, like most archaeologists, is overlooking a couple main points here. First, he acknowledges that they tracked the sun to predict the solstice, but how did they track the sun if they did not have solar markers to do so? It would be impossible to predict the very day of the solstice without fixed markers or observatories, to track the sun's movement. And each tribe would need their own markers. Otherwise, how would each tribe know the date of the Solstice? They didn't have almanacs. So, solar observatories must have been as common as grinding stones among the tribes. There must have been hundreds, even thousands, of such observatories throughout North America.

Secondly, he mentions the Mourning Ceremony at the winter solstice but completely misses the connection between the two; their ritual for the dead was not held at just any old time. It wasn't held in the springtime or in the middle of summer. No, it was held at the peak of the season of death. Here you see a clear connection between the type of ceremony performed and the time of year it is performed, but he, like most archaeologists, fails to see the connection. It's not his fault though, without a detailed knowledge of the Wheel of Time it might be hard to make that connection.

This kind of skepticism has been all too common in the past. Unfortunately, I've often heard this skeptical line of reasoning from scholars. In fact, last year I published an article on what I called *pathological skepticism* in the scientific community, and especially among archaeologists. [2] But, that trend may be changing.

In 2014, I presented some of my original research at a national archaeological conference to professors, researchers, and professional archaeologists. My presentation was on an ancient Native American solar observatory, documented through time-lapse photography.[3] To my surprise, many archaeologists came up to me afterwards and congratulated me on my research, and many said that they too knew of similar monuments in their home state. But, often these archaeologists still do not understand why tracking the sun was so important to ancient people. Nor do they understand the connection between these solar events and their ceremonies, such as the mourning ceremony being held on the winter solstice.

Now that many observatories and solar markers are starting to be recognized for what they are, the only thing missing, the missing link if you will, is the Wheel of Time. This is the one piece of the puzzle that meaningfully connects the archaeology to the ethnography. By understanding what the ancients were thinking, what their beliefs were, and what the seasons meant to them, suddenly a great many mysteries in archaeology are solved.

Now, let's look at a few of the more famous of the Native American observatories. To be clear, in a time before telephones, telegraphs, newspapers, or almanacs, each tribe would have to have their own solar markers to know when the solstice or equinox would occur. And, each tribe only needed to mark one solar event, because they could then count the days to the next solar event. So, just one marker could allow them to recalibrate their calendars and know when to celebrate each ritual on the appropriate day. The following monuments are only a few of what were probably thousands of such monuments and solar markers across North America.

BIG HORN MEDICINE WHEEL OF THE GREAT PLAINS

High atop the Bighorn Mountain Range, in northern Wyoming, there stands a Native American monument known as the Bighorn Medicine Wheel.[4] It is a circle of stones about 80 feet across, with lines of stones forming 28 spokes, which converge on a doughnut-shaped pile of stones, called a cairn,

Sites: Big Horn Medicine Wheel

Location: Big Horn Mtn., Wyoming

Date: 1200 CE

Site Description: A circle of stones, 80 ft. in diameter, it has 28 spokes radiating from the center. They are aligned with both the sunrise and sunset on the Summer Solstice, as well as the Orion constellation..

Points on the Wheel: Summer Solstice

that is 12 feet across and 2 feet high. There are also 6 cairns around the perimeter of the circle

Interestingly, the site is only free of snow for a few months during summer, as it is at an elevation of 9,462 feet, on a desolate and inhospitable spot in the mountains. As such, this was clearly not a village or community used year round. Rather, this was the site of an annual pilgrimage to celebrate a specific ritual or rituals each summer.

Not surprisingly, it is also an observatory, which marks the summer solstice sunrise and sunset, as well as the heliacal rising of certain stars such as Sirius, and Rigel in the constellation Orion. The site was believed to be 300 to 800 years old, but a careful study of the archaeo-astronomy of the site tells us that the alignments are most accurate for the year 1200 CE.

These particular alignments of these stars are important because they also mark the days before and after the solstice, and hence when to come and when to leave the mountain. Keep in mind the area is only free of snow during the summer months, and the heliacal rising of these stars actually marks off the 3 months of summer.

For instance one alignment marks the rising of the star Fomalhaut, which occurs exactly 28 days before the solstice. Aldebaran would rise 2 days after the solstice, while Rigel would rise 28 days after the solstice, and Sirius would rise 28 days after that, marking the end of summer. But, only two of the alignments bisect the circle and cut straight through the center cairn, and that is the solstice sunrise, and the solstice sunset.

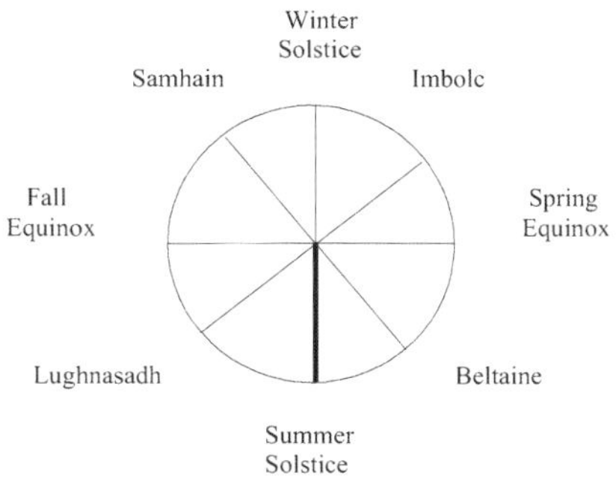

Excavations show that this center cairn is the oldest part of the monument, and that it may well have had a center pole in it originally, casting shadows on the cairns around the rim at solstice sunrise and sunset. This is important because it mirrors the construction of ceremonial buildings such as the Lakota sun dance lodge, which always includes an entrance to the east (rising sun), a central pole and 28 rafters, spread out in a circular fashion like the Bighorn Medicine Wheel.

Many may ask, why 28 spokes to the medicine wheel? The number 28 was sacred to many Indian tribes because it signifies the 28 days of the lunar month. And, notice the alignments that mark the rising of the 3 stars were each 28 days apart. By the way, the lunar month is 29.5 days long, not 28. So, why did they count the days of the month as 28? We know through ethnography that they did not count the 1.5 days that the moon is not visible. They said that the moon "lives" for 28 days. Also 28 is divisible by 4 and 7, and the numbers 4 and 7 were also sacred numbers.

This preoccupation with the number 28, for the days of the lunar month, is exactly what we would expect to find if the culture was not just observing the phases of the solar year, but also the lunar cycle as well, and it is a clear indication that the builders of this site most likely observed a lunisolar calendar, which we have already explained is further confirmation of the use of the Wheel of Time (see chapter 2). But perhaps this site is an aberration. What evidence is there that this was widely practiced among Native American tribes in the area? In fact, there are hundreds of such sites in the Great Plains.[5] And this layout is also replicated in the construction of all of their sacred dance lodges.

Black Elk, a holy man of the Oglala Sioux explains the symbolism of the medicine wheel as follows:

"… in setting up the sun dance lodge, we are really making the universe in a likeness; for, you see, each of the posts around the lodge represents some particular object of creation, so that the whole circle is the entire creation, and the one tree at the center, upon which the twenty-eight poles rest, is Wakan-Tanka, who is the center of everything."[6]

So we see that the wheel was a representation or model of the universe, in which each aspect in the various cycles of heaven and earth, of life, the moon, sun, and stars were all represented in the wheel, and there was a meaningful connection between these different aspects of the wheel.

This is the very same concept found in the Wheel of Time that we discovered in Britain and also seen throughout the world. And, as mentioned earlier, the correlation of celebrating the Mourning Ceremony at the winter solstice, among tribes in the far west, indicates that they attributed precisely the same meaning to the seasons that we see in monuments such as Stonehenge and Machu Picchu.[7]

This indicates that these are not different wheels of time, with different meanings for each culture, but rather it represents very much the same concept across different cultures. In spite of regional differences, each culture seems to align the seasons of the year and the phases of the sun and moon to exactly the same phases of life on earth. This concordance of cycles is precisely the same as in the Wheel of Time, as shown in Chapter 2.

WOODHENGE AT THE CAHOKIA MOUNDS

Sites: Woodhenge, Cahokia Mounds

Location: Collinsville, Illinois

Date: 900 CE

Site Description: A near perfect circle over 400 ft. across, made of 48 upright posts. The alignments mark the sunrise and sunset at all the solstices and equinoxes.

Points on the Wheel: All Solstices and Equinoxes.

Near Collinsville Illinois, just across the Mississippi River from modern-day St. Louis Missouri, lies the ruins of an ancient Native American city, called Cahokia.[8] Dating to approximately 1,100 years ago, there was a vast urban center, with many ceremonial mounds, some over 100 feet high, and an immense solar calendar called Woodhenge. The site is a near-perfect circle, 412 feet across, with 48 upright wooden posts, and each post was as much as 3 feet across, making this a mammoth monument that probably stood for well over 600 years before the site was abandoned.

The site was clearly a solar observatory with four posts marking the cardinal points of north, south, east, and west, two of which mark the sunrise and sunset of the equinoxes. There are posts that align with the sunrise and sunset of the summer solstice, as well as the sunrise and sunset of the winter solstice. What is most interesting here is the presence of 2 ceremonial mounds placed around the perimeter of the circle (numbered Mound 72 and Mound 96 by archaeologists). Actually, there are 3 mounds, because Mound 72 appears to be broken into two sub-mounds (Sub 1 & Sub 2). One mound (Md 72 Sub1) is right under the post that is aligned with the summer solstice sunrise. Another (Md 96) is under the post that marks the winter solstice sunset. This is a very specific but not a unique alignment. We've seen similar patterns at Stonehenge, Machu Picchu and elsewhere.

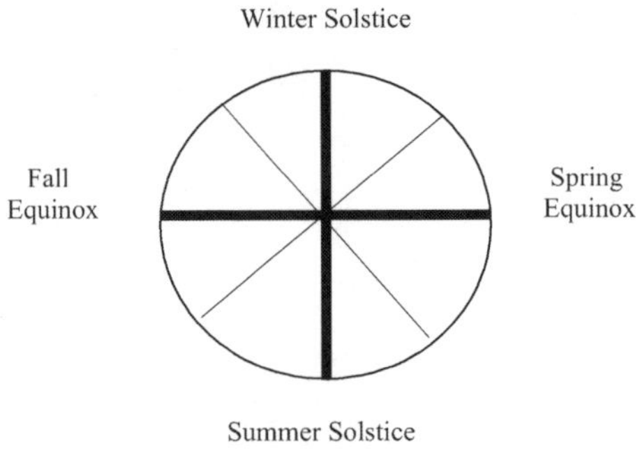

If you will remember the diagram of the Wheel of Time from Chapter 1, figure 5, sunrise represents birth and life, while sunset represents dying and death. Likewise the summer solstice represents life, and winter solstice represents death. So, it is not surprising that, while the Woodhenge marks both the sunrise and sunset at both solstices, it is only the concordance of sunrise on the summer solstice and the sunset on the winter solstice that are marked with ceremonial mounds. So, once again, we see a very specific pattern, consistent with the Wheel of Time. This time, the correlation is between the times of day and the times of the year, and both are correlated with the cycle of life and death.

There is one inconsistency between this site and others. The mound that marks the sunrise on the summer solstice, is also a burial mound with one very special burial of a figure called the "birdman" and 250 other skeletons, all dating to around 1000 years old. What is puzzling about this is that, in other similar sites, they have intentionally marked burial sites with alignments to the sunset, winter solstice, or even Samhain, all symbolic of death. Here, however, they mark a burial mound with sunrise on the summer solstice, symbolic of life.

I think this shows how different cultures can all be using the same cosmological schema but with local variations. For instance, we know that Egyptian mummification and burial practices were to insure life after death for the pharaoh. Perhaps they had a similar idea here, insuring eternal life for the very special and beloved chiefs and shaman who were buried here. The symbolism of the sunrise on the summer solstice might have insured that their souls would always be blessed with eternal life.

One might think that all Native American solar observatories are giant wheels with posts or cairns, located around the perimeter, and a large post or cairn at the center. That is true for these sites, but that is not always the case. These two sites are geographically and culturally connected to each other, as they are on opposite ends of the Great Plains region. But, when we venture off to the Northeast or the Southwest, we find that different tribes came up with different ways to accomplish the exact same goal, to mark the sunrise and/or sunset of the solstices and equinoxes. Case in point, Serpent Mound.

SERPENT MOUND

OHIO

Sites: Serpent Mound

Location: Adams Co., Ohio

Date: 0 CE

Site Description: A giant serpent shaped mound, over 1300 ft. long, contains multiple alignments.

Points on the Wheel: All Solstices and Equinoxes.

In southern Ohio, there is a most remarkable and interesting solar observatory located atop a plateau above the Ohio Bush Creek. This is the famed Serpent Mound.[9]

The site is much older than previous Native American sites we've explored. It is believed to have been built by the Hopewell culture, about 2,000 years ago. The site is a mound, not unlike at Cahokia, but this one is in the shape of a giant serpent 1,348 feet long and three feet high. The form consists of both a serpent figure and an egg, with the serpent swallowing the egg. We are not sure what this means, but this is not the only instance where a serpent swallowing an egg is used at a Native Americans' solar observatory, as we shall see.

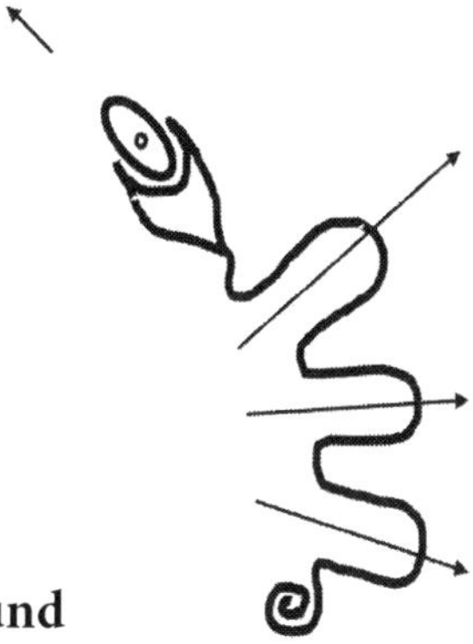

Serpent Mound

Its age is interesting because the Hopewell culture was contemporary with the Classical Mayan civilization. Ironically, the solar alignments of the Serpent Mound are reminiscent of the classic Mayan E-Group architecture. This is because the three dramatic curves in the serpents body each are aligned with the three phases of the sun; summer solstice, equinox, and winter solstice, all aligned with the rising sun. But, there is one more interesting alignment; the head and egg shape are both oriented to point to the summer solstice sunset.

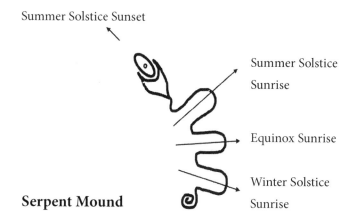

The summer solstice sunrise and sunset, also appear to be a Native American theme, also seen at Bighorn Medicine Wheel. Perhaps this was a major feast of the year, at the apex of the season of life. But, some researchers have also noted alignments with four standstill positions of the moon.[10]

This is important since it also indicates that they were using a lunisolar calendar. And, as we've shown, almost any evidence that a culture was attempting to find concordance of cycles between both the sun and moon, indicates that they were using something like the Wheel of Time.

SUN DAGGER OF FAJADA BUTTE AT CHACO CANYON

Sites: Fajada Butte

Location: Chaco Canyon, New Mexico

Date: 10,000 - 1000 BCE

Site Description: Petroglyphs on a cave wall are perfectly aligned with all solstices and equinoxes, as well as the phases of the 18.6 year-long lunar cycle.

Points on the Wheel: All Solstices and Equinoxes.

We now turn our attention to the Southwest, and here we find quite a different type of solar observatory. In Chaco Canyon, New Mexico, there is a most interesting solar alignment on the Fajada Butte, sometimes called the Sun Dagger petroglyph.[11] Chaco Canyon is a very impressive ancient city, consisting of 15 major complexes, which were the largest buildings in North America until the 19th century. The nearby sun dagger petroglyph is believed to have been made by the Chaco Anasazi people or their predecessors, and is at least 1000 years old if it was created at the time of the Chaco Canyon complex. But it may be much older than that. We know that there were hunter/gatherer tribes in the area during the Paleo-Indian period, from 8,000 to 13,000 years ago. Some Southwestern rock art has been dated to as much as 10,000 years old.

This is a most ingenious and dramatic solar marker. It

consists of three giant slabs of rock, which were placed there or naturally fell there. These slabs contain two narrow slits between the slabs, and on the rock wall below them are two spiral-shaped petroglyphs. At noon, the openings above creates two shafts of light shaped like daggers, or perhaps snakes, shining on the rock wall below. On the summer solstice, and only on the solstice, a dagger of light crosses the very center of the larger spiral petroglyph.

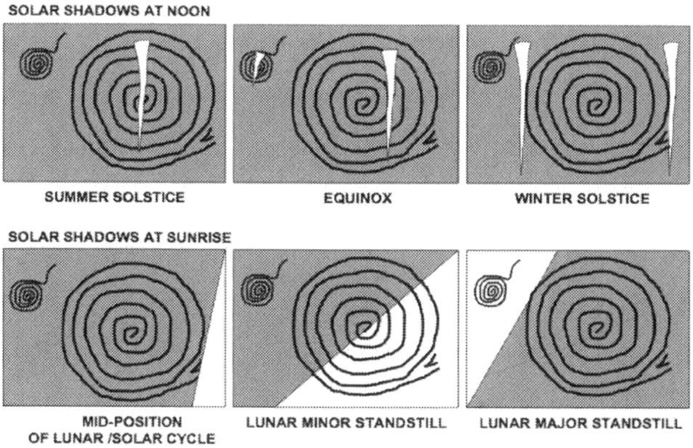

SUN DAGGER AT FAJADA BUTTE

On the equinox, and only on the equinox, the second dagger cuts right though the very center of the smaller of the spirals. Both of the daggers of light continue moving until the winter solstice, when they both stop precisely on either edge of the larger spiral. This is the one time of the year when neither light touches either spiral, symbolizing the maximum darkness at the winter solstice. It is really quite clear and striking to watch.[12]

In addition to these striking solar markers, as seen at noon, on both the equinoxes and solstices, there are also a number of lunisolar alignments, which are seen at sunrise, both at the minor standstill, major standstill, and mid-position of the lunisolar cycle. These same lunar alignments are also seen in the orientation of the kivas (houses) of Chaco Canyon village as well.[13] Again, this clearly indicated that these people were not only tracking the sun, but the lunar cycle as well. And when we say lunar cycle, we don't just mean from new moon to full moon, but we mean the entire 18.6 yearlong lunar cycle. This clearly indicates that they too were probably observing a lunisolar calendar.

OTHER SOUTHWEST ROCK ART SITES

There are many such solar markers and alignments found throughout the Southwest, perhaps hundreds of such markers. And, there are some very subtle patterns of the Anasazi rock art in this area that can easily be missed without careful observation. One of the patterns that you can observe is that there appears to be a yang/male vs. yin/female dichotomy that is reminiscent of ancient Taoist shamanism.[14]

For instance, there is a pattern to the many summer solstice markers, which differs sharply from many of the winter solstice markers. The summer markers are usually on rocky hilltops or cliffs, sometimes with serpent petroglyphs that are uncoiled, and carved in relief (raised), with 6 ½ turns. In contrast, winter solstice markers are more likely to be found in valleys, often with the petroglyph serpents coiled up, and the rock art carved deep into the rock (grooves), also with 6 ½ turns.[15] Here you see a pattern that is symmetrical yet opposite.

If you are familiar with the oldest Taoist writings, the above differences very clearly represent yin vs. yang symbolism. Yang is male energy; it is associated with white, brightness or light, as in sunlight. In fact, the Chinese character *yang* depicts the image of a sunny day. It is all things hard and rugged; it protrudes like a phallus, erect, symbolized by a snake or pillar.

On the other hand, yin is female energy; it is associated with black, or darkness. In fact, the Chinese character *yin* depicts the image of a cloudy day. It is all things soft and yielding, receding like a crevice or an opening, and symbolized by a circle.[15] So, we see in the familiar *taijitu*, the Chinese symbol of yin and yang, that black represents yin, darkness, and white represents yang, light. Curiously, in much of the traditional Southwestern pottery and weavings, these taijitu-type images are quite common.

One unique feature of Southwestern solar markers is that the round spiral petroglyph is more often used for all solar markers (equinoxes and solstices), such as with the sun dagger shown above. A petroglyph of an uncoiled serpent is common, but less frequently used as a solar marker. Perhaps this is because the dagger or serpent of light represents the yang/male, and the round spiral represents yin/female, so the sun dagger on top of a spiral, shown above, represents both the male and female, a type of Anasazi yin/yang image.

Clearly, these correlations are beyond coincidence. If

it happened once or twice it could be seen as a coincidence, but the pattern is seen over and over, throughout Southwestern rock art. Here we see that the ancients who made these petroglyphs perceived all the same dichotomies, values, and meanings that the ancient Taoist shaman did. But, over the centuries, Taoist beliefs in China evolved and changed in subtle ways. What we see with ancient Native American cosmology is consistent with the earliest meaning of the Taoist dichotomy of yin vs. yang.[16] And, this is what you'd expect to find if these were Asiatic peoples who left their homeland thousands of years ago, and retained the some of the original cosmology of their Asian ancestors.

Clearly, the summer solstice is the longest day of year with the maximum of daylight, and light represents yang/male energy. Winter, on the other hand, is the shortest day of year with the most hours of darkness, and darkness represents yin/female energy. And, this is exactly the pattern we see in Southwestern rock art.

Here we see another dimension to the Wheel of Time, a gender dimension, female vs. male, or yin vs. yang. This dimension is already seen very graphically in The Wheel of Time, as it is shown in the phases of the monthly lunar cycle, from pure light/full moon, to pure darkness/new moon (as shown in Figure 7).

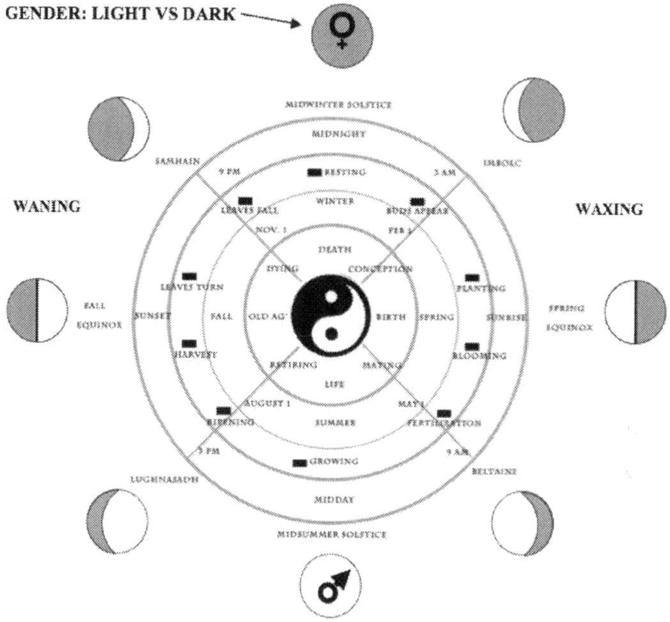

Figure 7

The above model of the Wheel of Time is actually over-simplified, since the ancient astronomers from around the world actually tracked not only the monthly lunar cycle but also the lunar nodal cycle, which is nearly 18.6 years long, as we see at Fajada Butte, and as we previously saw in the Golden Hats of prehistoric Europe. Prehistoric people all over the world were keenly aware of the lunisolar calendar, and thought it was important to observe it and schedule their feast days and holy days around it.

DOLOMITE LOOP PETROGLYPHS: ORIGINAL RESEARCH

Sites: Dolomite Loop Petroglyphs

Location: Lone Pine, CA

Date: Approx. 2,000 BCE

Site Description: Shadows on a flat rock reveal the image of serpent striking and swollowing a spiral petroglyph at dawn on the Equinox.

Points on the Wheel: Both Equinoxes.

Doing research for books, such as this one, usually involves two types of research, either library research, now aided by the internet, or revisiting sites that others have already researched, such as Stonehenge or the Great Pyramid of Giza. I am reminded of the very first Indiana Jones film, in which Dr. Jones is advising his students that archaeology is not as glamorous or adventurous as one might think; "most of our research is done in the library," he said. Of course, for the rest of the film we never once see him in a library, but rather we see him traveling around the globe, being the first to discover amazing archaeological finds. And, this is what we'd all like to be doing as archaeologists, but it's usually reserved for summer fieldwork, and even then it's only when we can get a grant to do such fieldwork.

There is nothing as exciting as being the first to discover something that might well have been buried for thousands of years. Though as an archaeo-psychologist, even when doing fieldwork, my research is usually confined to a reinterpretation of existing or well-known sites. But, every now and then I make a discovery of a site that is either unknown or not well known in the archaeological literature. Well, I'm happy to say that a few years back I was lucky enough to be able to do such fieldwork.

There are many Native American petroglyph sites in the Owens Valley of eastern California, and I have visited almost all the well-known sites at one time or another. But, I continually hear from locals about less-known sites that they have discovered. Archaeologists have catalogued almost all of these sites at one time or another, often in obscure texts, going back over a hundred years or more. However, there are thousands of petroglyphs that may have been cataloged, but not really studied in depth. Once in a blue moon one of these sites turns out to be somewhat important. And, a few years ago, I found one such site.[17]

There is a site near Lone Pine, CA that is well known by locals as a petroglyph site, on a bluff overlooking the now-dry Owens Lake, near the Dolomite Loop. It's very hard to date precisely but, judging by the patina, it is certainly quite old. Rock art with a similarly weathered patina in the nearby Coso Range have been dated to up to 10,000 years old. This site is estimated to be at least 4000 years old, similar to the date of the Little Lake petroglyphs nearby. Many locals know or have heard rumors that somewhere at this site is a solar calendar, but they are usually hazy on what solar event it marks or when.

It is not easy to find, even if you know where to look; and it's even harder to know which petroglyph is the one to look at, and when to look, sunrise, sunset, or noon? Does it mark the equinox or perhaps the winter solstice, or summer solstice? Try as I might, I found very scant information about this site in the archaeological literature. Local travelogues sometimes mentioned it, but seemed vague about what it did or where exactly to look. Fortunately, I was directed by a particularly astute local who showed me what he thought was the right rock and when to study it, which was at the equinox sunrise.

Since there were so many rumors about different alignments, and different petroglyphs at the site, I had no choice but to stake out several petroglyphs and photograph each of them, both at sunrise and sunset at both the solstices and the equinoxes. This was painstaking research that could not wait for the summer fieldwork season. Fortunately, it was less than 4 hours drive from my house. So, I packed my gear and headed out for a few days at a time, 4 times per year, camping out near the site.

I found that there is indeed a unique non-random lighting event seen on a couple of petroglyphs, at the equinoxes and the solstice. But it was not so impressive at first. At the winter solstice, there was no discernable alignment of any kind on the particular stone, which was the focus of our study. Three months later we were there again for the next equinox, and we had a better idea of which stone to study, and from what angle.

We awoke at our camp hours before sunrise, and got our cameras ready. We had a general idea of what to expect based on observations of the last equinox, but that had been several days past the equinox. So, this time we didn't know exactly what to expect and did not know the best position to set up our cameras, or how fleeting the shadow event would be. Would we have time to move the camera, if necessary? We had one camera on a tripod, to capture every moment, from what we thought would be the best angle. I also had one handheld camera to walk around and snap shots from different angles and of different petroglyphs, if we saw something interesting appear.

Once we had set up, we had a lot of time to wait. The site is at the very foot of a high ridgeline, on the eastern rim of the valley. So, as the sun rises, it first will light up the top of the snow-capped mountains to the west with a dark pink glow. Then it will begin to slide down the mountain and light up the opposite side of the valley floor.

The sunlight will slowly fill the broad valley, and finally the sunlight will reach us last. The site will not be illuminated until about 8:30 am. So, for hours we sat and waited, drank coffee, and tried to keep warm, as it is quite cold this time of the year. I filled my time journaling every detail of the site and the petroglyphs, and taking survey photos of the general area and the many petroglyphs. Finally, the sun crested the eastern ridgeline, and I was holding my breath in anticipation.

As the sun came up and forms of light and shadows began to appear on the rock, I found that my camera was in the wrong place after all. I had positioned it directly facing the rising sun to catch both the sunrise and the anticipated alignment, which was a big mistake. The first rays of dawn were shooting straight into the camera lens, fogging and obscuring everything. At the same time, high winds kicked up just as the sun rose. I scrambled to reposition the tripod, and had to suddenly grab it as the winds were starting to literally blow it away. I took off my coat and used it to hold down the tripod while I looked for something to weigh it down.

For a couple minutes there was panic as I was missing the beginning of this rare solar alignment. I took my backpack and filled it with sand and rocks to create a makeshift sandbag to hold down the tripod. But, just a minute later all my efforts were rewarded. Fortunately, I was not too late and what I saw next truly astounded me. When complete, this rock art ended up being just as astonishing as the sun dagger at Fajada Butte. No, even more astounding! What follows is a summary of what we witnessed on that cold windy morning (shown in the diagram on the next page).

The rock, which is quite large and flat on the ground, is gradually illuminated as the sun rises. A rugged, raised ridge on the east side of the rock casts shadows across the face of the rock. I found two very exciting features about the rock and its sunrise shadows. First, there is not only a mere dagger of light, but it is more precisely the moving image of a serpent! Secondly, there is a large spiral petroglyph strategically placed on the rock, just as at Fajada Butte. On the sunrise of the equinox, the serpent crawls up the side and across the top of the rock, just as the serpent of light does on the temple of Kukulkan at Chichen Itza.

Then the serpent gradually opens its mouth. Out of

the serpent's mouth comes what looks like a dagger-shaped tongue. This dagger of light extends out of the serpent's mouth and gradually pierces the rings of the spiral, until it pierces the very center of the spiral, like Fajada Butte but even more dramatically. Eventually, the dagger-shaped tongue is replaced by the serpent's head, as it lunges over a crack in the rock. Then, as the serpent of light gradually moves from west to east, the open mouth appears to swallow the center of the petroglyph, which may be meant to symbolize an egg.

Eventually, the mouth begins to close and as it does, the open mouth of the serpent of light forms an arrow pointing back to the center of the spiral petroglyph. This is shown in the diagram on the next page, panel 6, with the spiral drawn on top to see the alignment more clearly. At the very end, just as the entire rock face is becoming illuminated by the light of day, the serpent appears to morph into a bird, with outstretched wings, then disappears.[18]

Honestly, I can't make this stuff up. No one would believe me, anyway. This was one of the most incredible events of its type that I've ever seen. It was like a combination of the Equinox serpent of the temple of Kukulkan, and the Spiral Petroglyph at Fajada Butte, but even more dramatic to watch.

But, one question remained. How good is it at predicting the very day of the equinox? Perhaps this event happens everyday for a month or more. To answer that, I had to know what it looks like in the days and weeks before and after the event. And, that was even harder to discover.

Time-lapse progression at sunrise on the equinox

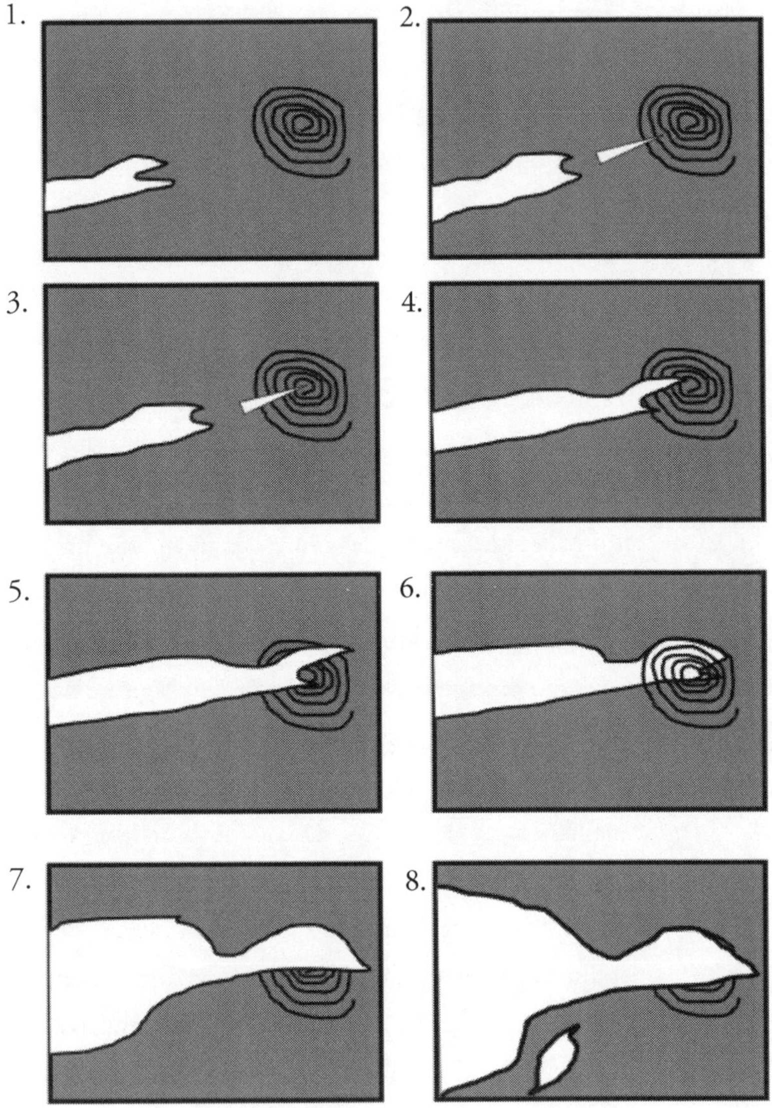

Dolomite Loop Spiral Petroglyph

To discover how well the petroglyph distinguishes between the very day of the equinox vs. other days around the time of the equinox, I had to camp out at the site from 2 weeks before the equinox until 2 weeks after the equinox, much to the frustration of my family and my other career obligations. But, this too paid off.

I discovered that the event is actually quite discriminating. One month prior to the autumn equinox, something appears, but it looks more like a desperately gasping turtle, and as it crosses the rock it moves below the spiral. Eventually it expands so that the spiral becomes the eye of the turtle, warning of the coming of the equinox.

Two weeks before the autumn equinox it is starting to take shape, but there is still no clear tongue, and it still looks like just a narrower version of the turtle's neck and head, with the spiral again forming what looked like the eye of the turtle, albeit lower on the face. Finally, only on the days before and after the equinox, the full image takes its final shape. And only on the day of the equinox does its tongue point to the very center of the spiral (Frame 3), and after swallowing the spiral center, possibly symbolizing an egg, its open mouth points back to the very center of the spiral (Frame 6).

About a week after the equinox, the serpent does not even exist. Two weeks past the fall equinox, there is no snake, and no turtle, but there is a bird image that remains, with its head forming just over the spiral. The bird of light gradually expands until the entire rock is illuminated. [19] So, it turns out that the image precisely indicates the very day of the equinox.

In fact, it is just as accurate as it is striking to watch.

This site and its spectacular solar alignment, raises a couple of important questions, though. The first question is, how much of the above phenomena was human-made vs. coincidence? In other words, how did they ever figure out how to chip the edge of the rock to create that precise serpent image? Or perhaps the image of a snake appearing around the time of the equinox was just a coincidence, which the local shaman was lucky enough to discover. Perhaps they were there looking for a good place to put an equinox marker and saw the naturally occurring serpent image.

This last scenario seems like the most probable explanation to me, and this is probably true for the Fajada Butte site as well. It would be almost impossible to make the spiral petroglyph first, and then to create a complex shadow image that aligns with the center of the petroglyph on the sunrise of the equinox. And, just like seeing images in the clouds, it is easy to spot all sorts of complex images in the shadows cast across the rocks at almost any time of day, on almost any day.

All they had to do was to find an interesting shadow on the dawn of the equinox and then mark it, and later they can take their time in creating a spiral petroglyph, positioned as marked. Though, to perfect the spectacle, they might have even used charcoal to make time-lapsed marks of the shadow's boundaries at various stages, as it crept across the rock. Then they could accurately plot the best place to put the petroglyph and how big the petroglyph should be. They could even add secondary spirals to mark other solar alignments, as in the Fajada Butte equinox marker.

Another interesting feature is the recurring use of a spiral petroglyph. It could, as previously mentioned, symbolize a coiled serpent. Or, it could also represent an opening, like water spiraling down a drain. What is it about a spiral that relates meaningfully to the sun and the various solar alignments during the year? Well, to understand the meaning of the spiral image, you need only add an arrow, or multiple arrows, along the course of the spiraling lines to see the movement of a reoccurring cycle in motion.

Just think of the international symbol for recycling. It's a circle in motion. Like the term 'a vicious circle.' It is a cycle that moves in a progression from one cycle to the next. The annual solar cycle is a sequence of events that repeats every year, but it's not exactly the same because every year is a little different. Children get bigger every year, trees grow taller every year, and the old get older every year, moving ever closer to death, to the very end of life. And, each year new babies are born, so the cycle repeats all over again.

If you look at one end of the spiraled line as birth, and the other end as death, then you see that this image represents the annual cycle in movement from one annual cycle to the next, from beginning to end. I think that this is clearly an abstract image designed to represent the Wheel of Time. And, the fact that we know local Native American tribes celebrated their annual Mourning Ceremony at the winter solstice indicates a concordance between life cycle and the life of the year.

So, we can be sure that this is not just any wheel of time; it is the same as the Wheel of Time shown in Figure 7. And, it is not really so different conceptually from the Taijitu (yin/yang) image, seen at the very center of Figure 7, which also represents a cycle in motion.

SUMMARY

In this chapter we have shown that North America contains one of the greatest concentration of ancient solar markers and observatories of any place in the world, and some of the most interesting and ingenious designs. Also, they are among the oldest such solar markers in the world. And, some are not merely static monuments that contain solar alignments, but rather they sometimes contain dramatic images that move, change shape, and can even point with precision to the center of a target, only on certain days of the year.

We have only included a few of the more interesting and important North American solar markers, but there are many, many more. Some are somewhat controversial, for instance, the Newport Tower in Newport Rhode Island. It is a stone tower with 8 pillars, which marks the main points of a compass, and supports a round enclosed tower above. An alignment of a window and a niche inside the tower marks the sunset on the summer solstice. Other alignments mark the lunar minor standstill, in the 18.6 year-long lunar cycle. The history of the tower is unclear, but for a long time it was thought to be made by either Native Americans or perhaps early Vikings. But, it now looks as if it was built by early European settlers in the 1600s.

Another interesting site is the Anubis Cave in the Panhandle of Oklahoma. There are solar alignments with petroglyphs in the cave that mark the sunset on the equinox, and the cave is also said to contain petroglyph imagery consistent with both Egyptian and Celtic cultures. This is important if true, but has not been studied well enough to be sure.

Then there is also the White Shaman mural, in West Texas near the Pecos River. [20] An archaeologist at Texas State University, Carolyn Boyd, believes the mural not only documents the creation mythology of the people who made it, but it also marks the passage of the seasons and celestial events. Dr. Boyd says "Time is written into the White Shaman mural". [21] And she also notes a correlation found there between the setting sun in the west and the winter solstice, which is echoed in the Wheel of Time.

There are literally thousands of such individual petroglyph sites in North America, and many if not most have not been well studied. But, the trend is clear; Native Americans, just like their European, African, and Asian counterparts, carefully tracked the movements of the Sun, Moon, and stars.

Finally, it is important to observe that many of the Southwestern solar markers also include symbolism that correlates the cycles of the Wheel of Time with gender, where the lightest times include yang/male symbolism, and the darkest times include yin/female symbolism. This is consistent with the ancient Taoist beliefs, found in East Asia. Furthermore, this is also consistent with other dimensions of the Wheel of Time, such as a correlation between the new moon and the midwinter, both being at their darkest phase.

So, we can now add a new dimension to the Wheel of Time, gender. Light being male and darkness being female, this correlates with all the other dimensions of the Wheel, such as the life cycle, seasons of the year, phases of the moon, times of the day, and the annual cycle of agriculture and plant life.

This is just the last chapter of what has been an exhaustive review of many ancient sites with very similar features, all of which reflecting some aspects of the Wheel of Time. They are found on every continent of Earth, and all are quite ancient. And, we have only looked at 30 sites in depth, but for every one site mentioned there are many dozens of other known sites, and perhaps hundreds that have yet to be discovered.

PART II:

HISTORICAL, LITERARY, & ETHNOGRAPHIC RESEARCH

CHAPTER 6

HOW TO SOLVE AN ARCHAEOLOGICAL PUZZLE

We all know what historical research refers to. The same is true for literary research. But, I have sometimes referred to the term *ethnography,* and some may wonder: what does this mean? What is ethnography and what does that have to do with archaeology?

Ethnography is actually a branch of anthropology which involves the observation and description of cultures. This is when an anthropologist lives with a tribe to learn their customs and traditions first hand. But, in archaeology, we can't observe a tribe that lived 5000 years ago. But, we still want to get the same type of information. That's because this type of information fills in missing pieces of the puzzle.

An artifact from an ancient civilization often gives us little information about its cultural meaning. Ethnography fills in the missing pieces. It tells us how the sites and artifacts might have fit into the ancient culture that made them. That's great, but it still doesn't explain how we can learn about a culture that existed thousands of years ago. So, we have to get creative, and use whatever ethnographic data we have.

That is why, when I refer to ethnography, I might be referring to a 2000-year-old description of a Celtic tribe, by a Roman historian, or a first-hand account etched into a 3000-year-old stone tablet. No, it's not as accurate as eyewitness observations, but often it's all we have.

Unfortunately, if all we have is the ethnography or literary evidence alone, that is not very valuable either. It is important that we have both types of information in order to be certain of our findings. Why? Well, it turns out that, as a group, archaeologists are very skeptical people. If we discover some old writings, going back thousands of years, which tell the tale of a great and mighty city, archaeologists don't necessarily believe it; not without hard proof. Such was the case of Homer's epic poem, the Iliad, about the city of Troy and the Trojan War.

In spite of the fact that there was a town named Troia, in about the approximate location where Troy was said to be located, few mainstream archaeologists took the story seriously; they thought it was just a myth. That is until a businessman and amateur archaeologist named Heinrich Schliemann excavated near the town, guided only by Homer's writings, local folklore, and maps procured from a local farmer, which showed where to dig. To the astonishment of mainstream archaeologists, Schliemann discovered the lost city of Troy. Subsequent excavations revealed 8 other cities, which spanned 2,000 years of Trojan history.[1]

In the above story we see three types of research used. One type of research is done by interviewing the local people, revealing their stories, beliefs, and local folklore. When done in a scientific manner, this type of research is called ethnography. A second type of research is when you discover an ancient document, a scroll, or a clay tablet from the distant past. This would be like discovering Homer's poem, the Iliad, written on an old dusty parchment scroll, perhaps buried in an ancient tomb. This type of research is usually referred to as *historical* or *literary* research, and it actually consists of a combination of archaeology and ethnography since it is an ancient artifact, and it also tells a story of the local people, their history, beliefs, and folklore.

Finally, there is the physical archaeological research, which consists of excavating ancient ruins and finding artifacts such as pieces of pottery, jewelry, clay or stone tablets, burial sites, and skeletal remains.

What we see in the excavation of Troy is that all three types of research are often necessary to understand past civilizations, especially when trying to locate lost sites or understand their culture. In this case, they did not need to find the Iliad as it was already a famous document that gives us an eloquent but unsubstantiated story about the city of Troy.

Local folklore then gives us the same story from a different perspective with missing pieces of information. Finally, the excavation gives us hard proof that the people in the story really did exist, and it gives us much more information about when they lived and what kind of culture they had. It tells us how big their cities were, their style of architecture, and so on.

Sometimes, however, it is the other way around. We might have a detailed excavation of an ancient site but no idea who the people were who built it or why. This is what we are dealing with when discussing ancient ruins that appear to be observatories or solar markers. At some sites, such as Stonehenge or the observatory at Chichen Itza, there was originally a good deal of skepticism about whether these sites really were built to mark the phases of the sun or not. For a long time, it was widely believed that Stone Age savages could not possibly have been so clever to do such a feat, to mark the solstices. And, seeing these sites as observatories implied that the ancients who built them were more scientific than superstitious, a notion that many people of the last century thought absurd.

This is why historical, literary, and ethnographic evidence is so important in this line of research. If we find a puzzling collection of stone slabs, such as Stonehenge, the first thought is that it must be an ancient building or a temple perhaps, someplace where they would chant and give burnt offerings for good luck on the hunt.

But, if you look at ancient texts and combine that with local folklore, you might get a very different story. It is very much like a detective investigating a crime scene. The physical evidence is at best circumstantial, then interviews and written documents fill in the gaps with a wealth of information. This extra information often helps to explain the physical evidence and what it means.

Only by looking at all three types of information can you get the whole story. If you only look at one or two types of information, you can easily be mistaken in your conclusion. Unfortunately, sometimes we only have one or two types of information. In the case of Stonehenge, the local people were fairly clueless about what it was or why it was built.

COMPARING APPLES TO ORANGES

There is another issue in the field of archaeology that I think deserves mentioning, and that is the practice of extrapolating information from one culture to artifacts or ruins of another culture. Most archaeologists would probably say this is a bad idea, since you are essentially "comparing apples to oranges." Ok, that's true enough. But, as is the case with fruit, identifying categorized items is a hallmark of science. For instance, all fruit contain seeds. So, even if you find a completely unknown fruit, you know that if you plant it, it will grow. You know this because this is true for all fruit. This is the same logic that we use when we take information from one culture and apply it to another culture.

So far in this book, we've already established that ancient observatories exist all over the world, mostly in the Neolithic and Bronze Age. And, most all of them have at least one or two features consistent with the Wheel of Time, and none have features that are inconsistent with the Wheel of Time. This means that all these sites have enough in common to establish them as a certain type of archaeological find. This is like saying a fruit is a certain type of food. In this way, these ancient observatories are by no means unique.

We have other examples of easily identifiable *types* of artifacts in archaeology, such as the so-called *goddess figures*.[2] We have found them all over the world, and all from about the same time period, stretching from the Paleolithic and throughout the Neolithic Age. And, these figurines are believed to hold the same general meaning and purpose for all who created them; the worship of an *earth-mother* goddess, and the promise of fertility. And there are many other identifiable types of artifacts, such as burial tombs and fortresses, which we find in many, if not most, ancient cultures.

I give this detailed explanation of what is a rather technical part of archaeology because if you're astute you may ask, what does the ancient astronomy of India have to do with Native American archaeological sites in the Southwest? And, what does the ethnography of Native Americans have to do with archaeological sites in China? The answer is that, if an ancient culture had the same type of archaeological finds as another culture, it might not just be a coincidence.

All burial mounds have a similar purpose, regardless of which culture had created it. The same is true for evidence of ancient kitchens, fortresses, swords, or goddess figurines. Therefore, if two different cultures both created solar observatories containing specific correlations to the Wheel of Time, then we may be able to infer other connections as well.

This is very important since, in some cultures, we have the ethnography from indigenous tribes with little or no ancient documents. In other cultures, we might have many ancient documents but, due to migrations, genocide, or cultural changes, we have no ethnography available from the locals who live there now. In some instances, we have neither; we only have the archaeological sites, with no explanation of what it was built for or why.

So if we can put together historical and literary documents, ethnography, and artifacts from different cultures, all pertaining to one *type* of archaeological find, we may be able to form a more complete picture the role that these types of sites and artifacts played in their culture.

Now let's apply this to the study of ancient solar and lunar observatories and the marking of certain days of the year. If we can identify certain patterns in people from different cultures, we may see connections between different observatories in different locations. Then we may be able to make some generalizations from one culture to another, even from different time periods or different continents. As we fill in the missing pieces, we may gain more insight into why the observatories were built and what they meant to the people who built them.

NEOLITHIC VS. NEO-PAGAN

The first issue that we can begin to resolve through ethnography and ancient records is the basic concept of the eight-pointed Wheel of the Year, as it's commonly known, which we call the Wheel of Time. It has been known for over a hundred years or more, and widely used by so called neo-pagans, those who follow the beliefs of paganism in the modern age.

There has long been a debate among scholars regarding the Neolithic vs. Neo-pagan origins of the eight-pointed Wheel. Neo-pagans claim that their concepts, such as the eight pointed Wheel, date back to before the time of Christ. Scholars, on the other hand, are skeptical and say that the Wheel of the Year is a fairly recent invention and probably has little or nothing to do with the actual pagan practices or beliefs of prehistory. Hopefully, if I do nothing else in this book, I can at least resolve this debate once and for all.

Not only have we seen ample evidence of monuments from around the world, which mark the solstices, equinoxes, and cross quarter days, but as we shall see later in this section there is actually documented evidence that early Celts in Briton celebrated all four cross-quarter days. We know this because it is documented by Roman historians, such as Diodorus (90 - 30 BCE), who identified 3 of their major holidays as being Beltaine, Lughnasadh, and Samhain, all cross-quarter days.

And, there were other Roman historians, as far back as 2000 years ago, who noted that these cross-quarter days were celebrated with a major celebration and bonfire. These were referred to as the fire festivals, and that makes them more than just astronomical observations. It makes them the four major holidays of the year in ancient Celtic culture.

We also have corroborating evidence of the four cross-quarter days because they were clearly listed as the start of the four seasons in the *Tochmarc Emire*, or the *Wooing of Emer*.[3] The Tochmarc Emire is one of the longest epic poems contained in the *Ulster Cycle,* which is the oldest known collection of Irish literature. The stories are set in the 1st century, and it is believed that they were passed down for generations through oral tradition. The oldest written versions probably date to the 8th century.

Keep in mind, these cross-quarter days could only be determined by monitoring the solstices and equinoxes, since they were the midpoints between them. There is no other way. This, combined with the monuments that we have researched, proves that the ancient Celts regularly identified and marked all eight points of the solar year.

And, the Celts were not alone. The Roman scholar Marcus Terentius Varro (116 - 27 BCE) also conceptualized the year in eight parts, as defined by the solstices, equinoxes, and the four midpoints between them.[4] He then adjusted them only slightly to fit key turning points in the annual agricultural calendar.

For instance, he reasoned that October 31st was too early to mark the end of the harvest season and so he extended it another week and a half, to accommodate late ripening fruits. It is not clear if Varro had learned this type of calendar system from the Celts of Europe, or if it was perhaps an ancient indigenous practice among the Etruscan pagans in the area, who predated the Romans.

Therefore, we can now say with some certainty that the use of a repeating annual calendar divided into eight sections, such as the Wheel of Time, is absolutely not a modern invention. Rather, this eight-pointed Wheel is nothing short of a window into the mind of ancient people. And, it enables us to understand how they conceived of the cyclic nature of life and time itself.

FILLING IN THE MISSING PIECES

We have already collected a large and rich database in the first section, just by looking at the physical, archaeological sites and artifacts themselves. This has yielded a conceptual framework we call the Wheel of Time, but there are still many questions.

Hopefully, by using historical and ethnographic evidence to fill in the missing pieces in the archaeological record, we can complete our understanding of ancient observatories, and their role in ancient civilizations and their beliefs. And, there are four important issues to be explored here.

1) Astronomy: Just how sophisticated were the ancient astronomers, who created and used these observatories? Ancient written documents may fill in gaps of information, especially in cultures where we find no ruins of observatories.

This is also important because there are still archaeologists to this day who are skeptical of ancient astronomers and their knowledge. Some even doubt that known observatory sites were really used to track the sun and moon. They suggest that any alignments discovered there might just be a coincidence. Is there any evidence that ancient people had any knowledge of Astronomy?

2) The Wheel: A lot of the interesting interconnections that we have seen are much more apparent when we plot these different cycles (solar, lunar, daily, nature, and life cycles) as concentric circles on a round diagram. If you plot

them on a straight line, many of the connections disappear. But, is there any evidence that ancient cultures conceived of these cycles as points on a wheel, or in any kind of a round image or diagram? If not, it certainly undercuts our thesis. We have already shown the use of a spiral in Native American petroglyphs related to time, and the same is true for the Golden Hats of Europe. But, we need more evidence.

3) Ancient Holidays: We know that they marked certain phases of the sun and moon, but were those days considered their holy days? We have already partially answered that question for the ancient Celts, regarding their four fire festivals. But, in other parts of the world, what were the holidays that people celebrated in ancient times?

We cannot tell what people were celebrating just by looking at the archaeological sites. Is there any ethnography, historical records, or local folklore to fill in the gaps in our knowledge about regional holidays? Also, are there any correlations between the holidays of different cultures, celebrated on the same day or at the same time of the year? And, if so, are these holidays also correlated with the Wheel of Time?

4) How Holidays Evolved: Finally, it's worth exploring just how the ancient celebrations of the equinoxes, solstices, and cross-quarter days evolved into the holidays that we now celebrate. And, is there a connection between our modern holidays and the ancient pagan Sabbaths of the Neolithic? What happened to the ancient Celtic fire festivals? Why aren't they still celebrated? This can only be found by looking at the written historical, literary, and ethnographic records.

CHAPTER 7

EVIDENCE OF ARCHAEO-ASTRONOMY & CYCLIC MOTIFS

In this chapter, we will look at ancient writings in order to hear the ideas and beliefs of ancient people in their own words. Our goal is to examine the ethnography of several ancient cultures to give us insights and a deeper understanding of what they were thinking when they built their massive observatories and stone markers. In their own words, how did they conceptualize time? And, what was the meaning of the different phases of the sun, moon, and stars? We begin in a country with one of the oldest written languages on earth, India.

Earlier in the book, we briefly discussed just one ancient solar observatory in India, but this is misleading because there are actually as much or more ancient astronomy documented in ancient Indian texts than in other ancient cultures. In the Vedic scriptures, the oldest writings from India, there is one book of special importance, the Vedanga Jyotisha.

VEDANGA JYOTISHA OF THE VEDIC TEXTS

The Vedanga Jyotisha is believed to be 3,400 years old. It is an appendix to the Vedic texts, and one of the six

Vedanga, the *limbs* of the Veda. The Jyotisha is known as the *eye of the Veda*, meaning the science that *helps one see the life path*. The Vedanga Jyotisha describes the rules for tracking the sun, moon, and stars. It includes astronomy, mathematics, cosmology, as well as the study of omens, the setting of auspicious times, and so on. As such, it is very consistent with what we see in other cultures, where they not only tracked celestial movements, but they imparted meaning onto certain phases of the sun, moon, and stars, just as we've seen in the Wheel of Time.

One important detail of the Jyotisha is that it describes the winter solstice corresponding to the period of approximately 1400 BCE. Its primary importance among academics has been to accurately date the Vedic texts of India. Since it is an appendix, it follows that it was the last of the texts to be written. If the appendix was written 3400 years ago, then we can assume that the other Vedic texts are even older, dated to as much as 4,000 years old and possibly much older. We know its date, in part, due to the precession of the equinoxes.

Precession of the equinoxes is the movement of the stars around our solar system that follows a predictable path, which takes 24,000 years to complete. The stars appear to move backward around the zodiac, in reference to a fixed point, when observed at the same time of year, each year (usually the equinox). If we know where a particular star was on either the equinox or solstice of a particular year, then we can calculate what year that was, based upon the movement of precession. It is because of this predictable movement of the stars that we know that the Jyotisha was written 3400 years ago, based on observations recorded in the text. Also, it is the phenomenon of precession that underlies some of the most fantastic writings from ancient India.

Swami Sri Yukteswar, in his book The Holy Science, written in 1894, claims that the 24,000 yearlong cycle, which we call precession of the equinoxes, is actually the revolution of our sun around our sun's binary companion star.[1] Furthermore, this is divided into two 12,000 year journeys that our sun makes, from apogee to perigee with our binary twin star, and back again. This is all based on the ancient Vedic texts of India. He wrote: "*...the sun, with its planets and their moons, takes some star for its dual and revolves around it in about 24,000 years of our earth – a celestial phenomenon which causes the backward movement of the equinoctial points around the zodiac.*"[2]

We know from archaeological research that the ancient people of India had observatories to mark the movement of the stars, sun, and moon, but the idea that they had discovered the procession of the equinoxes is truly impressive. This was something not detected by astronomers in the West until it was discovered by Hipparchus in approximately 120 BCE.[3] And, the theory that precession is caused by our sun, being part of a binary star system, whether true or not, is pretty amazing. It was not until the 1600s that astronomers in the West discovered so-called double stars. And it wasn't until the mid-eighteenth century that astronomers began to theorize that two stars could get caught in each other's gravitational field, creating such a double star orbit.[4] This gives us some idea of just how sophisticated ancient Indian astronomers might have been. In fact, there are several prominent researchers today that agree with this binary theory and are currently looking for our binary twin star, which could be a black dwarf star or Jovian mass, too dim and distant to detect unless you know exactly where to look.[5]

There is no doubt that the ancient Indian astronomers were far ahead of their time. But, their beliefs about the meaning of the movement of the stars is even more interesting. They perceived a much bigger cycle than anything we have imagined thus far, in the Wheel of Time. They envisioned a cycle that was 24,000 years long, each phase of which was imbued with meaning, similar to the Wheel of Time, but much greater.

Keep in mind that the only movement caused by precession is seen in the stars and their position, marked at a fixed point in time during the solar cycle, usually the equinox. But, as you will note on the Wheel of Time, there is no cycle for the phases of the stars, except the annual heliacal rising of a star, like Sirius. Precession is the very slow movement of all the stars in relation to our solar system. It takes 67 years to move just one degree. It appears they saw this as another dimension of the Wheel of Time, the precessional star cycle. In India it is called the Yuga Cycle

THE YUGA CYCLE

The Yuga Cycle is what they call the procession of the equinoxes. They further divide this cycle into 8 Yugas, 4 ascending and 4 descending. And, just like the Wheel of Time, this is usually depicted on a wheel, with the peak of the Yugas on one pole and the depth of the Yugas on the opposite pole (see Figure 8 below). On either side of the wheel is the midpoint between the maximum and minimum of the Yuga cycle. What did they mean by maximum and minimum? This is analogous to the Wheel of Time, except it relates to phases in human civilization and evolution.

The peak of the Yuga cycle is the peak of life, light, knowledge, and culture. They believed that, at the peak of Yugas, people will have almost superhuman powers, we will live longer, be healthier, wiser, and we will have no wars or violence. The last peak was 11,501 BCE, the next one won't be until 12,499 CE. The opposite position in the wheel is the middle of the Kali Yugas, at 499 CE, our Dark Ages, filled with ignorance, greed, and lust for power, when most lived a short life of poverty and violence (see Figure 8 below). The peak of the cycle is associated with day and light, and the depth is associated with night and darkness. So the Yuga cycle is really another dimension of the Wheel of Time. This dimension of the wheel corresponds to the cycle of the stars. By the way, this too is a wheel divided into 8 sections, though not as symmetrical as the Wheel of time. Coincidence?

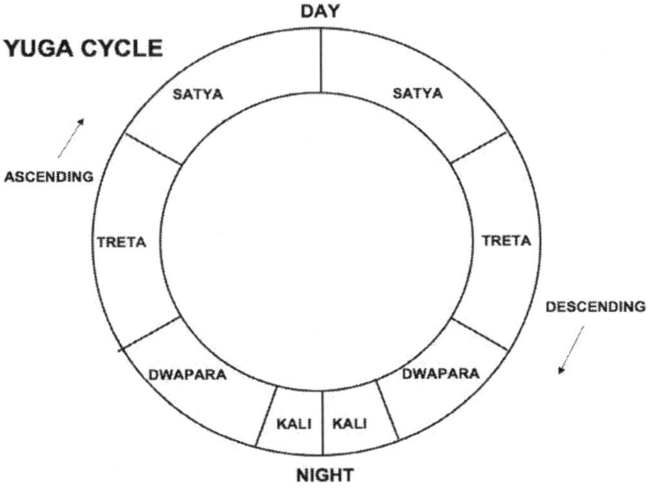

Figure 8

Notice that the wheel of the Yuga Cycle is the opposite of the Wheel of Time that we've constructed thus far, in that it is upside down. We put midnight on top and noon day on bottom. On the other hand, they put the peak (day) on top and depth (night) on bottom. This makes sense if you think of the wheel going from the very bottom and climbing its way up to the peak, only to descend again to the pit of the cycle. But, whether you put day on top or bottom means little because it is a circle; it has no beginning or end. Any way you turn it, it still aligns with the Wheel of Time. This is another version of the same familiar wheel that we've seen over and over again. The only difference here is that here we see mental and spiritual achievement associated with light, and a lack of mental and spiritual development associated with darkness, literally enlightenment vs. ignorance.

There is one more difference between the Yuga Cycle and the Wheel of Time; the Yuga wheel is not symmetrical. The Yugas start off very small at the bottom of the cycle; each Kali Yuga is only 1200 years long, or 2400 years total. Then each of the Yugas get progressively larger, until you reach the Satya Yugas, each of which is 4,800 years long. Both Satya Yugas combined are 9,600 years long. This is 4 times the length of the Kali Yugas. If you examine the progression it may remind you of something. This reflects speed differentials during a typical elliptical orbit. This is very meaningful when we realize that they believed that the Yuga cycle is actually caused by the sun's orbit around another star.

If the sun is in an elliptical orbit with its companion star, then as it whips around the binary twin it would be traveling very fast, due to the force of gravity. As it moves away from the massive star, it loses speed until it is traveling very slowly. Eventually, it is moving so slow it gets caught by the gravitational field of its companion star and begins its path back toward the companion star. As it moves toward it, it picks up speed until its rendezvous with the binary companion star, and then the whole orbit repeats.

Now let's look at the Yugas again. If every Yuga contains the same miles traveled by the sun in its orbit, then the Kali Yuga, the shortest, would reflect a very fast velocity. Likewise the Satya Yuga, the longest, would be the slowest. If you compare this to a computer simulation of two objects in motion in an elliptical orbit, then the match of the velocities with the length of the Yugas is uncanny. The Yugas accurately predict the speed of the earth in motion during the 24,000 year orbital cycle. In fact, recent investigations into the precession of the equinoxes have shown that it does, in fact, change speed over time.

Below, I have included another version of the Wheel of Time with the Yuga star cycle included. Though few other cultures that we know of recognized the phenomenon of precession, at least a couple of cultures, as we will see later, did observe precession as part of the Wheel of Time. Note that we have taken the Yuga cycle and turned it upside down to be aligned with our model, where light/day on the Yuga cycle lines up with light/day/noon on the Wheel of Time (see Figure 9 below).

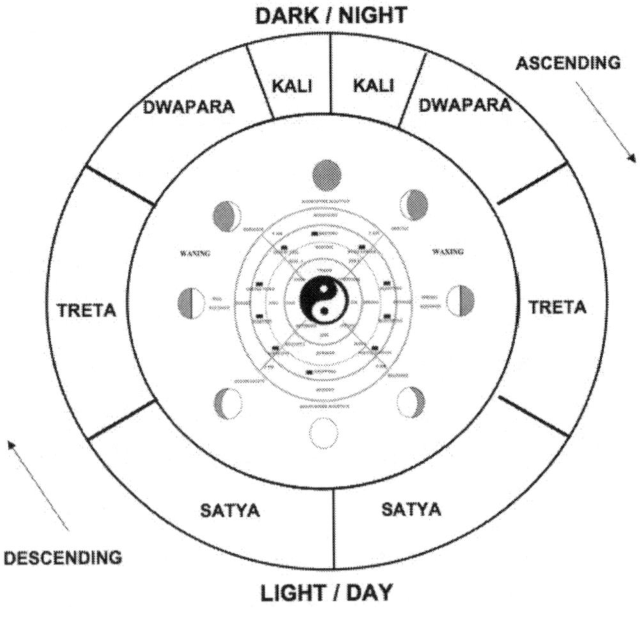

Figure 9

ANCIENT MANDALAS & THE WHEEL OF SAMSARA

What we are starting to see, in Figure 9, is rather complex; there are circles within circles spiraling ever inward. You cannot even read the letters on the inner rings. This is starting to look like a mandala. A mandala is a spiritual and ritual symbol in Hinduism and Buddhism, and it symbolizes cycles within cycles, with radial balance and harmony.

There are often very specific elements in a Buddhist mandala, such as four prominent cardinal points of the wheel, which is often seen as a circle within a square. These four points are seen as gates. But, the more general concept has been depicted in a myriad of ways.

More commonly, a mandala is any circular diagram or chart that symbolically represents the metaphysical universe. It is almost always some type of wheel pattern like the Wheel of Time. This is a deep and moving symbol of eastern mysticism that has been used in ancient spiritual practices and cosmological conceptions for thousands of years. Mandalas are perhaps the best evidence that the Wheel of Time, or something very much like it, was the very basis of ancient people's conception of the time, life, and the cosmos.

Mandalas are general templates for any diagram symbolizing a system of cycles within cycles. Each cycle lines up with one another and propels itself into future generations, while always repeating the same cycle. The famous psychiatrist Carl Jung recognized this and believed that it also applied to psychological growth as well.

There is a great quote that sums up the meaning of both the mandala and the Wheel of Time; "The process is that of the ascending spiral, which grows upward while simultaneously returning again and again to the same point."[6] This also explains the meaning of the curious spiral shapes used for marking the solstices and equinoxes in the desert Southwest, as well as at Newgrange in Ireland. The Mandala is first and foremost, not just a wheel, but a moving wheel; it is a spiral.

So significant is the mandala for ancient Buddhists, that there was a specific type of mandala used to depict the wheel of rebirth, called Samsara (*bhavacakra* in Sanskrit), also known as the Wheel of Life.[7] This is yet another cycle, which could easily line up with other elements on the Wheel of Time. In the Buddhist concept of Samsara, we see that there is not only a life cycle, where we are born, grow old, die, and are born again, but there is also a larger cycle, made up of many, many lifetimes, that we travel through reincarnation.

Not surprisingly, this is similar to the Yuga Cycles, except it relates to an individual soul, not to human civilization as a whole. In the Samsara depiction of cyclic existence, we see different levels of the wheel of spiritual evolution. Just as in our Wheel of Time, in this diagram there are circles within circles, each with different meanings and different segments.

At the center of the wheel is the three poisons, which hold us captive to the wheel: ignorance, attachment, and aversion. The second layer represents karma. The third layer represents the six realms of Samsara: this is like the Yuga cycle in that it is a progression that includes the realms of hell, ghosts, animals, humans, demi-gods, and eventually the god realm. The forth layer represents the twelve links of dependent origination, which is the causal links to karma. And, there are other figures around the wheel that represent other things as well, such as impermanence, liberation from Samsara, and Buddha pointing the way and telling us liberation is possible.

The Wheel of Samsara is very similar conceptually to the Wheel of Time that we've constructed, but quite the opposite philosophically. It's the opposite because the Wheel of Time that we have seen elsewhere around the world seems to be a celebration of the Wheel. The goal is to joyously and lovingly engage in and celebrate the turning of this wheel of life. It seems implicit that each aspect of the cycle is sacred and beautiful in its own way. The wheel of Samsara is the exact opposite.

In the Buddhist belief, the wheel of Samsara is something to be escaped from at all costs. The goal is not to celebrate the wheel but to get off of it, and not return, except to save others. Perhaps this is because an essential concept in Buddhism is that life is suffering. And our suffering comes from our attachment to life. To escape the wheel of rebirth is liberation. It is what we might call *heaven*. This is almost an anti-wheel of time, but nonetheless it is still based upon the same cyclic notions of life and time, seen in the Wheel of Time.

It's interesting that the Wheel of Time, as constructed earlier in the book, is mostly based on archaeological sites from the Neolithic Age, thousands of years before the life of Buddha. And, according to the Vedic scriptures, the Neolithic Age was a great Yuga; it was a golden age, when life was good and virtue reigned supreme on Earth. And, as we have seen, it was during that time that the Wheel of Time was celebrated, and it was probably hoped that our continual reincarnation would continue forever.

According to the Yuga cycle, by the time that the prophet Siddhartha Guatama Buddha was born (approximately 490 BCE), the world had descended into the Kali Yuga, a dark time when virtue was non-existent and life was suffering and misery. Perhaps this juxtaposition of periods on earth explains why Neolithic people seemed to celebrate the repeating cycles of life on the Wheel of Time, and yet Buddha saw the Wheel of Life as an endlessly repeating prison, not to be celebrated but to be escaped.

At any rate, one thing is certain. The wheel, or mandala, is exactly how ancient people conceived of time, specifically the cyclical movement through time. A wheel of time is definitely a most ancient concept. So, our Wheel of Time, or something very much like it, is exactly what we would expect to see in an ancient diagram depicting time and the movement of time.

THE STAR OF ISHTAR & THE ZODIAC

India is not unique in having great ancient astronomers. There are written records that indicate very sophisticated astronomical observations in the Middle East and in Mesopotamia as well. The Sumerians and Babylonians developed the science of astronomy and they invented astrology as we know it today.[8] The earliest star catalogs date to about 3200 BCE, about the same time as the oldest Sumerian cuneiform clay tablets. The Sumerians invented much of our modern science. They were the first to divide a circle into 360° degrees, and they divided an hour into 60 minutes.

Only fragments of Mesopotamian astronomy have been discovered, but it is still the oldest mathematical description of astronomical events in the Western hemisphere, and it laid the foundation for all the Greek, Roman, Arabic and European scientific thinking that followed. The ancient Sumerians also had a mandala seen in their artwork. Like the Wheel of Time, it was an 8-pointed wheel, called the Star of Inanna, also known as the Star of Ishtar (see below). It was so ubiquitous in the history of that region that it is also featured in the current flag of Iraq.

Star of Ishtar

It is worth noting that the ancient depictions of the astrological zodiac were also presented in the image of a wheel, consisting of 12 constellations, each constellation corresponding to a month of the year. These are the 12 constellations that the sun travels through each year. So, the ancient zodiac was another wheel of time that represented one solar year. But, it also represented the Yuga cycle. Because, due to the precession of the equinoxes, the sun goes through a cycle of movement through all 12 constellations, backwards, every 24,000 years.

The Zodiac

Just as in every other major civilization that we have studied in the ancient past, the ancient Babylonian calendar was also a lunisolar calendar, consisting of 12 months (or 12 moons), plus an intercalary month consisting of the left over days of the solar year. This was based upon the Sumerian calendar, which preceded it, dated to approximately 4100 years ago. Like native Americans, each month began with the sighting of the new, barely visible, crescent moon, and ended when the moon completely disappeared at the end of the month.

The Babylonians were also the first to count 7 days to a week, with the 7th day being a holy day. So, you see that much of our current calendar we owe to the Sumerians and the Babylonians who followed them. The name Sabbath, which comes from the Hebrew *shabbat*, is widely believed to have originated with the Sumerian word *sa-bat*, which means mid-rest, or *a day of rest*.[9]

THE DRESDEN CODEX

One of the most spectacular ancient books on astronomy comes from Mesoamerica, and it is referred to as the Dresden Codex. Out of thousands of books that are believed to have been written by the ancient Mayans, only a handful of books survived to this day. Most were burned by the missionaries as they were not Christian in nature, therefore they were believed to be Satan's work. The Dresden Codex is one such book. It consists of just 39 pages. Its name comes from the city where it is located today, in Dresden Germany.

The ancient Mayan book is actually a series of astronomical tables. They predict lunar eclipses and the transits of Venus far into the future. The codex also contains astrological tables and ritual schedules based upon them. For instance, the book contains specific instructions for rituals and ceremonies to celebrate the New Year. We've already shown in previous sections the widespread use of solar and lunar observatories in the Americas, but the Mayan astronomical charts, mathematical calculations, and even their calendar are all astonishingly more impressive than anything we could have imagined.

THE MAYAN CALENDAR ROUND

The Calendar Round is one of the most impressive calendar systems ever devised. It is quite complex and involves several interlocking calendar cycles or wheels.[10] The two main sub-calendars are the Haab cycle and the Tzolk'in cycle. The Haab is simply the 365 day solar calendar, divided into 18 months of 20 days each, plus a short, 5-day, 19th month. The Tzolk'in calendar is a 260 day long cycle, composed of 13 months, each 20 days long. Why 260 days? No one is quite sure, but it could be the period between the zeniths of the Sun or the period during which Venus is visible. It is also exactly one third of the synodic period of Mars. [11]

The two cycles interlock with each other to produce a unique combination. This combination only repeats every 52 years. This would be not unlike our own calendar, where Tuesday, July 15th might only occur only once every 7 years. But, the Mayan calendar is far more complex. Because of this 52-year-long cycle called the Calendar Round, it is able to avoid leap year and still accurately measure one year to be 365.24 days long. This is even more accurate than the current

365.25 days in a year that we use today.

The most important unit of time for the ancient Mayans was the tun. This is how they marked important dates in the past and future. A tun was the 360-day period of the Haab cycle without the 5 days leftover at the end. To keep track of time, they primarily counted tuns. 20 tuns was called a katun. A bak'tun is made up of 20 katun or 400 tun. And the long count was a series of 13 bak'tun or 1,872,000 days. That comes out to 5,200 tuns or about 5125 solar years. The last long count ended in 2012. If you remember, this was the event that was predicted to be the end of an age and the beginning of a new age, possibly marking the coming of a global cataclysm.[12]

The Popol Vuh is another Mayan codex. It contains the history of the Mayan people. In the Popol Vuh, it tells that the earth has been created and destroyed a number of times, 4 times in the past and one more to come. The Aztec calendar also contains 5 ages of existence each of which ends in destruction. So, this is where these apocalyptic theories of world destruction come from. The idea is that each age is one long count. Then as we come to the end of a long count, we come to the end of an age of humanity, and possibly a time of global destruction. This is where much of the 2012 prophecies of destruction came from. But, according to most scholars and according to my own research on the topic, it was generally predicted to be more of a New Age of humanity rather than the end of the world.[13]

The 5 ages of humanity, when combined, creates

another long cycle of life and time. If you do the math then 5 long counts would equal a 25,625 yearlong cycle. This cycle is a similar time span as the Indian Yuga Cycle and may, in fact, result from the Mayan calculation of a complete cycle of precession. And, the Mayans may have been correct, given their observations.

Remember that I previously mentioned that the speed of the precessional movement is changing, just as objects in an elliptical orbit change speed. Well it appears that precession is speeding up. It is quite probable that 2,000 years ago the movement of precession was much slower than today. At that time it would have appeared that it would take approximately 26,000 years to complete one cycle, which is approximately equal to 5 Mayan long counts. As the speed of the movement has accelerated, we now calculate that it will take approximately 24,000 years to complete, which is the same time period predicted in the ancient Vedic texts of India. Both were likely referring to the same star-cycle, the precession of the equinoxes.

Look at the Aztec Calendar (on the facing page). Notice how there are arrows equally spaced all around the wheel? Now, count the number of arrows. There are exactly 8 arrows on the wheel. Coincidence? No. This is an 8-pointed wheel, exactly like our Wheel of Time.

Most people are familiar with the Aztec calendar stone[14] What is so important for our study of the Wheel of Time is that the famous Aztec Calendar is very much like the Wheel of Time, more specifically, it is like the Yuga Cycle and the Wheel of Time combined. This is because it depicts their calendar within the context of a very long cycle of time, their 5 ages of humanity, or as the Aztecs called it, *the 5 Suns*. This is yet another wheel, from yet another culture, designed to conceptualize time and life itself in all its repetition and progress in one concrete and useful model of a mandala or wheel.

Aztec Calendar

What is important in this Aztec wheel of time is how they conceived of the cyclic progression of time and life. This, once again, shows us the power of the concept of a wheel in prehistory people's perception of time and life. They saw all aspects of the universe as being able to be plotted on a giant mandala, one which has cycles within cycles, corresponding to the earth, moon, sun, stars, phases of life, phases of creation, and phases of humanity. And, the Aztecs, like the Sumerians, specifically chose an 8-pointed wheel, as their mandala.

SUMMARY

In this chapter we have sought to fill in the gaps in prehistoric archaeology with actual written texts to more accurately reveal what the ancient people were thinking when they constructed their stone monuments to the sun and moon. We have seen that the astronomical observations, as well as the mathematical calculations by ancient people as far back as 4 thousand years ago, were far more sophisticated than anything we might have suspected by looking at their crude monoliths and observatories. They may not have had advanced equipment and technology, but they certainly had advanced mathematics, scientific ideas, and astronomical records.

The conclusions they came to were nothing short of astonishing. They observed the precession of the equinoxes, calculated it quite accurately, and conceived of fantastic and brilliant ideas to explain what this phenomenon was and what it meant for humanity. Some even went so far as to postulate that our sun was part of a binary star system, and that one cycle of precession was equal to one orbit around our companion star. That's not bad for a 4,000-year-old scientific theory.

Another thing that is abundantly clear now is the prevalence of the concept of a wheel depicting the cycles of time, life, humanity, and even the cycles and phases of the human soul. While each culture has their own specific wheel of time that they have constructed, they all appear to think of time as a wheel, and they all see that we and all life are progressing through different phases and cycles on that wheel.

The whole notion that *time is like a wheel* was a near universal concept among pre-history people on opposite sides of the planet. Perhaps this concept is simply derived from being a human on earth with an endless cycle of days, months, and years, and similar patterns in nature and all life; we are born, grow up, grow old, and die, and then new babies are born all over again. But, for whatever reason, this concept of the Wheel of Time appears to be the main foundation for people's concept of life, time, and the universe, all over the world, for much of the last 10,000 years, until just the last millennium.

In fact, it is primarily in Western culture, just in the last 2,000 years, that we have begun to move away from a cosmology based upon the Wheel of Time. Next, we will explore how that change occurred. What happened to make us go from believing in a deeply mystic and complex concept of cyclical progress to a simple linear narrative of existence? How did we go from celebrating the winter solstice and all that it symbolizes in the vast dimensions of life and time to celebrating Christmas with Santa Claus and Rudolph the red-nosed reindeer?

How and when did we lose the lunisolar calendar? Even though some lunisolar holidays still exist, millions of people who celebrate Easter, Passover, and Chinese New Year have no idea that they are lunisolar holidays or exactly how those dates are determined. As we shall see, it was a long and interesting process that led us to lose the Wheel of Time.

CHAPTER 8

HOW OUR HOLY DAYS EVOLVED: AMONG THE ENGLISH: PART I: 55 BCE TO 731 CE

So far we have explored how ancient people carefully tracked the cycles of the sun, moon, and stars and they sought to see a connection between all these various cycles, often creating elaborate mandalas to represent the cyclic nature of time itself. This also led them to create elaborate lunisolar calendars and to hold rituals and ceremonies at auspicious times of the year, such as solstices, equinoxes, cross-quarter days, and certain lunar events coinciding with these times.

We have created a working template of the Wheel of Time for understanding the connections between these different astronomical events and their relationship to nature, agriculture, the human life cycle, and even society. Finally, we have shown just how widespread this practice was and how people on every continent and hemisphere practiced something like this for thousands of years. So, if the Wheel of Time was so widespread and omnipresent in human history then where did it go? Why aren't people using it now? What happened?

To answer this question, we go back to where our

investigation began, to Britain. Wouldn't it be wonderful to go back 2,000 years, observe the people there, learn their beliefs, their customs, and ask them about their cosmological concepts? Well, maybe we can. Fortunately, there was someone who did that. He was a learned man, and he wrote in a language that we understand very well today.

Julius Caesar

JULIUS CAESAR

His name was Gaius Julius Caesar, he was the Emperor of Rome, and he made a detailed record of his conquests, the people he encountered abroad, their customs and cultures. In his book, *Commentarii de Bello Gallico*, known as *The Gallic Wars* in English, Caesar chronicles his efforts to fight the Gauls (Celts) and conquer the land of northwest Europe and a large island off the coast of Europe, which they named Britannia.[1]

So, how did Caesar see these people and their beliefs?

Unfortunately, most of his writing is devoted to military strategy, battles, alliances with Gallic leaders, rebellions, sieges and so on. He did, however, make some observations that prove to be illuminating. Much of his observations may seem trivial, but they are nonetheless interesting. For instance, he writes that in addition to bronze and gold coins they also used iron rods as currency. They also considered it wrong to eat rabbit, chicken, or goose.

He writes that the people who live in Kent are more sophisticated and they grow corn-crops (wheat and barley), but the people who live inland survive on meat and milk, and clothe themselves in animal skins. He talks about how they would paint themselves with woad, a fermented plant extract, which turned their skin dark blue. This was especially done for battle, and probably made them look more terrifying to their enemy. They also fought in the nude, even when it was cold, which was also quite startling to Roman soldiers.

One peculiar item appears to be the practice of polyandry, which Caesar appears to have misunderstood. He writes that men often share their wives with other men, especially their brothers. Coming from a patriarchal society, he could not possibly have understood what he was witnessing. He writes about it as if the women were the property of the husband, and her body was freely given to his brothers out of his generosity. But, we now know that the women of Briton were nobody's property and were often great leaders and even generals of armies, such as Queen Boadicea, who led an army of 100,000 Iceni (a Briton tribe) against the Romans.

Queen Boadicea

Queen Boadicea burned the Roman city Londinium (London) to the ground and killed 70,000-80,000 Roman soldiers and Britons loyal to Rome. So, it's unlikely Briton men could order their wives to sleep with other men. More likely, they practiced polyandry just as it is still practiced in other parts of the world today, such as in the Himalayan region of Ladakh.

There, women often take multiple husbands, usually brothers, but it is the woman who does the choosing. Women would marry the oldest of several brothers first. Then, as his little brothers come of age she would take them as additional husbands to create something like a harem of husbands.[2]

Like many matriarchal societies, in Ladakh the elder women are the leaders and property is passed from mother to daughter. This practice likely ended in Britannia when the patriarchal Romans conquered the island.

Caesar also infamously described their public executions in giant human figures made of wicker. The wicker man was a giant flammable cage, into which they would put criminals condemned to death or sacrificial victims and burn them alive. This was a practice that was continued by Christians in one form or another well into the 1600s, by the practice of *burning at the stake*. In spite of the fact that the Romans practiced crucifixion, Caesar seemed absolutely horrified by the wicker man executions.[3]

Druids

ANCIENT DRUIDISM

The Pagan religion practiced by the ancient Britons was called Druidism. The druid priests, according to Caesar, occupied a special status above all others. They had multiple roles; they were the priests, the physicians, the wizards, the poets, the diviners, theologians, scientists, astronomers, historians, and record keepers. Interestingly, he says that they purposely do not write down any of their knowledge but use oral tradition and memory instead.

This seems to preserve their teachings as secret and sacred knowledge, so as to not let it fall into the hands of foreigners. Instead of written records, all knowledge is contained in epic poems, which are ritually repeated and memorized by the priests and initiates. Being intensely patriarchal, Caesar believed that druids were exclusively male, but we now know that women were priestesses as well.

Caesar goes on to describe the gods that druids worshipped. Unfortunately, he used only the Roman names for these gods, drawing a parallel to similar gods in Rome. He said essentially that the druids worshiped much the same gods as the Romans. He said that the main god was Mercury, by which he meant Odin. He also referred to Apollo, Mars, Jupiter, and Minerva, by which he probably meant Bragi, Tiw, Thor, and Fri. One of the reasons we know the importance of these gods is because of the English names given for the days of the week.

While the Romans named the days of the week after the sun, moon, and planets (Sol, Luna, Mars, Mercury, Jupiter, Venus, and Saturn), the English used the corresponding ancient Norse gods instead. For instance, Sunday is named for Sunna the Norse Sun goddess and Monday for Mona, the Norse moon god. But, few know that Tuesday was originally Tiw's day, and it is named after the Norse god of war, Tiw, which Romans call Mars. Wednesday was originally Wodin's day, a phonetic spelling of Odin's day, named after Odin, similar to the Roman god Mercury. Thursday was originally Thor's day, named after the Norse god Thor, which corresponds to the Roman god Jupiter. Friday was originally Fri's Day, named after a Saxon goddess, similar to the Norse Goddess Frig, which has elements of both Minerva and Venus.

Of all the days of the week, only Saturday was left unchanged and named after a Roman god, *Saturn*, god of agriculture. Ironically, the Romans themselves changed the name of Saturday from *Sāturni Dies,* which means *Saturn's Day,* to the Latin name for the sabbath, *Sabato.* This is thought to be in reverence to the Judeo-Christian faiths and to discourage the worship of the popular pagan god Saturn, which is better known today as *Satan*.

Caesar went on to discuss many fascinating details of Gallic life but, unfortunately, there is not much that would directly relate to our study of the Wheel of Time. But he did make one interesting observation about druids. He said that the druid priests would study and train for up to 20 years, and what they studied included "the stars and their movements, the size of the universe and the earth, the nature of things."[4]

He goes on to say that they believed in reincarnation, which is essentially a belief that all life, including human life, is cyclic and repeats perpetually. He also documents the importance of the equinoxes and solstices as major holy days. This is important because it validates a couple of essential elements of the Wheel of Time. This confirms that they did see the human life cycle being echoed in nature and the changing seasons as marked by the repeating cycle of solstices and equinoxes. And, they believed that death and reincarnation are integral parts of the cycle of life and time. We already thought as much, but now we have an eyewitness account by Julius Caesar in 53 BCE confirming this belief.

DIODORUS OF SICILY

Another early Roman historian, who lived about the time of Julius Caesar, was Diodorus of Sicily (90-30 BCE). It is through him that we start to learn about the ancient Celtic holidays. He described three major holidays that they celebrated each year. One was celebrated when the constellation Pleiades first peaked above the horizon in spring, around May 1st.

The *Pleiades* constellation, also known as the *Seven Sisters,* or *Subaru* in Japanese, is not visible in the Northern Hemisphere for half the year, so the first sighting of Pleiades must have meant that it would soon be summer. Of course we know from the Wheel of Time that May 1st is also auspicious because it is a cross-quarter day, half way between the spring equinox and the summer solstice. In Gallic, it was called Beltaine. The rising of the Pleiades must have made this day doubly auspicious.

Another major holiday described by Diodorus was on the setting of Pleiades, six months later, around November 1st. Of course, this is another cross-quarter day called Samhain, the mid-point between the equinox and the winter solstice, and marks the beginning of winter, the season of death. Interestingly, because the Romans did not celebrate cross-quarter days, Diodorus referred to these holidays as celebrations of the equinoxes, but of course they are both a month and a half after the equinox. Likewise, he said that they celebrated the summer solstice by worshipping the Sun god Lugh, and they called the holiday Lughnasadh. But, again, we know from other sources that Lughnasadh was another cross-quarter day, celebrated at the beginning of August.

Though he may not have understood the concept of cross-quarter days, Diodorus does do one really important thing for us. He documents that 2000 years ago the Celtic people were not only marking all 8 solar points of the Wheel of Time (the solstices, equinoxes, and cross quarter days), but they actually celebrated the cross quarter days as the biggest holidays of the year. Just as we have Christmas, Easter, Halloween, and so on, for them, their major holidays were Beltaine, Lughnasadh, Samhain, and probably Imbolc as well. Of them, he reports that the two biggest holidays were Beltaine and Samhain as they also marked the helical rising and setting of the constellation Pleiades.

Interestingly, some historians nowadays believe that the cross-quarter days were not important in ancient druid beliefs and practices, and that this is primarily an invention of neo-pagans of the 19th and 20th century. But, we have already shown numerous ancient archaeological sites that mark cross-quarter days, and from Diodorus we have solid ethnographic information documented by a historian at the time.

Ironically, Diodorus didn't even know what a cross-quarter day was. He thought they were just marking the equinoxes and solstices at odd times. In fact, it is because of Diodorus' confusion that many modern scholars doubt the importance of the cross-quarter days among ancient people, quoting Diodorus that they only celebrated "the solstices and equinoxes". But, since he mentions that the Pleiades marks their holidays, and because Pleiades rises in the beginning of May and sets in the beginning of November, and because Diodorus calls the holidays by name, we now know that he was wrong. These holidays are not solstices and equinoxes, but rather they are the cross-quarter days.

We also know that these holidays were celebrated on the eve of each holy day. According to Caesar, they see the night before the day as the start of that day, and they always celebrate at night.[6] Though he did not specify it, I suspect that, just as today, they saw the start of the day as beginning at midnight. This is obvious when you look at the Wheel of Time because midnight is aligned with the start of the new moon and the start of the new year, so it follows that it would be the start of the new day as well. And, this is exactly what we do even today. That's why we celebrate the New Year at midnight.

That Beltaine and Samhain are the biggest holy days makes sense because on the Wheel of Time this corresponds to the start of the growing season and end of the harvest season. In the human life cycle, this segment of the wheel is what we might call adult life, from puberty to death. On the daily cycle it is also the most important time of the working day, from 9am to 9pm. You could also say that this divides the year in two parts representing life and death, just as we saw at Stonehenge. After all, we know that these were celebrations of light and dark, life and death, the binary components of the recurring life cycle and the phases of the solar day and year.

PLINY THE ELDER

The historian Pliny the Elder, born in 23 CE, probably gave us the best description of the Druids and their pagan beliefs and practices. He noted in his book *Naturalis Historia,* or *Natural History*, that the druid priests wore white robes, denoting their status among the Celts. And, they would carry with them a golden sickle. He wrote that mistletoe, a parasite that grows on oak trees, was regarded by the druids with religious awe.[7] They would use their sickle to cut off sprigs of mistletoe on the sixth day of the new moon. They called this day the All-Healing day, and mistletoe picked on this day could heal any illness. The 6th day of the moon is a waxing quarter moon, and on the Wheel of Time it corresponds to dawn, birth, and the spring equinox. This would be seen as a phase of the moon and a time of year associated with growing life energy. Thus, this would be associated with coming back to life and getting stronger.

Knowing how the Druids viewed mistletoe, this also helps to explain the connection between mistletoe and the midwinter celebration. The plant was probably picked not just because it's an evergreen, like pine and holly, but also because it is specifically associated with the waxing of life energy and the anticipated return of spring, which is the whole point of the midwinter holiday.

Finally, Pliny also mentions that they have a lunisolar calendar, with a repeating cycle that is 30 years long, which we might call an *Age* or an *Era*. At the time, this may not have been well understood, but we know such a system is necessary to reconcile the cycles of moons (months) with the annual solar cycle. Since there are 12.36 lunar cycles in a year, it takes many years to get a whole number of each. Then the cycle starts all over.

COLIGNY CALENDAR

One of the greatest discoveries for understanding the druid calendar has been the Coligny Calendar, found in Coligny France and dated to the late 2nd century CE.[8] It is an engraved bronze tablet, written with Latin letters, but in the Gallic language. It is, indeed, a lunisolar calendar, and it is huge. Originally in one piece, 5 feet by 3 ½ feet, it is now preserved in 73 separate fragments with some gaps. The calendar covers 62 months, over 5 years, arranged in 16 columns. And, it contains some fairly interesting features.

The fact that it is a lunisolar calendar is itself interesting. From the Golden Hats that we looked at in Chapter 3, we know that the Celts used a lunisolar calendar prior to the Roman invasion. And, there has been speculation among scholars whether the Gauls and the Britons were still using a lunisolar calendar as late as 1800 years ago. But, with the Coligny Calendar, we now know that they were indeed still using the lunisolar calendar, even a full 200 years after the Roman conquest.

One interesting feature of the Coligny Calendar is that the new year, literally the start of the calendar year, begins with the holiday they call Samonios. It is not clear what holiday this is. Many scholars think that this is the same as the old Irish Samhain (November 1st). You have to remember that while we spell Samhain and Samon differently, both spellings may have come from the same word in ancient Gallic, probably pronounced differently in Ireland than in France. The importance of Samhain has already been documented by Diodorus, so it is likely that they were referring to November 1st. But it also could have been the winter solstice as this corresponds to the new year on The Wheel of Time. In fact, you could argue that the winter solstice is the peak of Samhain (the season of death).

There are some other technical details to note in the Coligny Calendar. Each month was divided into 2 half-months or *fortnights*. The first half was always 15 days, the second half either 14 or 15 days, alternating each month. And they added a 13th intercalary month every 2 ½ years. The calendar only covers a period of 5 years, but based on this calendar it appears that they kept a 30-year cycle made up of exactly 371 moons, which is accurate to one day every 20 years.

This 30-year cycle is especially exciting because it validates Pliny the Elder's account of a *Celtic Age* being 30 years long. It's hard for us to know just how accurate Pliny was at the time. But, this finding lends credence to Pliny's other observations as well, and suggests that he was fairly accurate in his accounts of Druid culture. The use of a 30 yearlong calendar is a similar idea as that used in other cultures, such as the Mayan's 52-yearlong Calendar Round. In this way. The Celts observed that 30 years is a simple common denominator, the smallest period into which you can fit a whole number of both lunar months and solar years.

THE BARDS: THE BOOK OF TALIESIN & THE ULSTER CYCLE

With the exception of the Coligny Calendar, we have primarily relied on Roman records for descriptions of the Druids, their culture, beliefs, and practices. This is because the Celts kept few if any written records. Roman historians reported that the Druids did write in their native language, using Greek letters, and later with Roman letters, but we have very few such sources. Other than the Coligny calendar, the writings that did survive contain no astronomical observations, mathematical tables, or philosophical texts. According to Caesar, they studied such things but this knowledge was kept secret and, as such, was never written down, but passed down through oral tradition.

What we do have, however, are many epic stories

written by the Bards of that time. Many people think of Bards as simply medieval poets and minstrels. But, the Bards may actually have been the last remnant of the pre-Roman, learned and noble Celtic society. The Romans fought hard to stamp out the Druid religion. But, the Druids were more than just a religion. They were a privileged class among the Celtic people, like the Brahmins in India.

According to the Greek historian Strabo (20 CE), there were three types of professionals in Celtic society. There were Druids who were the priests, the Ovates who were the scientists, and astrologers. And, then there were the Bards who were the poets and musicians. The Druids and Ovates were banned by the Romans, but the Bards were allowed to continue their practice.

Even after the Romans broke up their religious order, the Druids and Ovates may have survived as Bards. Not unlike the description of Druid priests and Ovates, the Bards were educated, knowledgeable, literate, poets, musicians, and wise counselors to the native tribal leaders and kings. The Bards may well have preserved the old religion in secret but, of course, they did not write about that explicitly.

The Bards did not write about religion or science, but instead they wrote many epic stories. This is exciting because if they were the last of the Druids, then we can hear from them directly instead of reading Roman descriptions of them. The question is this: were these stories history or fiction? That's hard to answer.

In fact, the very question of whether a story is history

or fiction reflects a very Roman way of thinking, which we have inherited in our Western civilization. It appears that the ancient Celts didn't see the world that way at all. Most of their stories were populated by both actual historical figures and pagan gods. They contain stories of actual battles and events, but those stories were mixed with reports of magic, witches, and gods. Some are so far-fetched as to be almost comical.

Unfortunately, there are no manuscripts from the Roman times, but we do have several sources that date to the Middle Ages. Most of these manuscripts come from Wales or Ireland. And, scholars agree that some of these stories likely originated in the 5th century or earlier.

Remember, Caesar documented that the Celts did not write down their knowledge but rather memorized it and passed it down through oral tradition. As such, some stories that were set in the 1st century or earlier were probably passed down through oral tradition and written down centuries later. But, for the most part, the stories read like fanciful fairy tales, and in many ways resemble Greek mythology with their stories of gods, magic, and mortals.

Táin Bó Cuailnge, known in English as the *Cooly Cattle Raid*, is one that is set in the pre-Christian, 1st century, Briton; it is part of a larger collection of stories called the *Ulster Cycle*.[9] It features a protagonist named Cú Chulainn, who according the text was the son of Lugh, the god of light and Sun, and he was also a High King. In this story, Cú Chulainn is visited by Morrigan, the goddess of war, who comes to him first as a young woman to seduce him, but he rejects her.

Then, she turns herself into an eel and tries to trip him when he walks through a river. When that doesn't work, she turns herself into a wolf to cause a cattle stampede to trample him. Then, she turns herself into the cow at the front of the stampede. But, he fights her off again, wounding her. Finally, she turns herself into an old woman milking a cow and offers him milk to drink. He gratefully drinks the milk, and as he does so he blesses her for her kindness. Then, his blessing magically heals her wounds. The epic story goes on and on, but this gives you the flavor of this and many similar ancient tales.

Another interesting work is the Book of Taliesin.[10] It is believed that Taliesin was an actual historical figure, a Bard in the 6th century, and he may have written some of these stories. But, it appears that other stories about him were added to the collection in later centuries. The stories tell us that Taliesin was a great and magical Bard and an adviser to King Arthur. As such, there are connections between Taliesin and *Myrddin*, which is Old Welsh for *Merlin*. It is not clear if they are one and the same person or separate figures. They may well refer to the same person, and the name *Merlin* might have been more like a title rather than his actual name, just as being a Bard was also a Druid title.

The Book of Taliesin is also filled with magic, not unlike the *Táin Bó Cuailnge*. In fact, the 1938 novel, *The Sword in the Stone*, was loosely based upon the stories of Taliesin, among other sources.[11] Later, Disney turned the book into a popular animated feature film. In the film, the magical chase scene between Merlin and the witch Mim appears to be taken right out of a story in the Book of Taliesin.

The story goes that Taliesin was the product of an accident. The witch Cerridwen brewed a magical potion in her caldron to turn her hideous son Morfan into a great and wise Bard. The servant Gwion was in charge of stirring it. After brewing it for a year and a day, it was finally ready. Just then, some of it splashed onto Gwion's hand. It was hot, so he put his fingers into his mouth to soothe them. In doing so, he ingested the potion, and he stole all the magic that was in the caldron. Cerridwen was furious and chased him.

He ran away and, using his newfound magical powers, turned himself into a hare. She turned herself into a greyhound and gave chase. When he came to a river he turned himself into a fish and swam away, but she turned herself into an otter and continues to chase him. He leaped out of the water and turned himself into a bird to fly away, but the witch Cerridwen became a hawk and gave chase through the air. He flew to the ground, saw a pile of wheat, and turned himself into a single grain of wheat to hide. As she landed, she quickly turned herself into a hen, and ate him. But that was not the end.

Soon after this she became pregnant, though she had not laid with a man recently. She realized that the baby was Gwion. She became impregnated with him when she swallowed him. She wanted to kill him, but when he was born he was the most beautiful child she'd ever seen. But, she was still angry, so she put him in a bag and threw him into the ocean. A fisherman named Elphin found the bag caught in his net. When he found the boy, he named him Taliesin. And very soon it was clear that he was no ordinary boy, but a great and magical Bard. Much later, Taliesin went to the court of King Arthur where he became the king's Bard and a wise and trusted adviser.[12]

You see why I suggest that the Bards were an extension of the Druid tradition. In Taliesin's writing it is clear that, at that time, a Bard was considered much more than a mere writer or minstrel. The Bards and witches had magical powers. As such, it is also clear that they were seen as wizards and priestesses of the old religion. But, the stories are so fanciful that we can hardly glean much useful information from them. These stories are great literature but frustrating to historians. They are entertaining, and it does give us an appreciation for their story-telling ability, which was very impressive. But, if we wanted to know, for instance, how or when they celebrated their holy days, then we are out of luck.

There is only one exception to this dearth of information, and that is one story in the *Ulster Cycle,* set in the first century. In the tale of *Tochmarc Emire, (the Wooing of Emer)* there is a story where Cú Chulainn was trying to woo the maid Emire.[13] She gives him several tasks to fulfill in order to win her hand. One of them is that he must go without sleep for one entire year, literally throughout all four seasons of the year. And, it is here that she names the four fire festivals of the year; Imbolc, Beltaine, Lughnasadh, and Samhain, each of which was the first day of each of the four seasons.

This is useful information because it shows, yet again, that they actually observed and celebrated all four cross-quarter days, though Beltaine and Samhain may have been relatively bigger celebrations, according to the Roman historian Diodorus. It is interesting to note that while they had observatories to mark the equinoxes and solstices, according to multiple sources, the Druids clearly favored the celebration of cross-quarter days. Though, we can only assume that they acknowledged the other four points in the year in some way. After all, to find the cross-quarter days, you had to know when the solstices and equinoxes were. Only then could you find and mark the cross-quarter days as the beginning and end of each season. And, we know that, according to Julius Caesar, they celebrated the equinoxes and solstices as well. So, they must have observed all 8 days of the year on the Wheel of Time.

Seeing how the Bards were not great historians by our standards today, we must now turn to the other Roman and Christian accounts in order to piece together the evolution of the holy days from the time of the Roman occupation onward.

While the Bards occupied themselves and their audiences with fanciful tales of magic and mischief, it was becoming a dark time for the Roman Empire. From the 2nd century through the 5th century, Rome suffered a gradual erosion of power and influence. Corruption was rampant in Rome at the highest levels. Rome was first split in half and then repeatedly attacked by hordes of barbarians. Finally, the city of Rome itself was sacked. There was no choice. All Roman soldiers throughout the empire were ordered to return to Rome to protect the capital. With the withdrawal of the troops, many Roman citizens and colonists decided to leave as well. They might have thought that it was just temporary. But, they never returned, as that was the beginning of the end of the Roman Empire.

This was the beginning of the dark ages. As a result, during the 5th and 6th Centuries we really know very little of everyday life or even major events in the British Isles. This was the time of the legendary King Arthur, which is shrouded in mystery precisely because of the lack of credible historical accounts. There are many stories of Arthur written by the Bards, such as Taliesin, but they are so filled with magical events, witches, and gods, that it's hard to look at these stories as historical records. Also, many stories contradict each other, so it's impossible to tell what really happened. But, there was one author at that time who created a credible history of events in the 6th century and attempted to recap events of the previous century, and that was the Roman historian Gildas (516-570 CE).

GILDAS THE WISE

By the time of Gildas, many changes had occurred since the writing of the Coligny Calendar. Probably the biggest change was that Christianity was now the official religion of Rome, and missionaries had spread the religion to every corner of the Roman Empire, including Britannia. *Gildas the Wise*, as he was known, was one such Christian monk. He was a great scholar, well known for his literary style and vast biblical knowledge. But, perhaps he is most famous for his work *De Excidio et Conquestu Britanniae*, which is a history of Briton prior to the Anglo-Saxon invasion and a scathing rebuke of the pagan practices of the native Celts and even the Anglo-Saxons, which he simply refers to as Saxons.[14]

It is because of Gildas that we have the earliest historical account of the battle of Mount Badon, which figured prominently in stories of King Arthur. Gildas claimed to have been born in the very year of that famous battle. The battle was between the Romanized Britons and the invading Germanic Anglo-Saxons. While the Britons won the battle, they lost the war. Later, in the 6th century, Briton was eventually conquered by the Anglo-Saxons.

We say Anglo-Saxon, but there were actually 3 Germanic tribes from across the channel that invaded southern Briton; they were the Angles, Saxons, and Jutes. The dominant tribe was the Angles, originally written Ænglii. It is from this name that we get the name of their land, England, and their language, English. Ironically, like Gildas, many just refer to them as Saxons.

Gildas was very critical of both the native Britons and the Saxons during his time, though he seemed to have an especially negative view of the native Celts. He very harshly criticized them for their wickedness and their pagan practices. He said that they had many idols, even more than in Egypt.

But what is more interesting is how he describes their worship of Nature.

He berates the people for paying divine honor to the mountains, springs, hills and rivers. Of course, as a Christian, he complains that this was an abomination and explains how the earth should be subservient to the use of men, not the other way around. This is important because it directly relates to the Wheel of Time.

We know that they revered the cycles of the sun and moon and saw a connection between that and the cycles of nature and the seasons. Now, we get a more nuanced view of their beliefs. They saw all of nature, even the mountains, springs, hills, and rivers, as sacred. This is very similar to pagan beliefs in North America and elsewhere.

There were many historians such as Gildas in the following centuries, almost all of whom were Christian monks. This should not be surprising since they were almost the only ones who were educated and literate, with the exception of the Bards. Furthermore, at that time, the only written language was Latin.

Remember, the Druids and early Anglo-Saxons shunned the use of written records, preferring instead the memorization of epic poems, such as *Beowulf* or *Sir Gawain and the Green Knight*. In the monks' historical accounts, we see not just an outsider's view of ancient paganism but also the proliferation of the new religion of Christianity among those same pagans that Gildas railed against.

ST. AUGUSTINE & THE FIRST CHRIST-MASS

St. Augustine was a Benedictine monk and the head of a monastery in Rome. He was sent to Briton by Pope Gregory in 595 CE on a mission to convert the pagan king who lived there.[15] He landed in the Kingdom of Kent, in what is now the southeastern tip of England. He went directly to Canterbury to the throne of King Æthelberht (Ethelbert). The king had married a Christian princess from Paris and it was thought he might be open to conversion.

Augustine was successful and King Æthelberht was not only baptized himself but he also allowed Augustine to convert all the people of Kent. Æthelberht then gave Augustine a parcel of land to found a monastery there. On Christmas Day, 597 CE, King Æthelberht officially made Augustine the first Archbishop of Canterbury. Augustine, in turn, converted thousands of pagans in a mass baptism.

It's important to note that this ceremony took place on Christmas day. In Rome, there was an ancient winter solstice celebration known as *Solis Invicti*, celebrating the birth of the god Mithra on December 25th. In about 354 AD, it had been officially changed to a celebration of the birth of Jesus instead. Evidently, in spite of Rome being officially a Christian Empire, they could not stop the popular winter solstice holiday from being celebrated by the common folk. So, the Church in Rome synchronized the celebration of the birth of Jesus with the birth of Mithra. Essentially they just replaced the old god Mithra with the new savior Jesus while keeping the celebration on the same date and with many of the same traditions.

Though the change had occurred nearly 250 years earlier in Rome, the Celts and especially the Anglo-Saxons of Briton still celebrated the winter solstice on December 25th, with the Feast of Yule, celebrating the rebirth of their sun goddess Sunna. So, this mass baptism by Augustine was the first time any of them had celebrated this pagan holy day with a Christian mass. Of course, they most likely kept many of their same winter solstice traditions, including the burning of the Yule log, gift giving, a feast, drinking ale, and decorations with boughs of evergreens, holly, and mistletoe. But, from then on, the day became known throughout the land as a Christian holy day.

And so we see it. Right here, on the winter solstice celebration of 597, the people of Kent celebrated this traditional pagan Sabbath for the first time with a Christ-mass. And over the centuries it simply became known as Christmas.

WHAT MAKES CHRISTMAS CHRISTMAS?

With the above story, we now see how evergreens, holly, and mistletoe became associated with the birth of Christ. But, there is a deeper issue here. Why were evergreens, Yule logs, and such things used to celebrate the pagan festival of Yule in the first place? To answer this, you need to examine the Wheel of Time. Let's look at Figure 6 below again. Notice that midwinter is associated with darkness. It is associated with the lunar phase of the totally dark, new moon, and the time of day associated with this place on the Wheel of Time is midnight.

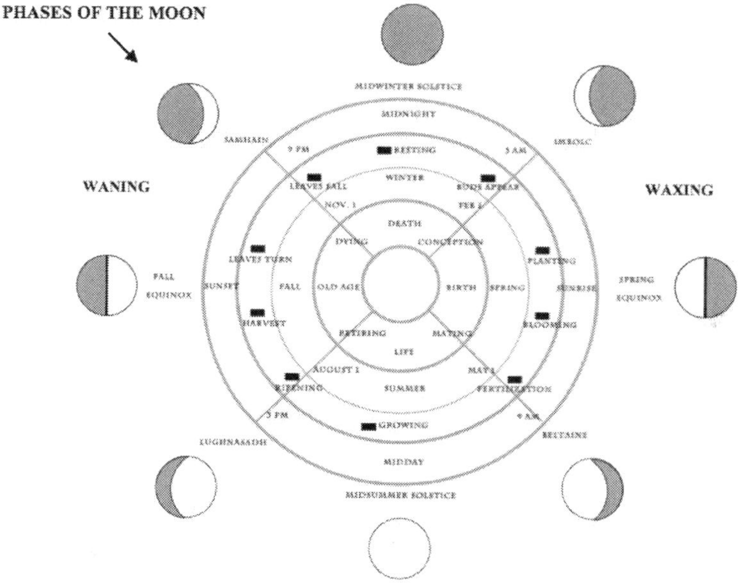

Figure 6

It's clear that this is why the Christmas mass is celebrated at midnight, even to this day. This comes from the Wheel of Time. This point on the Wheel of Time, midnight/midwinter/new moon, is the very end of one cycle and the beginning of a new cycle. This is most clearly seen with the cycle of the moon. It is the end of one visible moon, and the beginning of another visible moon. That's why we celebrate the New year at this time of year. And it is why midnight is the start of a new day as well. This point on the Wheel of Time ends one cycle and begins a new cycle. That's why it's important.

Of course, Christmas, like Solis Invicti before it, was on the 25th, but the solstice is actually around the 21st or 22nd. If they tracked the sun so well, why were they off by a few days? The Romans actually had 2 different holidays at this time; Saturnalia on the actual solstice and Solis Invicti on the 25th of December.

The reason why they celebrated three days after the midwinter solstice is because that was the first day that you could tell that the sunrise had changed directions and began rising a little further to the north each day. The annual cycle of the sun was moving back toward another spring and another new year.

Remember that they thought a new moon was not on the day when there was no visible moon, but rather the first visible sighting of a sliver of the new moon, which began the new lunar cycle. At the time of the solstice, the sunrise doesn't appear to change for a few days. Then, after 3 days, the sunrise appears to begin moving a little to the north again. So, the new year was not on the winter solstice but the first sighting of movement of the sun, after the solstice, which is about December 25th.

Like the sun and moon, all the plants that die in the winter are not actually dead after all; they are just asleep and will return in spring. Now we see that the evergreens are symbolic of this very concept. They too live on and in midwinter they remind us that the rest of nature is not dead but just asleep, and that it will return to life in the spring. They are proof of the persistence of life and, thus, the promise of renewal and a new spring.

For humanity, the symbolism is even deeper and more meaningful. It means that the death of a person is not the end, it is just a temporary sleep, and we will be reincarnated again. Remember that the Celts believed in reincarnation. So evergreens symbolize the idea that, though our bodies die, our souls live on, like the evergreens. So evergreens, like pine, holly, and mistletoe, represent life after death; they literally represent eternal life. Perhaps that is why the winter solstice and the traditions of Yule were so hard to stamp out of popular culture at that time. It is the most profound of all pagan holidays.

Despite the fact that the Druids of Briton preferred to celebrate the cross-quarter days, this was not the norm for most pagan cultures. From our study of Stonehenge, we know that much earlier the solstice had been a very important holy day among the Britons. As we shall see, for most pagan people throughout the world, the winter solstice is one of the biggest holidays of the year.

For Anglo-Saxon pagans as well, it was one of the most spiritual and reverent holy days of the year. It was a celebration of the Wheel of Time itself and a reaffirmation of eternal life. None of this changed with the conversion to Christianity. They simply imbued Christmas with all the same qualities that had made the Yuletide so special.

In fact, they never really stopped celebrating the Yule. For the most part, we still celebrate the Yule to this day. We just call it Christmas.

Father Christmas

DAGDA, ODIN, & FATHER CHRISTMAS

There were two different midwinter pagan mythologies in England in the middle-ages; one came from the native Celts and one from the Anglo-Saxons. The Celts worshipped the goddess Cilleach Bheur. She was the goddess of old age and death, and so she was also the goddess of winter.

Also the God Dagda (or Dagodeiwos) was also honored at the winter solstice. He was also known as the Eochaid Ollanthair, *All Father*. He was the god of time and also the god of the afterlife. As such, he was also worshipped at the winter solstice. He was described as having a long white beard, wearing long red robes, and he carried with him a cauldron of plenty, with gifts for everyone. He is usually depicted carrying a wheel in one hand, symbolizing the Wheel of Time, and a club in the other.

Among the Anglo-Saxons, there was the goddess Frī, also known as Frija, or Frīg, goddess of love and motherhood, who was honored at the midwinter solstice. And, Frī's husband, the Norse god Odin, was also honored at this time of year. According to Norse mythology, Odin had a long white beard, a fur lined robe, and he was believed to ride an 8-legged horse across the night sky on December 24th, throwing out gifts to the people, especially women and mothers, in honor of Frī.

Clearly, the early church fathers frowned upon stories of the pagan gods Dagda and Odin. So, sometime in the hisory of Britain we begin to see references to *Father Christmas* instead. Meanwhile, the mention of any goddesses appears to have been stamped out altogether by the patriarchal church fathers. But, it seems clear enough to us today that Father Christmas had elements of both Dagda and Odin. He had a long white beard, fur lined red robes, and he had a large sack of plenty (clearly a carry-over from *the caldron of plenty*).

And, Father Christmas rode through the night sky on Christmas Eve, giving out gifts. Of course, at some point his 8-legged flying horse was replaced with 8 flying reindeer. Notice the repeated reference to the number 8? Perhaps this is a sign that the holiday is the culmination of the 8 holy days of the Wheel of Time; the solstices, equinoxes, and cross-quarter days. Later we will see other references to the number 8 in popular holidays, which I suspect is not a coincidence.

Meanwhile, back in Rome, there was a holy day devoted to St. Nicholas every December, who had become the patron saint of children. St. Nicholas of Myra was a Christian bishop persecuted by Romans in the pre-Christian 3rd century. Due to a growing Christian ethos and a bias against the old pagan mythology, at some point, St. Nicholas either replaced or somehow merged with Father Christmas, making them synonymous in most people's minds.

Among the Dutch, St. Nicholas was known as St. Klaas, pronounced in Dutch as *Sinterklass or Santeclaus.* Many centuries later, in America, large numbers of European immigrants would make the name *Santeclaus* or *Santa Claus* interchangeable with St. Nicholas and Father Christmas.

And, so there are elements of the gods Dagda and Odin in our modern concept of Santa Claus to this very day. Now you know the rest of the story.

Father Christmas / Santa Claus

CHAPTER 9

HOW OUR HOLY DAYS EVOLVED: AMONG THE ENGLISH: PART II: 731 CE TO PRESENT

When we left off, we had shown how the pagan celebration of the midwinter solstice had started to become the Christmas holiday we now know today. Next, we will show how a pagan feast for the fertility goddess, Ēostre, became our modern holiday, *Easter*.

THE VENERABLE BEDE & THE FIRST CHRISTIAN EASTER

Bede (672-735 CE), known as *The Venerable Bede*, was an English monk at a monastery in the kingdom of Northumbria in northern England.[16] He was a well-known scholar and was a famous author, but he is best known for his work *Historia ecclesiastica gentis Anglorum*, or *The Ecclesiastical History of the English People*, written in 731 CE.[17] In his book, he combined the writings of Caesar, Pliny the Elder, Gildas, and others in one complete history of Britannia from the time it was first discovered by the Romans until the 8th century. It is because of this book that he is known as the Father of English History.

Bede was an amazing scholar and linguist and translated many ancient Greek and Roman works, making them accessible to the English people. But, in addition to being a translator and historian, he was fascinated with how we perceive, record, refer to, and celebrate the passage of time. As such, he is a pivotal character in the history of the Wheel of Time.

Venerable Bede

Bede was a unique individual in that, while he was a Christian scholar, he was also a native of England, a celebrated historian of ancient Britain, and a student of ancient Greek and Roman writings about calendars and lunisolar calendar systems. More than most scholars of his time, he understood the ancient lunisolar calendars and various systems of time-keeping designed to reconcile the lunar and solar cycles. And, writing in the 8th century, he was considerably closer to the times of ancient pagan practices than any of the scholars who followed.

In 725, Bede wrote a book about time-keeping systems called *De Temporum Ratione*, which means The Rekoning of Time.[18] The book is quite amazing. He understood how the spherical Earth and moon created the lunar and solar cycles, over 800 years before Galileo. He had mastered the understanding of calendar systems and had created a macro-concept of the different ages of the Earth. Also, it is because of Bede that we use the designation of AD, meaning *Anno Domini* or *In the Year of the Lord*. Bede's view was that we were living in the sixth age of Earth, which began with the birth of Christ. By the way, AD is now referred to as CE, *Common Era*, so as to be used by all religions.

Bede's calendar used the same Roman Julian Calendar, but he numbered the years starting with the birth of Jesus. Anything prior to that date was the 5th age, and it was called BC or *Before Christ*. Nowadays we say BCE, *Before the Common Era*. It was an obscure monk, Dionysius Exiguus, in 525 CE, who actually devised this system, but it was Bede who popularized it and convinced the Church in Rome to make it standardized throughout the Holy Roman Empire. Prior to that, there was no standardized way of referring to a specific year which made it somewhat confusing.

But, Bede contributed something else even more important to the study of the Wheel of Time. Because he was an expert on lunisolar calendars, it was Bede who simplified the calculation for the date of the resurrection of Jesus, as an annual holiday. This had long been calculated based on the Jewish lunisolar calendar. They knew that the resurrection was three days after the crucifixion, which was believed to be the day before Passover. But Passover was a lunisolar holiday, using the Jewish calendar, which was nothing like the Julian

Calendar used by the Romans. This created some confusion among early Christians.

It was Bede who resolved the matter once and for all. He argued that Passover was simply a lunisolar holy day, associated with the spring equinox, similar to that celebrated by the Anglo-Saxon pagans. In England, they called it the Feast of Ēostre, the goddess of fertility, also known as the goddess of the dawn, literally goddess of the East, hence the modern name for the holiday, Easter.

Bede argued that they do not need to use the Jewish Calendar, they can use the Julian Calendar. They can simply celebrate on the first full moon after the spring equinox. Of course, they need to celebrate it on a Sunday, the Christian day of worship. So, he said that the true date for Ēostre is the first Sunday after the first full moon after the vernal equinox.[19] And, we still do this today. For instance, in 2017 Passover began on the eve of the first full moon after the equinox, April 10th, and Easter was on the Sunday after that, April 16th.

What's so interesting is that he didn't call it the Resurrection Day or Pasqua, as they do in Rome; he actually called it *Ēostre*, named after the pagan goddess of fertility, which we now spell Easter. This is also where we get the words east, estrus, and estrogen, all relating to fertility and the new dawn. From then on, the feast of the Goddess Easter was synonymous with Christ's resurrection. Now we have solid documentation of the second major pagan holy day to become Christianized.

There are a couple of interesting things about this. First of all, we see that the date of the Christian holiday we call Easter came from the ancient celebration of Passover, which it turns out was also a lunisolar celebration of the spring equinox. That is not the meaning traditionally associated with Passover. But, then again, that's not the meaning traditionally associated with Easter either. So, we see that over time different cultures overlay different specific meanings and associations with days that were originally pagan holy days on the Wheel of Time.

Secondly, it is interesting to note that the goddess of fertility, Ēostre, was also the goddess of the new dawn. Of course, you can see in figure 6 below that the spring equinox is associated with sunrise on the daily cycle. Not surprisingly, even today Christians celebrate Easter with a sunrise ceremony. So we are still using the ancient Wheel of Time and we don't even know it.

But, what do rabbits and eggs have to do with crucifixion and resurrection? To understand this, we need only to remind ourselves that it was originally a celebration of fertility, and then it all makes sense. We celebrate with Easter bunnies because rabbits are seen as very fertile. We celebrate with Easter eggs because eggs are symbolic of fertility and new life. And, of course, we celebrate with all the things we see in nature at this time of year: new spring grass, flowers, baby chicks, birds nesting and singing, colored eggs, and so on.

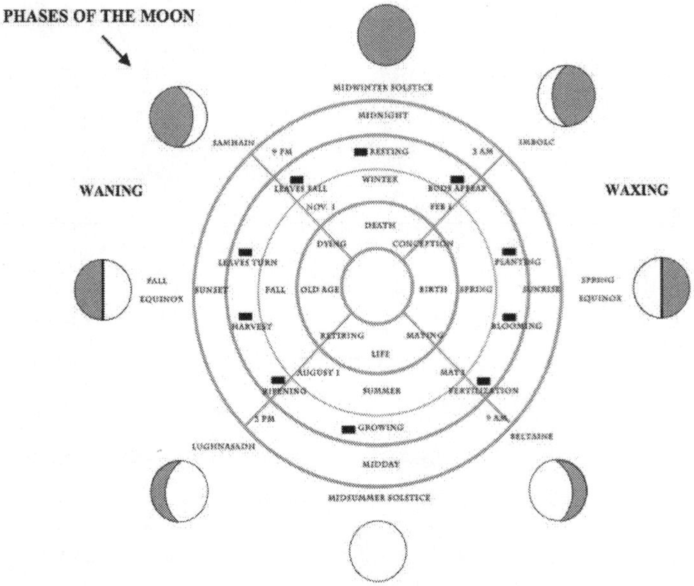

Figure 6

THE ANCIENT HEBREWS

If you are really paying attention, you may ask why they celebrated Easter on a full moon and not on a waxing quarter moon? If you look at Figure 6 above, you will note that the spring and sunrise are associated with a new quarter moon. So, why celebrate it on a full moon? Did The Venerable Bede get it wrong? Well, kind of. Remember he wasn't really concerned with identifying the pagan spring holy day, but rather the Jewish holy day of Passover. And, he accurately identified the lunisolar holiday of Passover as being on a full moon after the spring equinox.

Actually, on the Jewish lunisolar calendar it is the 15th

day of the month of Nisan, which corresponds to the month of the spring equinox.[20] On any lunisolar calendar, the new moon always occurs on the first of the month. Two weeks later, the 15th falls on a full moon. Therefore, the 15th of Nisan is always a full moon. According to the Jewish Calendar, Bede was fairly accurate. For instance, in 2017 Passover indeed fell on the first full moon after the equinox, and Easter was on the very first Sunday after that.

So, that begs the question: why did the Hebrews celebrate the spring equinox with a full moon and not a quarter moon? Were they not using the Wheel of Time? Good question. Remember in Chapter 2 when discussing the phases of the moon on the Wheel of Time, I said that the Wheel of Time is a circle, with no beginning and no end. So, you could independently dial the moon cycle to correspond to any point on the solar cycle in order to start the new year whenever you wanted to. So, the Chinese chose to celebrate the new year on the second new moon after the winter solstice, which is the midpoint between the winter solstice and spring equinox. And, other cultures choose to celebrate the new year at other times of the year. We choose to celebrate it on the first day of the first month after the winter solstice which most closely corresponds to the Wheel of Time in Figure 6.

Well, to understand why we celebrate Passover on a full moon we have to ask: when do the Hebrews celebrate the new year? If you're Jewish you know that Rosh Hashanah (Jewish New Year) corresponds to the fall equinox! So that is where they dial in the new moon. It is literally celebrated on the first day of the month of Tirshei, which occurs around the fall equinox.[21] Again, they celebrate the new year on the first day of the month, and that corresponds to the new moon, just as the 15th corresponds to the full moon.

If they were being consistent with the Wheel of Time, and they celebrated the new year with a new moon in the fall, that means, according to the Wheel of Time, they would celebrate the peak of the year with a full moon in the spring. And, that is exactly what we see with the Jewish Calendar. Rosh Hashanah is their new year celebrated on a new moon in the fall, and Passover is on the opposite side of the wheel, celebrated on a full moon in the spring.

You may ask, do they celebrate Passover at sunrise, just like Easter? No, that would be inconsistent with the Wheel of Time. Just look at Figure 6 and ask, what time of day corresponds to the autumn equinox? Sunset! So if the Autumn is the new year, then they celebrate the new year at sunset, and in fact they celebrate each new day, including Passover, at sunset. Similarly, we in the Western culture marks the new day at midnight, and the new year at midwinter. All they did was move the dial of lunar cycles to correspond with the time of year that they wanted to celebrate the new year, just as the Chinese did, and that becomes the top of their Wheel of Time.

Everything about the Jewish holidays, the beginning of the day, phases of the moon, and so on, are all perfectly consistent with the Wheel of Time. And we see that they, like the ancient builders of Stonehenge and even like the ancient druids, had two major holidays, one at the beginning of the year and one at the opposite position on the Wheel of Time, probably stemming from the same basic dichotomy of life vs. death and light vs. dark.

By the way, one might ask, why did they make fall the beginning of the year? I suspect that it was because of their own unique annual cycle tied to nature in their unique region of the world. If you've traveled to the Middle East, you know that the summer is unbearably hot and the winter is one of the nicest times of the year. So their summer is much like our winter, a time when not much is done, and people are mostly holed up and out of the elements. If that's the case, then the fall would be like our spring, a time when people would start spending more time outdoors and start being more active, and the beginning of a new year.

Also, I know from the bible that raising and shearing sheep was an important part of their culture. So, based on the Wheel of Time, I would predict that the shearing months would be around May or June because that's their harvest time. I really didn't know if that was true, but it was my prediction based upon the Wheel of Time. So, I looked it up and guess what? May and June were indeed the shearing months for the ancient Hebrews of the Bible.

So, now you see that even the ancient Hebrews used the Wheel of Time. As for the Celts and Anglo-Saxons in Briton and Northern Europe, there is very little documentation of when they celebrated the lunisolar holy day associated with the spring equinox but it probably wasn't on a full moon. Based on the Wheel of Time, it was most likely on the first quarter moon after or closest to the spring equinox. Indeed, this is confirmed by writings of Pliny the Elder (79 CE), who recorded that they celebrated the equinox on the 6th day of the moon, which would be a waxing quarter moon, just as predicted by the Wheel of Time.

NENNIUS & THE EVOLUTION OF KING ARTHUR

We are going to switch gears for a while and discuss the legends of King Arthur. In part, this is because for the next 300 years the historical writing about England and the British people was dominated by stories of King Arthur and a host of characters associated with Arthur. Another reason we are going to examine King Arthur is because of what Arthur represents to the British people.

Arthur was like a Rorschach test. People from different times in history saw different attributes in Arthur, and he became an evolving identity that changed as the people of Britain changed. I will argue later that this evolution in the zeitgeist of the English people is echoed in how they celebrate their holidays of the year. This will then help us to understand the changes that occurred over time in the holidays, and how they were celebrated.

We start with Nennius and his work, the *Historia Brittonum*, the History of the British People, which begins to rewrite the history of Briton in the 9th century.[22] But, before we get to Nennius, I want to first remind you that Gildas, writing in the 6th century, never even referred to King Arthur at all. He just said that there was a huge battle between Britons and Saxons at Mount Badon, in the year of his birth, 516 CE. Then, he went on to excoriate both the Britons and Saxons as godless, idol worshipping pagans. Later, in 731 CE, Bede also referred to the famous battle of Mount Badon, but he did not mention Arthur either. He said it was Ambrosius Aurelianus who lead the Britons to victory that day.

Finally, in 828 CE, it was Nennius who wrote that it was the legendary Arthur who won the battle of Mount Badon. He was likely influenced by the stories of the Bards who wrote extensively about King Arthur. Nennius went on to list 12 other famous battles of Arthur, who fought the invading Anglo-Saxons, and created a peace that lasted a generation.

Nennius fills in gaps missing in previous histories. He refers to King Vortigern, who invited the Anglo-Saxon warlords Hengist and Horsa to come to Briton as mercenaries to help defend the Britons from the Scotts and Picts from the north, after the Roman army left. As part of the deal, Hengist's daughter was promised to be Vortigern's bride. But, the Anglo-Saxon warlords betrayed Vortigern and made war upon the Britons, killing Vortigern's son, and paving the way for an Anglo-Saxon invasion.

Ambrosius Aurelianus, according to Nennius, was a precocious lad who helped Vortigern and later became king himself, as Bede had claimed. In fact, Ambrosius Aurelianus is described as a king among kings in Briton, like an emperor or Caesar. His brother and successor, Uther Pendragon then became king. And it was King Uther Pendragon's son who became the legendary hero, Arthur. According to Nennius, it was Arthur who was the hero of the battle of Mount Badon, a prominent military leader, and held the Saxons at bay in the decades that followed.[23] But, he doesn't refer to him as a king, only as a military leader.

King Arthur

In addition to filling in gaps in previous histories, Nennius adds new information that changes previous narratives. For instance, Nennius tells us that Arthur, the good and just leader of the Britons, was a Christian, with the image of the Virgin Mary on his shield, upon his shoulder. So this good Christian leader was fighting the pagan savages that threatened to invade Briton.

Notice how the narrative had changed since Gildas? Arthur, the victor of the battle of Mount Badon, has gone from a nameless pagan warlord to a great and noble Christian leader, fighting off the pagan Saxon invaders. And, he now has an impressive and complete pedigree as well as a prince and the rightful heir to the throne. The Saxons, according to Gildas, were painted as a somewhat civilizing influence in Briton, but by the 9th century they are now the pagan savages. This constitutes quite a change in the view of the British about native Britons, invading Saxons, and the role of Christianity. It is clear that the English are now identifying all that is good and true about their people with this figure Arthur who is, of course, both British and Christian. Nennius has almost completely edited out the Britons' paganism following the Roman conquest.

ANNALIS CAMBRIAE

Next, we move forward one hundred years and we find the next evolutionary mutation of British History in the form of the *Annalis Cambriae* or the Annals of Whales, probably written in the 10th century.[24] Here are added other characters that are central to the Legend of King Arthur. Mordred, Arthur's son, and Merlin, Arthur's mentor and wizard, are introduced in this version. By all accounts, Merlin appears to be very much like a Druid priest. Arthur is now said to be a great King, not just a military leader as described by Nennius. And, King Arthur is again said to be a Christian, bearing the image of the Virgin Mary upon his shield and/or on his shoulder.

Notice how Arthur has been promoted to King, and he is given a Druid wizard as a mentor? As the story evolves, we begin to see shifting perspectives of the English people and how they may be romanticizing their history. Now, there is no doubt in the minds of the English that all Britons were Christian, and we begin to see that the Druids, once an abomination to Christianity, are being romanticized as magical wizards.

What's more important is that we are seeing a confluence of two different lineages of history in England. There were the Bards with their historical but somewhat fantastic tales. These stories read like dramatic, fictional epics. Then there were the Roman historians like Pliny the Elder and Gildas, which may be more accurate but are not nearly as interesting or dramatic. And, now we are starting to see a combination of these two types of histories. The objective histories are being combined with fanciful tales of these same people and events. What we get in the end is a hybrid mythology, part history and part a Bard's tale.

THE NORMAN CONQUEST

Something very interesting happens at this point in British history. In 1066, at the Battle of Hastings, a Duke from Normandy named William I, aka William the Conqueror, aka, William the Bastard, defeated the Saxon forces to conquer all of England. This is known as the Norman Conquest. William brought with him his Norman culture and language. And, since Normandy was originally a part of the Carolingian Dynasty of France, their language and culture is essentially a form of French language and culture. What might surprise many people today is that, for the next 400 years after the Norman Conquest, the official language of England was a dialect of French. And, if you have read the legends of Robin Hood, you know that the Saxon peasantry was vilified among the Norman nobility. What you may not know is that the French and Norman people were themselves Celts.

The French people were originally Romanized Celts who were then conquered by the *Francs*, a Germanic tribe. The Francs, or *Franks* as it's commonly spelled, named their land after themselves and they ruled the land but they did not change the culture. The Celts kept their culture and language as it was. Their language was basically Latin but with a heavy Gallic pronunciation and some Gallic vocabulary. Their country was named Francia in Latin, which means *Land of the Francs*. They also named the language Francia as well, though it remained unchanged, a Celtic form of Latin, and had nothing to do with the Franks.

The same was not true for the Saxons in England. The Saxons were also a Germanic tribe, and they conquered the Romanized Celts of Briton. The difference is that the Saxons all but wiped out the Celtic culture in Southern Briton. By the time the Normans arrived, there was no Celtic culture or language left in Southern England. The culture was entirely Saxon, and their language was closer to German than anything we might recognize as English today. So, when the Normans conquered England, there was a clash of cultures. It was the Romanized Celts vs. the Germanic people again, but this time the Celts won.

The reason why this is so important is that the resulting culture clash between the Normans and Saxons dramatically changed the way the English saw themselves and their history. Their language changed overnight. In the year 1066, Old English ended and Middle English (a hybrid of English and Norman French) began. English history was revised as well. And, this revised history completed the trajectory already started by Bede, Nennius, and others.

They say that history is written by the victors, and by the end of the 12th century, nobles and educated people in England were taught that King Arthur was a Celt and a Christian and a brave and valiant king. His closest advisor was a wise Druid priest who had converted to Christianity, named Merlin. King Arthur fought off the invading Saxons, who were evil, vile, and disgusting heathens. After the death of Arthur, the country had fallen into a dark time, the age of Saxons, until the good and noble French Normans came to save them and civilize them.

THE VULGATE CYCLE

It is in the context of the Norman Conquest and resulting cultural changes that the *Vulgate Cycle* (1210-1230) was written. This is really the completion of the King Arthur legend.[25] This is a series of 5 volumes, which again repeats and clarifies the story of Vortigern, Ambrosius Arelianus, Uther Pendragon, and King Arthur, and their relationship to each other. But, this series tells us of the quest for the holy grail, how Merlin educated and mentored Arthur, about the Knights of the Round Table, and about the love affair between Lancelot and Arthur's wife Guinevere. It told of how Galahad took on the quest for the holy grail, and finally how Arthur died at the hands of his own son Mordred. It now has all the drama and grandeur of a Greek tragedy. And, now the story leaves no doubt that Briton was a shining beacon of knowledge and Christendom prior to the invasion of the crude, heathen Saxons.

Here the myth is fairly complete. Of course, according to the Vulgate Cycle, Britons are the most Christian of any people on earth. Also, we see that some Druid priests, such as Merlin, were capable of being very wise teachers as well as great and magical wizards. Now, with the grail quest and the love affair between Lancelot and Queen Guinevere, there is even more drama, idealism, and romanticism than ever.

AS ARTHUR GOES, SO GOES THE HOLIDAYS

So, you may wonder why we are going into such depth on these writings about King Arthur and the Norman Conquest. What do they have to do with the Wheel of Time, Christmas, Easter, and the other holy days of ancient paganism? Well, as I mentioned before, it appears that while these shifts in English identity and perception of history were taking place there was a similar transition occurring with the ancient holy days of the annual calendar. We see that the story of Arthur had evolved a great deal. And, this evolution resulted in a total transition of his character, from an unknown pagan warlord to a wise and benevolent Christian King. At the same time, there was a similar transition of the ancient Druids from savage witch-doctors to wise and magical wizards.

Meanwhile, the Yule and Ēastre celebrations had also evolved to become synonymous with Christianity. To the English people of the middle-ages, these holidays were clearly Christian holidays, and always had been. Of that, there was increasingly no doubt. At the same time, as the pagan beliefs and practices drifted further into the past, they took on an almost magical and romantic quality. It was almost as if the pagan mysticism of the past left an indelible mark on the psyche of the people in the middle-ages. It seemed to burn bright in their imagination, beckoning them to romanticize the past and wonder at what they had lost.

Though they were certain that Christmas had begun with the birth of Christ, there must have been a very attractive and magical aura surrounding their many folk tales of ogres, fairies, and wizards. And, this was probably true for their ancient customs at Christmas as well, such as Father Christmas, the Yule log, the holly, and mistletoe. Perhaps they saw a magical quality to those things that seemed to transcend their hum-drum existence and boring church liturgy. Perhaps they could not help but imagine a time in the distant past when wizards and dragons roamed the land. And, I'm sure it was not just Christmas that evoked these feelings. The same could probably be said for Easter and all the other church holidays, such as Candlemass (Imbolc), May Day (Beltaine), and All Hallows Eve (Samhain).

King Arthur

Sometime around 1470 CE, Sir Thomas Malory completed his epic *Le Mort d'Arthur*, and with it the Arthurian legend was set in stone.[26] It was now complete with all the trappings of the 15th century, including gleaming armor, spectacular castles, noble steeds, royal heraldry, wise wizards and evil witches, magical swords, romance, betrayal, and finally the tragic death of King Arthur. And, as we mourn Arthur, we mourn all that has been lost in our ancient past.

With Malory, the foundation of the post-renaissance psyche was crystallized. And, in Western culture, we have not really changed our collective psyche since then. Though we have progressed scientifically and technologically, at the dawn of the 21st century, our culture is still populated with the same images and characters that were conceived in the middle-ages.

One could argue that our culture has changed dramatically in the last few centuries. But, just look at our children. My son, like most kids, loves everything from Disney, and his favorite stories were always about kings, castles, knights, dragons, and princesses. Like most people, our family celebrates Christmas, Easter, and Halloween in the usual fashion. And, while I try to tell my son about the pagan origins of our holidays, he cannot help but absorb the influence of the dominant culture all around him.

Case in point, when my son was eight he informed me that our Christmas traditions were actually started by St. Nicholas who was a bishop, and that he was the first to give gifts to children at Christmas time. And, he said that he knew this was true because he had learned it in school. Between Disney, schools, churches, and the rest of our culture, history and science is no match for the perennial zeitgeist of legends, myths and fairy tales. Though we live in the 21st century, much of our fantasies and beliefs still live in the Middle Ages. And that is probably more true for our holidays than anything else in our culture.

Think about it. Just look at Santa Claus and his elves, their outfits, his workshop and his sleigh. It is clearly not from the 20th century nor even the 19th century. If Santa was from the 1700s, he would look more like George Washington than an over-grown elf. Even if the story was from the 1600s, he'd look more like Oliver Cromwell or the Pilgrims. No. Santa is from further back in history than any of those other people. Santa is from the Middle Ages or before.

Santa Claus circa 1889

Santa is Father Christmas; he is a combination of the Celtic god *Dagda*, the Saxon god *Odin*, and the Christian *Saint Nicholas*, all combined and set in the age of King Arthur. And, along with his elves and his sleigh and his workshop, that concept has never really changed, not even to the present day. Santa, like all other traditional holiday concepts, was fairly complete, set, and crystalized in our cultural imagination by the time of the Renaissance.

THE PROTESTANT REFORMATION & WITCH HYSTERIA

Of course, there have been some twists in the evolution of the holidays since the Renaissance. The Roman Catholic Church, the only church for 1500 years, was not entirely hostile to pagans and their holiday practices, and even adopted pagan holidays and traditions to celebrate Christianity. They saw pagans as ignorant, misguided, and in need of salvation. But, they saw the pagan holiday traditions as perfectly fine so long as their holidays were used as an opportunity to worship God and to remember the life of Jesus. But, all that changed after the Protestant Reformation beginning in the 16th century. Martin Luther is famously credited for starting what would become a major revolution in the Christian faith. This revolution would also have profound implications for the celebration of the former pagan holidays.

Martin Luther and all those involved with the 16th century movement of Protestants (literally meaning *Protestors*) knew full well that Christmas, Easter, and Halloween were all pagan holidays, as was Candlemas, St. Valentine's Day, St. Patrick's Day, May Day, and all the rest. They knew this because they were part of a literate society that had read the bible and read the history of the church. Previously, most Christians were not able to read the bible because the bible had never been translated from Latin. Martin Luther translated the bible into German in 1522, and later Henry VIII had the bible translated into English in 1539. Once they knew the truth, they were right in saying that these holidays really had nothing to do with Jesus or Christianity.

The Renaissance was a wonderful time of knowledge and exploration of science and history. The printing press had just been invented and everything from Plato's *Republic* to *Le Morte d'Arthur* was available to the masses. People, especially noblemen, were encouraged to learn to read, and not just the bible but philosophy, history, mathematics, and science. Part of this was the Druid/Celtic influence which had always valued such knowledge, even if the Church said such knowledge was unimportant for average people to know.

Ironically, the Protestant movement was also a Renaissance movement. I say *ironically* because the Protestants' stance on religion and holidays was anything but enlightened. In fact, it was downright barbaric. This was the time of the now infamous witch hunts. Between 1500 and 1800, it has been estimated that over 200,000 witches were tortured, burned at the stake, or hung. Of course, the term *witch* was applied to anyone practicing anything like paganism, including herbology, or any other non-Christian folk traditions or beliefs.

Oliver Cromwell

Christmas and all the other Christian holidays were all but stamped out by the end of the 1600s because of their pagan history. In fact, in the 1650s Oliver Cromwell and the English Parliament outlawed Christmas in England and he had the soldiers go through the streets and into homes, tearing down any Christmas decorations that they found.

I imagine if you partied too much or put up too many decorations, you might have been accused of witchcraft. Many were, and many good, innocent people were hung or burned alive as a result. Imagine what they did to you if you celebrated Halloween!

What began as an age of enlightenment in the Renaissance had to overcome the darkness of the Reformation and narrow-minded brutality in order to be considered truly *Enlightened*. But, that is exactly what eventually happened. The 18th century saw what is known as the Age of Enlightenment, as well as the American Revolution and the French Revolution. Freedom was in fashion; freedom from the Church and freedom from the Crown. In fact, people wanted freedom from any superstition or prejudice, including anti-pagan hysteria. The witch-hunts were over, and it was once again safe to celebrate. Then, the traditional holidays seemed to get a real boost.

THE 19TH CENTURY & THE AGE OF FAIRY TALES

It was in the 1800s that tales of sin, sorcery, and the supernatural became the fodder of popular novels and poems like never before. Not since the time of the Bards of the 5th century had people become so enamored with the stories of pagan magic and fantastical tales of all types. Of course, this correlated with a renewed love and celebration of the traditional pagan (now Christian) holidays.

Vampire

Halloween, long seen as an especially evil pagan Sabbath, got a boost with a new genre of novels called *horror* stories. Washington Irving published *The Legend of Sleepy Hollow* in 1820, and Mary Shelly wrote her classic tale of horror, *Frankenstein,* in 1818.[27] Lord Byron, a friend of Mary Shelly, was the first to write about vampires.[29] Later in the century, Bram Stoker would write his classic novel, *Dracula*, based upon Lord Byron's work.[30]

But, it was Charles Dickens who is credited for bringing back the vigorous celebration of Christmas and the traditions of the Yuletide season, with stories such as *A Christmas Carol* (1843), *The Chimes* (1844), *The Cricket on the Hearth* (1845), and a dozen other short stories about Christmas.[31]

As far as I know, Dickens didn't write explicitly about the pagan aspects of Christmas, but he did write more than a few Christmas stories that involved ghosts.[32] I find this interesting because in the Christian liturgy and even in Jewish traditions, this time of the year is not usually associated with death. So, what made Dickens think of ghosts?

The Ghost of Christmas Present

But, to the pagans, midwinter was the apex of the season of death. It represented survival of life after death. Dickens didn't write about that, but I just find it interesting that, of all the holidays, he associated ghosts with Christmas. Perhaps, telling ghost stories at Christmas was a nearly extinct, last vestige of paganism that was still smoldering in the traditions of the English common folk in the early 1800s.

Throughout the 1800s, echoes of Malory and a fascination with the mystery of our ancient pagan past continued to grow. It was as if our holidays along with our pagan cultural heritage were simply in hibernation during the Reformation. Then, in the 1800s, English and American culture picked up right where it had left off, from the 1500s. And, all of our cherished customs of Santa and his elves, of the Easter hare and painted eggs, and jack-o'-lanterns at Halloween returned just as we left them, hundreds of years eariler.

The Tales of Mother Goose circa 1800s

In the 19th century, stories such as *Ivanhoe* (1819) about the adventures of Robin Hood,[33] as well as the Brothers Grimms' (1812) tales of *Cinderella, Hansel and Gretel, Snow White,* and *Sleeping Beauty* were all wildly popular.[34] In fact, we get the name *Fairy Tales* because of the popularity of stories about fairies and other magical creatures in the 19th century. Of course, to our ancient ancestors, elves and fairies were no laughing matter. They were part of our pagan ancestor's mythology and part of a deeply held and widely believed spiritual faith. But, after the Age of Enlightenment, people were able to embrace these stories as quaint remnants of a bygone era, without any deeper meanings or beliefs.

Santa Claus circa 1900

By the end of the 19th century most people in the Western world began to associate Christmas with magical elves and flying reindeer, thanks to Clement Clarke Moore's famous poem *'Twas the Night Before Christmas* (1823).[35] From then on, whether you called him Father Christmas, St. Nick, or Santa Claus, a magical, fat, little man in a red suit with a white beard became the figure most associated with Christmas. By the 20th century even witches were sometimes seen as good, such as Glinda the good witch, in *The Wonderful Wizard of Oz*, by L. Frank Baum (1900). And, Baum later wrote *The Life and Adventures of Santa Claus* (1902), further cementing Santa Claus into our modern celebration of Christmas.[36]

As we have Christianized our ancient pagan holy days and, in the process, lost sight of the Wheel of Time, we increasingly yearn for magic and mystery. I think this explains the popularity of the New Age movement, the Goth movement, Eastern religion, and so many other trends and fashions of today. We seek our birthright as descendants of our Neolithic pagan ancestors.

No wonder we preserve stories about Santa Claus, the Easter Bunny, and the Tooth Fairy for our children. We want them to have the magic and the wonder that we feel we've lost in our modern world. Unfortunately, what is left of ancient pagan magic and wisdom has thus been reduced to a child's fairy tale.

Rudolph the Red-Nosed Reindeer & Hermey

At Christmas time, in America and elsewhere in the world, we can choose to celebrate the birth of Jesus, the Maccabean Revolt, other traditions such as Kwanzaa, or we can celebrate Santa Claus and Rudolph the red-nosed reindeer. But, we can't help but feel that there is something else, something missing, something truly reverent and mystical about this time of year that we can't quite put our finger on. There's a magical quality about the short days, long nights, and the Yule log that never goes out, even in the midnight hour of the longest night of winter.

There's something about rounding the midwinter mark and starting a new year, all over again. It speaks to us because it is a basic part of nature, and we evolved from nature; it's in our DNA. This is something that has nothing to do with red-nosed reindeer, nor babies being born in the desert of Israel. This has to do with the magic and miracle of life itself, and how it never goes out but continues to be reborn. This is something that we may not think about consciously, but it is still dormant in our collective unconscious. It still calls to us. This is our current relationship to the Wheel of Time.

SUMMARY

In this chapter and the previous one, we have only focused on the pagan sabbaths that became Christian holidays in the Western World. Even then, we have left out a lot of holidays celebrated in Europe and the Americas, such as

Groundhog Day, May Day, Lughnasadh, and Halloween, all of which evolved from the ancient pagan cross-quarter days, and all of which have their own quaint modern versions, still celebrated to this day.

Of course, there are many other holidays around the world not covered in this section. We have only briefly looked at Jewish holidays but I'm sure their holidays have endured a similar transition as that of Christmas and Easter. At some point in history, the ancient Hebrews went from celebrating the first full moon of the spring equinox to celebrating the exodus out of bondage in Egypt, but it was still celebrated on the same day, probably with a Seder. The date is the same, but what was the original meaning of their spring equinox Seder before they left Egypt or even before they arrived in Egypt?

In all the countries that we've looked at so far in this book, China, India, Peru, Guatemala, Mexico, and in the desert Southwest of America, there must be similar stories for each of these cultures, spanning thousands of years.

We know this because they all had ancient observatories that are thousands of years old, and yet today they all have very different religions and cultural beliefs than they had when those observatories were built. Yet, if we look carefully, just as we've seen in this chapter, I'll bet many of their ancient traditions and the lunisolar dates of their holidays have remained the same, while their cultural meanings have evolved.

Just look at the Chinese New Year; it is a lunisolar holiday, celebrated on the new moon closest to the cross-quarter day, Imbolc, yet I'll bet most Chinese Americans have no idea of that. We know that throughout the world, in all different cultures, people mostly celebrate holidays on the equinoxes, the solstices, or the cross-quarter days, or a specific phase of the moon closest to these days. Furthermore, if we look at their traditions, the time of day of their celebrations, and the phase of the moon that their holidays fall on, I am sure we will see many connections to the Wheel of Time.

We have focused mostly on Christmas and Easter in the Anglo-Saxon world as an example of how the ancient pagan holy days have gradually morphed into our modern holidays. There are so many holidays in the world that it would require a 24-volume set of books to show the evolution through archaeology and ethnography of each holiday, from the Bronze Age to the present. Hopefully, in the last chapters you have acquired a good overview of the often puzzling and convoluted evolution of holidays just by looking at some of the more famous holidays in the Western world.

By looking at the evolution of these holidays, we also get a good idea of how that complex evolution is a reflection of the changing culture and history of the people celebrating the holidays. We continually rewrite history as we change our beliefs and our perceptions, and this is most poignantly reflected in how we perceive and celebrate our holidays. So, a sacred pagan ceremony, marking an astronomical event with deep spiritual and philosophical ramifications, becomes a celebration of Santa and his flying reindeer. Either that or it's the birthday of a Jewish religious leader in Israel, who sparked a new religion in Rome.

One thing we know for sure, holidays are hardly ever what they seem. Most people have no idea why they celebrate the holidays the way they do, or when they do. They don't know the meaning or origin of their favorite holidays.

They might think that they do. They have certainly been told stories about their holidays, what they mean, and how they started. But, as we have seen in the last two chapters, those stories are usually incomplete, altered over time, or just plain fiction. Now, at least, we do have a tool to help us decipher the history and the original meaning of our holidays, and that is the Wheel of Time.

CHAPTER 10

THE WINTER SOLSTICE: A GLOBAL SURVEY

In this chapter, we continue our historical and ethnographic research by investigating the holidays of the world and throughout history. This time we are going to focus on one holiday in depth, the midwinter solstice. We will look at the winter solstice holidays throughout history, such as in ancient Babylon, Egypt, and Rome. And, we will look at various cultures from around the world and how they celebrate these holidays, both in the past and today. With few exceptions, we will not go into how these holidays evolved and changed over time; we've already shown detailed examples of that in the last two chapters.

The purpose of this and the next chapter is to illustrate the major themes of the World's holidays and how they are all related to the Wheel of Time. We will also reveal the historical roots of what often appears to be arbitrary traditions of our holidays today. We will eventually discuss all 8 Sabbaths of the Wheel of Time, made up of the equinoxes, solstices, and midpoints between them, the cross-quarter days. Each holiday will start with a chart of the basic facts of the holiday, and the moon symbol that represents it. But, we start with the great grand-daddy of all holidays, the winter solstice.

MIDWINTER SOLSTICE

Point on the Solar Cycle:	The Winter Solstice
Pagan Sabbath Name:	Yule (meaning Wheel)
Approximate Solar Date:	December 21st
Dates of Lunisolar & Other Holidays:	Mid December through Early January
Time of Day to Celebrate:	12 Midnight
Symbolic Meaning on the Life Cycle:	Peak of Death / True Reincarnation
Corresponding Modern Holidays:	Christmas, Hanukkah, Kwanzaa, New Year's Day, Dongzhi, Pongal, Soyal

We have already discussed this holiday a great deal in the last chapter, but just to recap, the midwinter celebration is really the end of a period of about 6 days, centered around the shortest day of the year, the winter solstice. If you were looking at the shadow cast by the rising sun every day, throughout the year, you'd see that, in the fall, it would move a little south each day (in the northern hemisphere).

As it moved, the days would get shorter, the nights longer and, as it gets progressively colder, almost all living things would appear to wither and die. Then, about three days before the solstice, the sun's movement would slow to a stop.

For six days it would rise at about the same place each day.

Then, on about the 3rd day after the solstice, you would notice that the sunrise is starting to move a little bit further north each day. Of course, this means that you've rounded the midwinter low tide of the solar year and are headed back toward another spring and summer. The solstice is around the 21st of December, and three days later would be eve of the 25th of December. And, for people all around the world and throughout history, this has been a holy day and a day of great celebration.

It marks the virtual return of the sun and the light of day. I say virtual because it is still in the middle of winter, but the movement of the sun tells us that longer, warmer days will soon return and we know that in 3 months it will be spring again. So, symbolically, the holiday represents the concept of reincarnation and the promise of salvation.

By the way, when I say reincarnation, people often think of someone dying and then being born all over again as a baby. But, on the Wheel of Time, birth, conception, and reincarnation are all separate points on the life cycle. So, there are three separate points corresponding to the annual solar cycle as well. If November 1st is death, and February 2nd is conception, and the space between them is the domain of death, then the winter solstice, midwinter, represents mid-death. That is the point where the soul is reincarnated and begins moving back toward the realm of life.

Another issue people often ask me is: did ancient people really get so worried during the winter when plants appeared to die? After all, they knew that in a few months spring would come again, right? The answer is yes; I think that they did get a little worried. You have to remember just how important their crops and orchards were to them. They didn't have a supermarket to go to. To us, in the modern world, it would be like if all the supermarkets closed for 3 months out of the year, and we had no guarantee that they would all reopen in the spring. And, we didn't know which would reopen and which wouldn't.

I'll give you an even better example. I own a vineyard, and after I planted my vineyard and nurtured my baby vines all season, I saw them dry up, wither, and die in the fall. I knew it was normal for them to go dormant in the winter, but I couldn't help but worry. These are my babies, and they looked like they were dying. I knew that an unexpected late hard freeze could kill a young vine, so how could I tell if they would survive the winter or not? All I could do was wait and worry.

Well, it's been over 10 years since I planted my vineyard, and some vines have died from time to time. So, each year I still get a little worried when I see them wither in the fall. I wait and I worry, hoping they all will survive the winter freeze. Perhaps the ancients had similar feelings about winter. Plus, today we have an extensive knowledge of science. Back then, they mostly believed that the world was controled by supernatural forces. They probably believed that if their god or goddess cursed them for some reason, then they might very well take away the sun forever.

And, that is why it was so important for ancient people when they saw the sunrise starting to move back northward toward spring on the dawn of December 25th. To them it was probably like a miracle. Life itself was like a friend dying of an illness. All they could do is and wait and pray for a miracle. Once they saw the sun moving again, back toward spring, they knew that they were over the hump, and it was cause to celebrate. At that point, they could all breathe a little sigh of relief. You might say that December 25th was hump day. From then on, they were just waiting for spring.

So, the winter solstice is the peak of the season of death and the point where we begin to make our journey back to spring and new life. Likewise, if you believe in reincarnation, this phase of the solar year represents the moment of re-incarnation, the point after death when we begin our journey back toward rebirth. As a solar event, this is the start of a new solar cycle. In a way, it is like the birth of a new sun.

And, the lunisolar holiday associated with midwinter is celebrated on the new moon. If you look on the Wheel of Time, this is the midnight of our year. Midnight, midwinter, and the black, new moon are all lined up on this section of the Wheel of Time. This holiday represents the pit of death and darkness, and the promise of new life and light. This, more than anything else, represents the survival of the soul, literally life after death.

This holiday celebrates eternal life, that death is not the end, as the soul is not even dead but only sleeping, to be reincarnated again and again. This is a celebration of the spiritual miracle of reincarnation, in human life just as it is in nature. This marks our first Sabbath on the Wheel of Time and the pinnacle of all eight Sabbaths of the year.

The Sun God, Marduk

THE BABYLONIANS & THE BIRTH OF MARDUK

The winter solstice was celebrated in ancient Mesopotamia by some of the oldest cultures in the world, the Babylonians and the Sumerians.[1] They saw it as the birthday or rebirth of their sun god, Marduk. Over the centuries, in Mesopotamia and the surrounding region, they had many different names for the god of sun and light; Shamash, Bel, Tammuz, Utu, Nergal, and most commonly Marduk were all names for the Babylonian god of light and sun. Marduk was associated with the winter solstice, and was the son of Utu, the Sumerian sun god that preceded Marduk. Nergal was another Mesopotamian sun god, though he became associated with the Summer Solstice.

The symbolism of the birth of a new sun, at the winter solstice is clear. Just as a new moon is the birth of a new month (lunar cycle), likewise the sun is also at its nadir during the winter solstice. Hence, it represents the birth of a new year (solar cycle), and a new sun.

Unfortunately, though we know that the Babylonians, and likely the Sumerians before them, observed the solstice and its meaning regarding the solar cycle, we actually know very little about how they celebrated it. We know that they had a 12-day long festival for the birth of Marduk, at the winter solstice, which predated the 12 days of Christmas by thousands of years. But we don't know about their solstice decorations or traditions. Fortunately, there are some other ancient cultures, however, which were contemporaries with the Babylonians, and are much better known.

THE VIRGIN ISIS, & THE BIRTH OF HORUS

In ancient Egypt, the god Horus was one of the main deities. He is mentioned in the Pyramid Texts, and has been worshiped for at least 5000 years. And, we know from the Roman historian Plutarch (46-120 CE), that the birth of the sky god Horus was celebrated three days after the winter solstice.[2] This celebration was on the date that we call December 25th.

If you think this is vaguely similar to the birth of Jesus, you have no idea how similar the two are.

Horus was born to a virgin, Isis, he was the son of a god, Osiris, and according to some legends, he was baptized by Anup the Baptizer in the river Nile. But that's not all. Horus was the god of light, and was called upon by the Egyptian people to heal the sick. He was depicted in a similar way as the Christian crucifix, except he was on the cross of Ankh. Then, after he died, he was resurrected on the 3rd day. Clearly this is a reference to the sun's shadow beginning to move again on the 3rd day after the solstice.

Virgin Isis and baby Horus

Virgin Mary and baby Jesus

And, there are even other Egyptian connections to Jesus as well. Jesus was tempted by Satan in the desert, while Horus did battle in the desert with the evil god Seth, god of the desert. Perhaps the most compelling parallel is the way the mother and child, Isis and baby Horus, are depicted in Egyptian paintings and sculpture. Aside from the typical Egyptian stylization, the image of a Madonna and child is immediately recognizable. In ancient Egypt, this was a favorite motif of the holiday season.

The nativity scene, the birth of our god of light, our savior, now so familiar in the Christian religion, appeared originally in Egyptian mythology. The ancient Egyptians celebrated the end of the winter solstice with depictions of baby Horus, just as we do today. And, while the attributes and stories about Horus changed and evolved over time, we know that the story of Horus existed in late Prehistoric Egypt, over 3000 years before Jesus.

But, many of the traditions we associate with Christmas were probably borrowed more directly from Roman mythology than from Egypt. What the story of Horus shows us is that the traditions and meaning that we associate with the Christian Christmas story not only existed in Rome prior to Christianity, but existed in Egypt over two thousand years before the founding of Rome.

ANCIENT ROME & THE BIRTH OF MITHRAS

Mithra was an interesting god of antiquity. He was also a sun god and a benevolent god of light, like all the other gods mentioned so far, but he had a long and curious history. Originally, there was a sun god mentioned in the Vedic religion, over 3500 years ago, and his name was Mitra. Over the thousands of years that followed, the worship of the sun god Mitra migrated to the Assyrian and Hittite kingdoms, in what is now Iran. This sun god became known as Mithra, and was regarded with the exact same attributes.

The Baby Sol Invictus, with a Halo of Light

The sun gave us light, life, and food, and all the gifts we needed to live. The return, or birth, of Mithra each December 25th symbolized the promise of our salvation, as it symbolized cyclic and perpetual life. Finally, the Persian god Mithra made its way to the Roman Empire, and he became known as Mithras: Sol Invictus, the *Unconquered Sun*.[3] He was seen as unconquered because, no matter what, he was born again every December 25th without fail. Nothing could stop or interfere with the return of the sun god.

Fortunately, we know very well how the Romans celebrated the winter solstice. There are actually two different Roman festivals associated with the solstice. The first, Saturnalia, was a week-long celebration of the god Saturn, from

December 17th through the 22nd. The Saturnalia celebration was one time of the year that the Roman elite would care for the less fortunate. They would not only give their slaves a day off, but the masters would serve the slaves a great feast.

Slaves were permitted to disrespect their masters at this time, without fear of punishment. This was also a time of gift giving, into which the Romans put a great deal of thought. They could be small, simple tokens of affection or very expensive and rare gifts. The masters also gave their servants gifts and perhaps some extra money, so that the servants could buy Saturnalia gifts for others as well.

Most of all, Saturnalia was a time to feast, drink heavily, and be merry. They drank a mixture of wine and honey, and they would light a candle or candles in front of a shrine to the god Saturn. They also decorated their homes with garlands and wreaths of evergreens with golden pinecones. They did not put up a tree indoors, but they decorated the evergreen trees outdoors, with symbols of the sun, moon, and stars. They also made cookies in the shape of the sun, moon, and stars. Basically, if you visited ancient Rome at midwinter, you would immediately recognize it as a Christmas celebration.

Three days after the end of Saturnalia, on December 25th, they would celebrate the second Roman festival of the winter solstice, the birth of the baby Mithras, the unconquered sun. They actually referred to this day as Dies Natalis Solis Invicti, or *Birthday of the Unconquered Sun*, which was also the patron god of soldiers. According to Roman mythology, Mithras was born of a virgin in a cave. Sound familiar? He was a savior-god, who performed miracles. He died, and was resurrected on the third day, to become a messenger god, an intermediary between man and god. The similarities between Mithras and Jesus are uncanny.

They celebrated Solis Invicti with lights, lots and lots of lights. They had candles, lanterns and lamps everywhere, adorning homes, in windows, and even in evergreen trees. And, they probably had a roaring fire, both to symbolize Mithras, the god of light, and to keep away the cold. And while I don't know if Romans had depictions of the baby Mithras on his mother's lap, this was a popular Roman motif anyway; all year long you could see depictions of the goddess Venus with baby Cupid on her lap. This was no doubt an inspiration for many early depictions of the Madonna and child.

It's quite possible that the Egyptian celebration of the birth of Horus had influenced the Romans and how they celebrated the birth of Mithras, and that might explain some of the similarities between the Egyptian and Roman winter solstice traditions. Nonetheless, the correlation between how the ancient Egyptians celebrated the birth of Horus, how the ancient Romans celebrated the birth of Mithras, and how modern Christians celebrate the birth of Jesus is simply astounding.

In the entire last chapter, we carefully explained how the pagan celebration of the winter solstice became Christmas, but now we see that the same thing had been happening for thousands of years prior to Christ.

Each culture, in each millennium, had created its own myths, mythical figures, gods, and stories about those gods. The names of their gods changed but almost nothing else did. For the last 5,000 years, people have been celebrating the birth of their god of light, in almost exactly the same way, with very much the same traditions, on exactly the same day each year, three days after the solstice, what we call December 25th.

ON VIRGIN BIRTHS

By the way, there is a side-note about the virgin births of these midwinter gods. The idea of a god or demigod being the child of a virgin mother is very common in different cultures. In fact, the birth of the baby Krishna was also supposedly a virgin birth. This is a curious feature. Why virgin? Well, one reason is to show that this little baby is really divine, the child of a god. This is not unlike the birth of Hercules, also the child of a god. But there is another reason. Think back to the pagan concept of reincarnation.

The soul is incarnated into a new life, but the new person being born is not just the product of the male and female who conceived the physical baby. There is another entity, a spiritual entity that impregnates the mother's egg with its soul. The mother and father may create the physical baby, but that is merely the vessel for its soul. The baby still requires a soul to reincarnate within it, to be a whole person with consciousness. So, the virgin birth represents the spiritual birth of the soul, for which there is only the mother and the soul; there is no father.

Think of it this way. On the Wheel of Time, you will see that there are actually three important dates in the birth of the new year: the reincarnation, the conception, and the actual birth. The reincarnation occurs in the middle of death, symbolized by the winter solstice. But, the year is only reincarnated, it is not yet conceived or born. The physical conception of the new year takes place later, at Imbolc, on February 2nd. This is when we begin to see trees and vines pregnant with buds that will not blossom for 6 more weeks.

Then, the actual birth of the new year takes place in the spring, at the spring equinox, or on the lunisolar holiday we call Easter, the first full moon after the equinox. That is when all of nature comes alive. So, the virgin birth symbolizes the idea that this is not a physical conception of a new year so much as it is a spiritual rebirth, or reincarnation of the new year.

Perhaps they believed that, with a symbolic celebration of reincarnation and the rebirth of the sun god on December 25th, our new physical solar cycle is also impregnated with the very life-giving spirit of the sun god, the soul of light. Otherwise, the physical sun may shine but not give warmth; it may blind but not give life to the plants. Perhaps, the ancients perceived that it's the soul of the sun god that creates the sun's life-giving magic. And hence, there is yet another parallel between the solar cycle and the human life cycle on the Wheel of Time. It is as if the ancients were obsessed with getting every nuance of each cycle reflected in how we ritualize and celebrate those cycles.

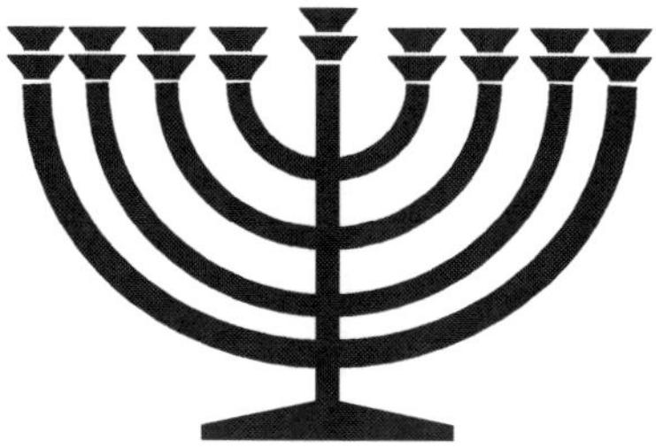

The Hanukkah Menorah

THE HEBREW CELEBRATION OF HANUKKAH

Among the ancient Hebrews, they celebrated the winter solstice with *Hanukkah*, the 8-day festival of lights, starting on the 25th of Kislev (December on the Jewish Calendar).[6] The story associated with Hanukkah is that of the Maccabees, who had only enough oil to light their lamps for one day, but it miraculously lasted for 8 days. Again, the story is different but the symbolism is the same.

It is the story of how the light miraculously spanned the breach of darkness. The menorah (candle holder) is the Jewish version of the Yule log, a visual representation of the miracle of light, surviving in darkness. Make note of the number 8; it will come up again in different holidays from around the world. Remember that this is really a celebration of the 8 pointed Wheel of Time, though that knowledge has been long forgotten.

Some people nowadays say that Hanukkah was a made-up holiday, created to compete with the popularity of Christmas. But, the story of the Maccabees predates the life of Jesus. And, as we see here, the symbolism and even the date is spot on for a midwinter celebration. Just as we've seen with Passover, they may have celebrated the winter solstice long before the time of the Maccabees.

Perhaps the story of the Maccabees came later and is otherwise unrelated to the original meaning of the holiday, which marks the winter solstice and the rebirth of the sun. Whatever the case, it is filled with the same symbolism and meaning as the other pagan traditions we've seen so far. And, of course, the giving of gifts each night of Hanukkah is at the center of this Jewish holiday tradition.

THE NORSE FEAST OF YULE

The Norse culture refers to the Germanic peoples of northern Europe, which includes the Anglo-Saxons who invaded and settled in southern Briton. We don't know how far back their culture goes, but we do have archaeological evidence of Germanic peoples in northern Europe as far back as 1200 BCE, over a thousand years before Christ.

The Norse people, including the Anglo Saxons, celebrated the winter solstice with a 3-day celebration called *Yule*, also spelled *Juul or Hjul*. It is sometimes referred to as the Yuletide for the same reason that we refer to the low or high tide of the oceans. The Yule was the low tide or nadir of the sun's light and the length of the day. The celebration started on the winter solstice and lasted for 3 days, concluding on December 25th, just as the other holidays we've seen. The word Yule comes from the Norse word Hjul, meaning *wheel*, referring to the wheel of the year. Unlike the more sophisticated civilizations to the south, such as Egypt and Rome, the Norse were consciously aware that they were celebrating the turning of the Wheel of Time.[4]

Most of us in the Western hemisphere are well aware of the traditions of Yule, as they have become incorporated into how we now celebrate Christmas. There is the Yule log, which is a giant log, lit on the eve of the solstice and burns all night, until the sun rises again. They would hang sprigs of evergreens, pine, holly, and mistletoe, over the door and around the house. The Yule log and the evergreens both have the same symbolism, the survival of the soul, spanning the breach between death and reincarnation. This is the very heart of the meaning of the midwinter solstice. They would also feast on boar (ham), drink ale or mead, and sing Yule songs. They would often walk around singing and drinking. This was called *wassailing*, or more commonly known as *caroling*.

The Norse did have a sun deity, the Norse goddess *Sunna,* which is where we get the name *Sun*. The Latin name for the sun is Sol. But, for the Anglo-Saxons, this time of year was more closely associated with the celebration of Môdraniht. According to the Venerable Bede, on the eve of the 3rd day of Yule, literally on Christmas eve, they would make votive offerings or sacrifices to maternal deities, such as the goddess Frī or Frige, and the goddess Hertha.

This somewhat echoes the theme of Madonna and child, but here the emphasis is on the mother not the child. The focus is still on birth, as in the birth of a new year, but they were specifically celebrating the mother. This could be due to the fact that their sun deity was a goddess. Perhaps they were thanking the goddess Sunna, for giving birth to the new year, and so celebrated the maternal spirit herself. Gift giving was also a Yule tradition but, in keeping with the spirit of *Môdraniht* or *Mother's-night,* gifts were given primarily to women and mothers in ancient times.

Hertha, perhaps originally called Nerthus by German tribes, was especially important at this time of year. She was the goddess of the home and hearth. At the Yuletide, they would construct a great alter of flat stones and build a fire of fresh evergreen branches, which of course would produce a lot of smoke. Hertha would then emerge from the smoke to give the gift of clairvoyance to the wise.

Hertha stones became known as the *hearth-stones*. This is why we call the fireplace a hearth. This fragment of old Norse mythology was also passed down through folk tradition, and managed to survive in the myth of Santa Claus; it is the reason why he comes down the chimney and emerges from the hearthstones, like Hertha, bearing gifts.

Another important figure in Norse Yule mythology was the god Odin. He had a long white beard and was believed to ride an 8-legged flying horse across the night sky on December 24th, throwing out gifts to the people. There's that number 8 again. Later, with the Christian influence, the god Odin was called Father Christmas.

Father Christmas with his Yule Log

According to the myth, he rode from the north, across the night sky on Christmas Eve, throwing out gifts to the children. Eventually, elements of Father Christmas survived in stories of Ol' St. Nick and Santa Claus, and the 8-legged flying horse became a team of 8 flying reindeer.

THE CELTIC MIDWINTER

The Druids of ancient Briton had their own celebration of the winter solstice, somewhat different from that of the Anglo-Saxons.[5] As we already reviewed in the last chapter, the Celts had their version of the Norse god Odin, and he was called Dagda or Dagodeiwos. He was also simply known as Eochaid Ollathair (*All Father*). He was the god of time, the god of the life, and the god of death and the afterlife. He had a long white beard, red robes, and carried with him a giant caldron of plenty with many gifts for everyone. Though the Celts did not call this holiday *Wheel*, as the Norse did, nonetheless Dagda was often pictured holding a wheel in one hand, symbolizing the wheel of the year, and a club in the other hand, symbolizing the power of life and death. And like Odin, elements of Dagda also survived in stories of Father Christmas and eventually Santa Claus.

Father Christmas

Just like the Anglo-Saxon pagans, the Celts also had a goddess at the center of their midwinter mythology. She was Cilleach Bheur, the oldest of the triple goddesses. Not unlike the holy trinity in Christianity, the three goddesses are actually three aspects of one goddess. Each one represents a phase of a woman's life, a phase of the moon, and a phase of the year.

As such, they mirror and symbolize the Wheel of Time. The three goddesses are the Maid, the Mother, and the Crone (also called the Hag). Of course, the Hag is associated with old age, death, and the afterlife, so she is also the goddess of winter.

And, just like the Anglo-Saxons and the Romans, the Celts decorated their homes with evergreens. Usually, throughout the other three seasons, they worshipped the mighty oak as a symbol of the earth's life-force and profound secrets. But, this time of year, when the oaks were dormant, they would cut the evergreen mistletoe from the oaks, and hang them in their homes and over their doors. It is believed that they would also do the same with sprigs of pine and holly, but the mistletoe cut from the oak was preferred, as it was believed to represent the afterlife of the mighty and revered oak. Literally, it was the soul of the oak that survived to span the breach between Samhain (death) on November 1st and Imbolc (conception) on February 2nd. In fact, the name *Druid* is believed to come from the Proto-Indo-European term *Oak-Knower* or *Oak-Seer.*

MIDWINTER TRADITIONS FROM AROUND THE WORLD

Another midwinter celebration that many people may have heard of is *Kwanzaa*. This week-long holiday is celebrated from December 26th through January 1st. This is actually a modern American holiday, created in the 1960s to celebrate African American's unique ethnic and cultural heritage. After all, the sub-Saharan Africans of old probably did not decorate pine trees or hang holly and mistletoe. The name Kwanzaa means *First Fruits* in Swahili, referring to the fruit harvest, since this is the phase of the agricultural cycle occurring this time of the year in Africa. So, even though it's a very modern holiday, it still relates to the Wheel of Time.

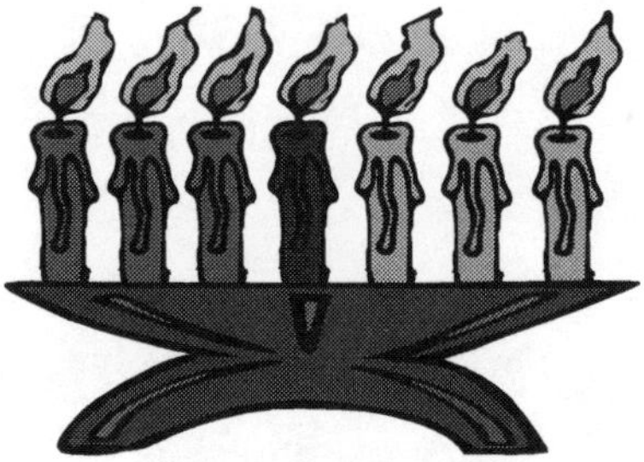

A Kwanzaa Kinara

Kwanzaa celebrates all aspects of the winter solstice as it is experienced in East Africa. There is also a lot of philosophical and political meaning to Kwanza. There are seven candles in the Kwanzaa candelabra, the Kinara, and they symbolize the seven principles that Kwanzaa embodies: Unity, Self-Determination, Collective Work, Cooperative Economics, Purpose, Creativity, and Faith. The purpose of the holiday and its seven principles is to create a sense of community and to promote *Kawaida*, the Swahili word for *the common good.*

THE SLAVIC FESTIVAL OF KOLEDA

We've spent a lot of time discussing the winter solstice as it was celebrated in Western culture, but, of course, there are solstice celebrations found all over the world.[7] For instance, the Slavic festival of *Koleda*. In Russia, Koleda is called *Kutuja*, and was later incorporated into Christmas. Originally, it was a celebration of the pagan god *Kolyada* and *Lada*, the goddess of beauty, love, and marriage. The themes and traditions are very similar to other midwinter celebrations. Each year, at this time, Lada was reborn. The family burned something like a yule log, that lasted all night, and children went from house to house singing, and they were given gifts.

DONGZHI FESTIVAL IN CHINA

The Chinese celebrate Dongzhi, their winter solstice festival.[8] The roots of this festival are found in ancient Taoism, in the duality of light vs. dark, and life vs. death. Of course, the winter solstice represents darkness and death. It is the nadir, low tide, of the annual solar cycle. This point in the year is symbolized by the I Ching hexagram *Fu,* which represents *returning*. They celebrate the positive life-energy, *Chi*, returning to the world, after the winter solstice and the peak of darkness.

THE HINDU FESTIVAL OF PONGAL

In the Hindu tradition, they celebrate Makar Sankranti, also known as *Pongal*, the annual winter festival.[9] This is the only Hindu holiday celebrated on the solar calendar. All other celebrations are on the lunar calendar. This celebration honors the sun god *Surya* and the beginning of the sun's 6-month journey to the north. Ironically, even though it is definitely a celebration of the winter solstice, the holiday is celebrated on January 15th. Presumably this is to coincide with their harvest time. If it were celebrated a month earlier, it would interfere with the harvest. Once the harvest is complete, they have time to celebrate and feast. So, this is also their feast of thanksgiving.

The festival lasts for 4 days. There are many stories associated with this holiday, just as in other cultures. There is the goddess *Sankranti*, for which the celebration is named. It is this time of year that she awakens from her slumber in a cave, to return love and abundance to the world. They tell of *Lord Shiva* and his bull, *Nandi*, and how *Lord Krishna* lifted the mountain *Govardhan* with his little finger, to protect the people and cattle from *Indra*, the rain god.

But, the second day is Surya Pongol day, and it is the most important day. Pangol means solstice. It is the day that they honor the Lord Surya, the sun god, and his long journey from one extreme in the north to the other extreme in the south. Obviously, this refers to the direction of the rising sun from summer solstice in the north, to winter solstice in the south.

Again, the stories, deities, and various legendary figures may change, but the purpose is essentially the same, to celebrate the winter solstice. And, in this case, they celebrate their harvest season as well.

THE HOPI CELEBRATION OF SOYAL

Among the Hopi, they celebrate *Soyal*, on the winter solstice.[10] This is a celebration of renewal and rebirth. There is a ritual to bring back the sun god from its winter slumber and mark the beginning of another phase of the great Wheel of the Year. It is at this time that the *Kivas*, underground ritual chambers, are opened up. And, this marks the beginning of the *Kachina* (spirits) dance season. The celebration lasts for up to 16 days, and it is a great celebration, especially on the exact day of the winter solstice. The solstice ceremony ends with a public Katchina dance.

The Hopi also have their own unique stories of gods and famous figures associated with the solstice, such as the *Palulukonuh*, a plumed snake that is similar to the Aztec god *Quetzalcoatl*, or the Mayan god *Kukulkan*, also known as *Gukumatz*. These are gods of renewal and creation, and are associated throughout Mesoamerica and North America with the winter solstice.

THE CHRISTIAN CHRISTMAS

Finally, I must add to our list the Christian celebration of the winter solstice, that we call Christmas. The pagan meaning of Midwinter echoes in Christianity as well. Just as other sun-gods are born or reborn three days after the winter solstice on December 25th, so too is the baby Jesus, the new light of the world. If you are a Christian, this holiday may represent the promise of salvation, eternal life, or symbolize the miracle of being spiritually born again.

In Europe and America, this is the best known winter solstice holiday, so I don't need to go into a lengthy description of this holiday. Suffice it to say, this is the most common midwinter celebration in Western society, and it is usually celebrated very much as it has been for thousands of years when it was called Yule, or Saturnalia, or Sol Invicti. And, not unlike Horus, at Christmas-time there are pictures of Jesus as a baby with his mother, the Virgin Mary. And, like in Ancient Rome, nowadays we celebrate by decorating trees, putting lights up everywhere, and baking cookies.

Ironically, while most Christians do celebrate Christmas in the traditional way, for much of the last 2000 years, the only people who didn't consistently celebrate Christmas were Christians. Let me explain. It was not until the 4th century in Rome that this day was officially recognized as the birth of Jesus. Prior to that it was simply a pagan holiday to be avoided at all costs.

Then, even after the 25th of December became *Christmas*, the celebration of this holiday in the traditional manner was still discouraged by the Church. People were only supposed to go to a midnight mass, maybe have a nice dinner the next day, read their bible, sing hymns, and not much else.

The true spirit of the season would not die, however, and the traditional Yuletide Christmas survived through the Middle Ages and Renaissance, right up until the Reformation. During the Reformation, the Protestants and reformers sought to purge Christendom of all things pagan, even executing people as punishment for practicing their pagan traditions, which were often seen as a form of witchcraft.[11]

As mentioned earlier, as late as the 17th century, Oliver Cromwell and the English Parliament outlawed Christmas in England, and Cromwell had his soldiers tear down any Christmas decorations they could find.[12] This was the real war on Christmas, and it was waged by devout Protestants.

Of course, traditional Yuletide celebrations have made a comeback since the beginning of the Victorian era and are hugely popular today. Yet, even to this day, there are still some Christian denominations that do not celebrate Christmas, such as Jehovah's Witnesses and other conservative Christian groups. Perhaps many Christians don't celebrate this holiday because it was a pagan holy day that existed long before Christ and is shared by many non-Christians.

It's true, as we have seen, that most of the traditions that we hold dear and associate with Christmas do come from pagan religious practices and mythology. So, it's no wonder some conservative Christians feel a bit squeamish about practicing what they see as pagan traditions.

The truth is that in modern-day America, for most people, Christmas isn't really a religious holiday so much as it is a cultural holiday, like the 4th of July or Superbowl Sunday. On a personal note, I'm not a Christian. Like many Americans, I was raised Christian, but I don't practice it as an adult. Yet, I still celebrate Christmas like most people do. I send out Christmas cards and I wish people a Merry Christmas. And, while I might sometimes refer to it as the Yuletide season, I don't call this holiday *The Yule* or *Alban Arthuan,* like the neo-pagans do. I just call it Christmas.

And, I know that I'm not alone in this. This is true for a lot of non-Christians. This is even true for some Jewish families as well as Hindus, Buddhists and others.

Most people, including atheists, celebrate this time of year, in one way or another. So it's ironic that there are still some Christian groups that don't celebrate it. For more thoughts on this topic, see the Epilogue at the end of the book.

SUMMARY

There are many, many other midwinter holidays all around the world, but at this point I think you see the pattern. People all over the world and throughout history celebrated the winter solstice as a turning point in the annual solar cycle. In many pagan traditions, the annual solar cycle is often times referred to as a wheel or the Wheel of the Year. In fact, Yule means wheel in ancient Norse.

And this phase of the wheel is associated with rebirth, renewal, and the miraculous survival of life, after its apparent death in the late fall. They are all recognizing that the sun has turned the corner, so to speak, and is heading back to summer, and this begins another solar year. Some cultures celebrate this on a new moon close to the winter solstice, but all recognize the solar solstice as an important day as well.

Curiously, each culture has their own stories of mythical figures, gods, and/or historical events to explain why they are celebrating this holy day, at this point in the year. Some stories are very clearly about the sun god being reborn or making his or her journey through the year. But, other stories are as varied as you can get. They include everything from the birth of a savior in the desert to the story of a small amount of oil lasting for 8 days.

The stories include feathered serpents, spirits who enter your home through smoke in the fireplace, gods who fly through the air on an 8-legged horse, or a similar figure that flies through the air on a sleigh pulled by 8 magical reindeer. It's interesting how often the number 8 comes up; perhaps this is due to the fact that there are 8 points on the Wheel of Time, and this holiday sums them all up.

Yet, at the heart of almost all these stories is an acknowledgement of the purpose of this holiday, a celebration of the winter solstice and all that it stands for on the Wheel of Time. This is the turning of the year; in a sense, it is the reincarnation of the new year.

And, regardless of which god you worship, this holiday is a celebration of god's eternal gift of salvation and renewal, and that death is not the end. This holiday literally represents the miracle of life after death and the promise of reincarnation, both in nature and for the human soul as well.

CHAPTER 11

THE EIGHT SABBATHS OF THE WHEEL: A GLOBAL SURVEY

Now that we've explored the winter solstice in some depth, we will more briefly describe the rest of the 8 major Sabbaths on the Wheel of Time. Again, the 8 points of the year consist of the two solstices, the two equinoxes, and the four midpoints between them, known as the cross-quarter days. For each of these, we will do a roundup of some of the more prominent holidays in Western civilization, in antiquity, and around the world that occur at these auspicious times of the year.

Needless to say, that is going to be a lot of holidays, so this chapter is more of an overview or general survey of the holidays. The purpose is to give you some context with which to understand and relate to each of the 8 major points on the Wheel of Time, and to see how they correspond to our modern holidays of the year.[1]

Having dispensed with the winter solstice, moving clockwise around the Wheel of Time, the next major Sabbath is Imbolc, the first mid-point, or cross-quarter day.

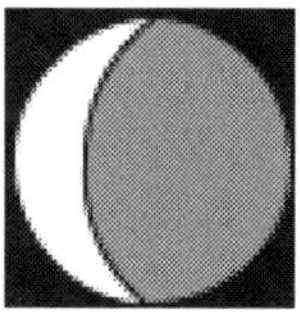

1ST MIDPOINT

Point on the Solar Cycle:	Midpoint between Winter Solstice and Spring Equinox
Pagan Sabbath Name:	Imbolc (meaning pregnant)
Approximate Solar Date:	February 2nd
Dates of Lunisolar & Other Holidays:	Late January to Mid February
Time of Day to Celebrate:	3am or Pre-Dawn
Symbolic Meaning on the Life Cycle:	Courtship / Fertility / Conception
Corresponding Modern Holidays:	Chinese New Year, Groundhog Day, Candlemas, Valentines Day

Imbolc is the Celtic pagan name for this holiday. It is the midpoint between the winter solstice and the spring equinox. And to many ancient pagans this was the start of spring. When I talk to people about this holiday, they usually say that they've never heard of it. I tell them that they actually have heard of it and they probably have celebrated it without even knowing.

Then I tell them some of the names that this holiday is called, like Groundhog Day, or Chinese New Year, or even St. Valentine's Day. Immediately there is an 'ah ha!' moment of recognition. Of course, we've all heard of these holidays.

Then people often ask, why are all these holidays on different days? How can they all stem from one point on the calendar? Good question. That is because there are a few different ways that the dates of holidays are determined. First, there is the actual solar midpoint between the winter solstice and spring equinox, but that is different each year. Because of our 4-year, leap year cycle, it might be anywhere from February 1st to the 3rd. So, throughout history people just picked an arbitrary date close to the actual date, and that is where we get the date of February 2nd, which is the date for Groundhog day, Imbolc, and the Catholic holiday, Candlemas.

Then there are the lunisolar holidays. This is a particular phase of the moon closest to or after Imbolc. Chinese New Year, for instance, is such a holiday. It is the second new moon after the winter solstice, that puts it anywhere from late January to mid February. One year it was on February 8th, just a few days after the solar midpoint of Imbolc. The next year it was on January 28th, just before Imbolc. Then, there are the other celebrations at other phases of the moon, such as the quarter moon or the full moon. Finally, there is the juxtaposition of holidays from a lunisolar calendar to a solar calendar. That's a little complex, so let me explain.

On a lunisolar calendar each new moon begins a new month. So, the 1st of the month is always on a new moon (no visible moon), and the 7th of the month is always a quarter moon, and the 15th is always a full moon. But, when they switched over to a solar calendar, as the Romans did with the Julian calendar, then the fixed dates of the holidays became independent of the phase of the moon.

So, if a holiday was originally celebrated on a full moon, it would have been on the 15th of the month every year. But when they switched to the Julian calendar, they may still celebrate on the 15th, even though that date is now unrelated to the phase of the moon. So, one year the 15th of the month might be a quarter moon and the next it could be a full moon, but it would always be February 15th. That is what we see with most holidays that fall on a fixed date each year. If, on the other hand, they chose to scrap the fixed date and stick to the lunar phase then the holiday would fall on a different date every year, like Easter or Chinese New Year.

What really makes it confusing is that there is no consistency from one holiday to the next. Each different holiday, in each different culture, was designated using a different system. Holidays like Groundhog Day and Candlemas are holidays corresponding to the phases of the solar year, and are on the same date each year. Holidays like Chinese New Year or Easter are entirely a lunisolar event, so the date changes from year to year, but the phase of the moon is always the same. Meanwhile, the ancient precursor to St. Valentine's Day was originally celebrated on a full moon in February, and then was switched to a fixed date on a solar calendar, February 14th.

Unfortunately, there seems to be no rhyme or reason why people saw fit to designate holidays the way they did. And, of course, each different culture resolved this issue in their own way, with no consistency. So we are stuck with a hodge-podge of holidays, some solar dates, some lunisolar.

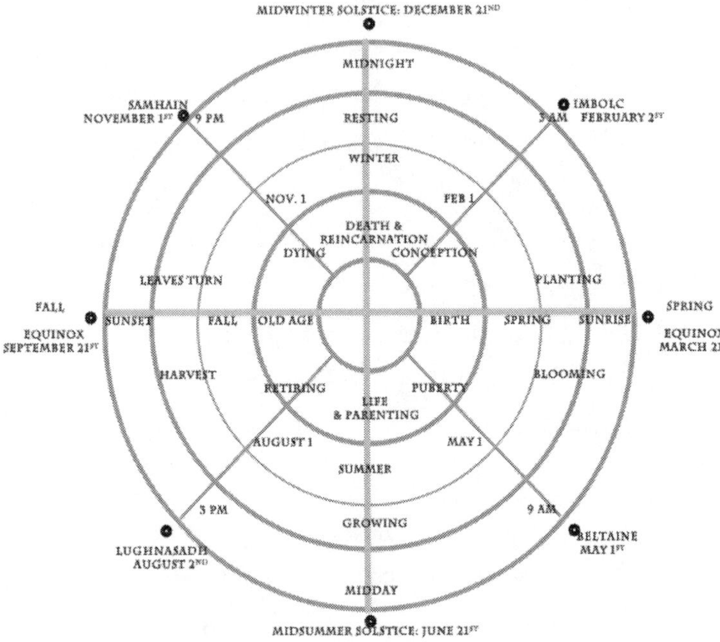

Figure 10

As we will see, the one thing all these holidays have in common is the theme of the season as indicated by the Wheel of Time, above. All the above holidays, at this time of year, Imbolc, are related to one thing: fertility. More specifically this time of year represents the physical conception of the new year. Literally, the Earth is becoming pregnant with new life. And, this corresponds to all the different levels of the Wheel, including the time of day (pre-dawn), the phase of agriculture (buds forming on vines and branches), livestock (becoming pregnant, and begin lactating), and the phase of human life (sex, conception, and pregnancy). So, all these different holidays really are manifestations of one single point on the 8 pointed Wheel of Time.

This explanation for the varying dates of the Imbolc holidays is also true for all of the other holidays of the year. So, this is something to keep in mind as we go through all the holidays from around the world and across the centuries. Now, let's look at each of the Imbolc holidays a little more in depth.

EGYPT: NUT AND THE CONCEPTION OF THE SUN GOD, RA

First, the Ancient Egyptians, just like the Celtic pagans, celebrated what would be February 2nd on our calendar. In their religion, it represented the birth of the Goddess Nut. Like most holidays this time of year, this celebration is related to the conception of the new solar year because, you see, Nut was the mother of the sun god Ra. Without Nut, the sun would never be conceived or born, and there would never be a new year. So, by celebrating Nut, they were celebrating the mother of the sun and therefore the conception of the new year.

CHINA: THE CONCEPTION OF THE NEW SOLAR YEAR

Among the Chinese, they saw this as not only the start of spring but, as such, they saw it as the official start of the new year. As mentioned before, the Chinese lunisolar calendar begins with the Imbolc new moon, the second new moon after the winter solstice, so it lands on a different day each year. For the Chinese, the fact that it is the *New Year Celebration* is the most important feature of the holiday. So, they celebrate it just as we celebrate the New Year, with parades, fireworks, and parties that last all night. There are, of course, special foods, stories, and traditions associated with this holiday, such as hanging red lanterns, eating sticky cakes, and watching the Lion Dance. And, to the Chinese, each year is associated with a different sign in Chinese astrology. They say that if you conceive a child at this time of the year (late January to mid February), it will have the characteristics of that astrological sign.

ANCIENT ROME: THE NONES AND IDES OF FEBRUARY

The ancient Romans also celebrated this time of year. They observed two holidays at this time. There was the Nones of February, which marked the start of spring, and the Ides of February, which was even more auspicious for fertility. You see, the original Roman calendar, like the Chinese and like most ancient calendars, was a lunisolar calendar.

On that calendar there were three auspicious lunar phases each month, and many if not most holidays fell on one of these days. The Kalends, Nones, and Ides. The Kalends was a new moon, on the first of the month. The Nones was the first quarter moon, on the 7th of the month. And the Ides was a full moon, on the 15th of the month. But, when they switched over to a strictly solar calendar, like the one we have today, they kept the holidays on the same dates, irrespective of the phase of the moon.

So, according to the Roman scholar Marcus Terentius Varro (116 BC – 27 BC), it was the Nones of February which marked the start of spring. But, by the time of Varro, this had nothing to do with the moon, but rather it was simply the 7th of February. This was a very important day for farmers and vintners, because it marked the arrival of the new buds on olive and fruit trees.

The Nones of February was a time when Favonius, the god of the west wind and servant of Cupid, would start blowing favorably, and that meant it was time to get back to work, clearing the debris, weeding the grain fields and pruning the grape vines. There was a close bond between religion and agriculture in ancient Rome. So, this date was likely marked with some religious ceremony or celebration, like a ground breaking ceremony in the fields, orchards, and vineyards.

But, the Nones of February was not so important for the average people of Rome. For them it was *Lupercalia* that was the big pagan celebration because that holiday was directly related to human fertility. Lupercalia was a 3- day celebration in honor of Lupercus, god of fertility, on the Ides of February. The Ides was originally on the full moon, I think you can see how the swelling of the moon, at the start of spring may have originally been seen as a good omen for women trying to get pregnant. But, when they switched to a solar calendar, it was simply the 13th - 15th of February.

Lupercalia also honored the Roman god Faunus. Like

the Greek god Pan, Faunus was the god of sexuality, and of all things wild. On the last day, the men of Rome would first slaughter a goat in a religious ceremony. Then the men would run through the streets naked or wearing only a loin cloth made of animal skin, carrying strips of the sacrificial goat's skin. Women who wanted to get pregnant, would line the streets. The naked runners would slap the female onlookers with a strap of skin from the sacrificed goat.

Getting slapped by the men was believed to make them fertile and pregnant in the coming year. There is even a story that Julius Caesar was concerned that his wife could not get pregnant. So he asked Mark Anthony to run for him at Lupercalia and to be sure to slap his wife as he passed her, to insure her fertility.

CELTIC CELEBRATION OF IMBOLC

Imbolc is one of the Celts four annual fire festivals and, like the Romans, the official start of Spring. In Gallic, Imbolc, or *i mbolg,* means pregnant, literally *in the belly.* That is because Imbolc, on February 2nd, is associated with the pregnancy and lactation of the ewes, who will give birth to the spring lambs.

Another related name for this holiday is Oimelc, which means *ewe's milk*. Among the Celtic pagans, this was the start of spring. Not surprising, imbolc is also the Irish name for *spring*. And, as such, it is traditionally a time to tend to the grain fields and orchards, and all the other tasks associated with the coming of spring. But, as with the Romans, it has another meaning corresponding to the human life cycle. It is also called St. Brigid's Day, a day to honor Brigid, the goddess of fire, poetry, healing and, most importantly, childbirth.

One folk tradition of Imbolc holds that on this day all the young, unmarried women of the village would gather together in a house, and they would create a corn dolly to represent Brigid, and it was called *Brideog*, meaning *Little Brigid*. And they would make a little bed for Brideog to lie in, and they would stay up all night, kind of like a slumber party.

At some point in the night, the young men of the village would come over to pay their respects to the young maids, as well as to Brideog. This symbolic courtship ritual reflects the underlying meaning of this holiday: courtship, fertility, and conception.

THE NORSE CELEBRATION OF DISTING

Among the Norse heathens of northern Europe, such as the Germans, Dutch, Saxons, and others, the holiday known as *Disting* was celebrated on the same day, February 2nd, with all the same associations to nature, the coming of spring, pregnancy and lactation of the ewes, preparing the fields, and human conception as well.

This date is dedicated to the Norse goddess Frige, goddess of beauty, love, and marriage, and it is also dedicated to all the *Disir*, the female ancestors. But, among the Norse peoples this was also a time to count your livestock and assess your wealth. It was said that if a calf was born during Disting, it was a good omen.

And, there is another feature to this holiday; the prognostication of the weather. Yes, there are many legends that certain ground-dwelling animals, such as a badger, a bear, or even a groundhog, can predict the coming of an early spring if it doesn't see its shadow at dawn on this day.

Many centuries later, among early German-American settlers, the curious legend of the groundhog predicting the weather became the overwhelming feature of the February 2nd holiday. People, mostly the young men and women of the village, would stay up all night drinking beer, eating bratwurst, and singing songs, waiting to see the groundhog at dawn. In truth, the groundhog has as much to do with Disting as Rudolph's red nose has to do with Christmas. Nonetheless, many still observe this ritual every year, even to the present day, the most famous of which is held in Punxsutawney, Pennsylvania. Nowadays, in America, February 2nd is simply called Groundhog Day.

It is interesting to note the tradition of staying up all night among both Celts and Norse pagans. Why is this a tradition of Imbolc? Well, in looking at the Wheel of Time you see that Imbolc corresponds to 3 am, or the pre-dawn hours between midnight and dawn. Given a choice of getting up at 1:00 or 2:00 in the morning to get ready to attend a gathering, or simply staying up all night drinking, and singing, and waiting for dawn, what do you think people would choose?

SCOTLAND: UP HELLY AA

In Scotland, they celebrate the end of the Yule season at the end of January with a festival that they call Up Helly Aa, which roughly translated means "Up Holy Day All". This was an ancient holiday that was celebrated with *tar-barreling*, the practice of dragging barrels of burning tar through the streets. This was done by squads of young men in the middle of the night, and probably involved a fair amount of drinking. This was originally done at the beginning, middle and end of the Yule season, which to the ancient Vikings, went right up until Imbolc. Nowadays, they simply carry torches through the town, which is much safer.

CHRISTIANIZING PAGAN HOLIDAYS

Of course, as with Christmas and Easter, the Christian Church incorporated these pagan holidays into their new religion. By the 4th century, Imbolc and Disting were replaced with the Christian celebration known as Candlemas, a festival in which all the candles to be used in the new year were brought in to be blessed by the priest.

As you may well imagine, there was some carryovers from the pagan traditions to Candlemas. Even to the present day, in Ireland, many continue their Imbolc celebrations but call them Candlemas, also known as St. Brigid's Day. And, not unlike Groundhog day, Candlemas also involved predicting of the weather.

There is an old poem that goes:

> If Candlemas Day be fair and bright, Winter will have another fight.
> If Candlemas Day brings cloud and rain,
> Winter won't come again.

Clearly, this is the same as the legend of the Groundhog. If he sees his shadow there will be 6 more weeks of winter. But, if it's cloudy and he doesn't, then there will be an early spring.

And, just as with other pagan holidays, the shameless pagan ritual of Lupercalia was seen as blasphemous to the Church. And, in the year 496, Pope Gelasius I finally banished Lupercalia, and replaced it with a feast in honor of the martyr St. Valentinus. Of course, we know this holiday as St. Valentine's Day.

Interestingly, the original holiday, Lupercalia, was from the 13th to the 15th of February, but St. Valentine's Day is just on the 14th. There are two possible reasons for this. First, according to legend, Valentinus was martyred on the 14th. Secondly, the Pope may have wanted to avoid a direct connection between the two holidays of Lupercalia and St. Valentine's Day.

The Church might have learned from their previous mistakes, such as with Christmas, and found that just renaming a pagan holiday was not enough to stamp out its pagan traditions. Pope Gelasius may have wanted to create a completely different holiday with new traditions so he could outlaw the Lupercalia traditions forever. There would be no more naked men slapping women with bloody goat skins in the streets of Rome.

And, it appears that Pope Gelasius was somewhat successful. Even to this day there are still scholars who doubt that the modern holiday of St. Valentine's Day is in any way related to the traditions of the pagan holiday Lupercalia. Scholars such as Henry Ansgar Kelly, author of *Chaucer and the Cult of Saint Valentine*, suggests that it was actually the English writer and poet Geoffrey Chaucer who first linked the feast of St. Valentine with romantic love in the 14th century, with his epic poem *Parlement of Foules*. In it, Chaucer clearly indicates that St. Valentine's Day is a day to celebrate romantic love and all that it entails.

But, as we've seen, this holiday had already been associated with fertility, conception, and even courtship rituals for over 1500 years prior to the life of Chaucer. And, the connection between fertility and romance is a natural one, since conception is often the result of romantic love, whether intentionally or not. I think it's summarized best by the single phrase: *The Mating Season*. So, it makes sense that we celebrate human conception with courtship rituals of love and romance, such as flowers and chocolates, decorated with little red hearts.

At any rate, one thing is for sure, by the time of Chaucer in the 1300s, Valentine's Day was a holiday for lovers. And, whether it was permitted by the Church or not, that much has never changed. Over the years, the holiday became more associated with the pagan god of love, Cupid, than the Christian martyr St. Valentinus.

Unfortunately, there was always some controversy in the Church over this holiday. It was probably the obvious pagan connections with the holiday that irked the Church leaders. But, there was another problem, and that was that we don't know which martyr is being honored on this day. There were 3 martyrs named Valentinus. Interestingly, they were all martyred on the same day, February 14th. Finally, in 1969 the Pope eliminated St. Valentine's Day altogether as an official Catholic holiday.

Alas, it was far too late to stop the popularity of Valentine's Day. Today it ranks right up there with Easter or Halloween in terms of the time, attention, and money that is spent on it. Ironically, it has become so commercial that many people believe that Valentine's Day was invented by the greeting card and candy companies. But, now you know the rest of the story.

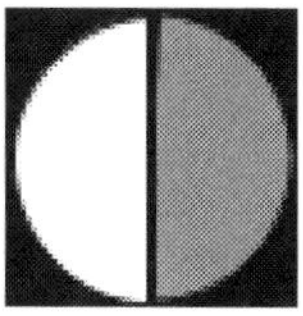

VERNAL EQUINOX

Point on the Solar Cycle:	The Vernal Equinox
Pagan Sabbath Name:	Ēostre, or Ostara
Approximate Solar Date:	March 21st
Dates of Lunisolar & Other Holidays:	Mid March to Mid April
Time of Day to Celebrate:	6 am or Sunrise
Symbolic Meaning on the Life Cycle:	Fertility/ Birth/ Rebirth /Resurrection
Corresponding Modern Holidays:	St. Patrick's Day, Easter, Passover, Holi

Nowadays, most people refer to this holiday as *Easter*, and the neo-pagans refer to the spring equinox as *Ostara*. But, the roots of both names are the same, Ēostre, also written *Ēastre,* the pagan goddess of fertility. Just like Imbolc, there are actually many spring equinox holidays. There is Easter, Eastern Orthodox Easter, Passover, St. Patrick's Day, Holi, and others. There is the solar equinox, and then there are multiple lunisolar holidays clustered around the equinox. The lunisolar holiday of the ancient Celts was on the waxing quarter moon, which corresponds to the same phase of the sun at the equinox. But, Christian and Jewish holidays are on the full moon after the equinox.

There are actually many lunisolar holidays on a full moon, stemming from different calendars: the Jewish calendar, Eastern Orthodox Calendar, Gregorian Calendar, and the Hindu Calendar. One year they fell on two different full moons, one in March and one in April, but that is rare. Actually, Christian Easter is celebrated on the first Sunday after the first full moon, after the spring equinox, on the Gregorian calendar.

It gets pretty confusing to keep track of all these. But, there is one unifying principal to all these holidays. The spring equinox is the meaning of the season of Easter. This is the time we celebrate the peak of the spring season, and all that it represents on the Wheel of Time: fertility, birth, rebirth, resurrection, and the annual return of new life in nature.

THE BABYLONIAN FESTIVAL OF AKITU

As we've seen with other holidays, the roots of this holiday stretch back to ancient antiquity. In ancient Babylon, 2000 years before Jesus, on the first new moon after the equinox, they celebrated the Goddess *Ishtar* on this lunisolar holiday, and they called it Akitu. Notice that they celebrated on a new moon?

If you've been paying attention you may remember from previous chapters that celebrating on a new moon meant that this was their new year. While other cultures may mark the beginning of their wheel of the year at midwinter or Imbolc, or even the autumn equinox, the Mesopotamians marked the new year with the birth of new life seen everywhere in nature at this time of year. Interestingly, in many middle-eastern dialects Ishtar was probably pronounced something more like *Easter*. In keeping with the spring theme, she was the goddess of love, sexuality and, of course, fertility.

As far as we can tell, the ancient Babylonians appear to have celebrated their Easter holiday very much the way we do today, with decorations of flowers, hot cross-buns (markng the four seasons of the Wheel of Time), painted eggs and egg hunts. They also had a feast of cured pork (ham), and probably a sunrise ceremony, which commemorates the concept of resurrection, life reborn.

EGYPT: SHAM EL NESSIM

In ancient Egypt, as far back as 4500 years ago, they celebrated *Sham El Nessim*, which literally means *Smell the Fresh Breeze*. This holiday basically meant *Spring Day* to the ancient Egyptians, and it still does. So as to not conflict with the Christian Easter, it is officially celebrated the day after Easter. And, since the Egyptian Christians use the Coptic Calendar, different from the Gregorian Calendar we use, this is not always on the same date as our Easter Day in the West. Now, as then, Egyptians of all religions, Christians and Muslim, go out into the country at dawn to witness the sunrise, and to take in the fresh, gentle, breeze, which marks the beginning of spring. They also worshipped their goddess *Isis* and her consort *Osiris* on this day, much as the Babylonians worshipped Ishstar and Tammuz on this day.

VERNAL EQUINOX THEMES IN THE ANCIENT WORLD

Isis and Osiris were the Egyptian versions of the Babylonian goddess Ishtar and her consort Tammuz (also known as Marduk). This pair of deities were among the most common gods in the region. Every culture had their own version of them. In Rome they worshipped the goddess *Cybele*, known as the Magna Mater or *Great Mother*, and her cosort *Attis*.

In Greece they had the goddess *Aphrodite* and her lover *Adonis.* Together, they represent the Mother Earth and her slain and resurrected lover and consort. This earth mother goddess is where we get our modern concept of *Mother Nature*. This goddess appears to have originated in Anatolia and was originally depicted as a fat, pregnant earth goddess in ancient artifacts found at Çatalhöyük (7500 BCE-5500 BCE).

As we've already discussed, the ancient Hebrews also celebrated a lunisolar spring holiday, on the first full moon after the spring equinox, with a Seder, a solemn feast, which they called *Pesach*, also known as *Passover*. Of course, according to Jewish tradition, it is not about fertility, rebirth, or resurrection from the dead, but rather commemorates their ancestors' liberation from slavery in Egypt. The story of the Exodus is told and retold each year at this time, at a *Seder* meal. This is clearly an important historical tale for the Jewish people, but it's not clear how it relates to the full moon after the equinox.

Interestingly, the Seder meal consists of, among other

things, an egg, which represents the freedom that hard labor gave birth to. The meal also contains parsley, which is a symbol of springtime. And, the Seder contains apples and walnuts as well as grape juice or kosher wine. Although these items have special meanings related to the Exodus, some of them, such as the egg and parsley, are also clearly symbolic of spring and fertility, and others are symbolic of the bounty of nature and the more universal meanings of springtime.

SPRING IN ANCIENT ROME

In Rome, they celebrated a very unique holiday, which in many ways is more specifically like the strictly Christian customs of Easter. In the Roman equinox celebration, March 22nd would commemorate the death of Attis' body, and it would be a day of mourning, not unlike the Christian Good Friday. Then, the next couple of days would involve different specific rituals for Attis or at the temple of Magna Mater (Cybele).

The night of March 24th was said to be a sacred night, when there would be a vigil for Attis' body, and this was a major holiday. Three days after his death, on March 25th, they would have a sunrise ceremony, celebrating the resurrection of Attis, which would be a time of great rejoicing and merry making. Notice that this ceremony was held at dawn, which corresponds to spring on the Wheel of Time.

What is fascinating about ancient Rome is that they had many different cults and religious sects, each celebrating the equinox and other seasons with their own unique traditions. For instance, another holiday in Rome took place a couple weeks later, specifically devoted to the worship of Cybele, the Great Mother. This was celebrated on April 4th and, as we've seen before in other holidays, this likely originated as a lunisolar holiday. Being on the 4th of the month, that date would be on a young waxing moon of the lunar month following the equinox. So, it may have evolved as a fixed date for what was previously a lunar holiday, on the 4th day of the April moon, which is a new waxing moon. And, as a celebration of the fertility goddess Cybele, it was probably very similar to the Babylonian Ishtar celebration, with painted eggs, bunnies, and all the rest.

Another Roman celebration that took place this time of year was *Bacchanalia*, on the 17th of March. This holiday was primarily celebrated by drinking and drunkenness, in honor of *Bacchus*, the god of wine. Bacchus was the Roman version of *Dionysus*, and the Greeks had the same holiday called *Dionysia*, which had been celebrated for centuries, long before Rome.

The holiday was later renamed *Liberalia,* in honor of *Liber,* the god of vineyards, winemaking, freedom, and fertility. This is where we get the word *liberal.* The change appears to have been an attempt to tamp down the cult of Bacchus, which had become excessively rowdy, and in some years even violent, going on drunken rampages through the streets of Rome every March 17th. As we'll see later, this eventually became known as St. Patrick's Day.

ÊASTRE: THE SAXON RITES OF SPRING

According to the writings of the Venerable Bede, we know that the ancient Anglo Saxon pagans in Early England and elsewhere marked this event with the worship of the Goddess of Fertility, *Ēostre,* also written Ēastre, which was probably pronounced more like *Easter*. And, they too celebrated with fertility symbolism, including flowers, bunnies, painted eggs, a sunrise ceremony, and other traditional features of the now familiar Easter celebration.

An interesting bit of trivia, the connection between Ēastre and the sunrise was so strong that we get the name East from the name Ēastre. Ēastre was the goddess of the dawn and the goddess of the East, which is exactly what we see on the Wheel of Time. If the winter solstice corresponds to midnight, and the summer solstice is high noon, then the spring equinox is right in between, and so it corresponds to dawn, which is when we celebrate it.

HOW BACCHANALIA BECAME ST. PATRICK'S DAY

We know less about the ancient Celts and Druids and how they celebrated the equinox. As far as we know the Anglo-Saxon pagans and Druid pagans of Briton had many similar customs. For instance, the Celtic version of Ēostre was the goddess Ostara. So it's reasonable to assume that they celebrated with sunrise ceremonies, painted eggs, bunnies, egg hunts, and wild flowers as well. We also know that the pagan Britons would build bon-fires, and would jump over the burning embers to give them fertility in the coming growing season.

The traditional Celtic celebration of the spring equinox may be best represented by the Saint's feast day, known as St. Patrick's Day. St. Patrick was a 5th century Roman missionary. He is credited for driving the snakes out of Ireland, and for bringing Christianity to the island nation. Ironically, we now know that there never were any snakes in Ireland. So, many think that by bringing Christianity to Ireland, he actually drove the Druids out of Ireland, and that is what was meant by *driving the Snakes out*. But, he may have unintentionally brought something else to Ireland. It may be because of him, though accidentally, that they celebrate the pagan holiday Bacchanalia, or something like it, in Ireland to this very day.

As we mentioned, in ancient Rome, March 17th was the festival of Bacchanalia, later known as Liberalia. It was a day of public drunkenness to celebrate wine and wonders of intoxication. As we've seen with other pagan Sabbaths, the Church was none too happy with this pagan drunk fest. So, they felt the need to create a Christian holiday on the same day as Bacchanalia, to facilitate conversion to Christianity and to stamp out pagan practices.

Bacchanalia was probably especially irksome to the Church as it actually celebrated public drunkenness. So, the Church in Rome made March 17th a feast day for St. Patrick, just as they had done with St. Valentinus because, according to legend, Patrick was buried on March 17th.

But, in making this a Christian holiday, the Church had created a day of feasting right in the middle of Lent. This period known as Lent is a solemn religious practice of purification and penitence that lasts for 6 weeks before Easter. During Lent, people were supposed to abstain from alcohol, overeating, and hedonistic pleasures. This was a brilliant move by the Church because it meant that the pagan celebration of Bacchanalia was effectively stamped out altogether.

And, they didn't even need to change the date of the holiday. They could not celebrate St. Patrick's Day the same as they had celebrated Bacchanalia or Liberalia because it was right in the middle of Lent. All they could do to celebrate was to go to mass and have a modest meal.

But, St. Patrick was the patron saint of Ireland, and the people of Ireland were very proud of their Saint. So, this holiday was very dear to them. As such, the Church of Ireland made an exception for St. Patrick's Day. Just this one day, they did not have to observe Lent, and they could celebrate the holiday as they traditionally had done, with parades, singing, dancing, and drinking as much as they wanted.

Eventually, the fun and festivity of St. Patrick's Day spread to America, where it is still celebrated to this very day, usually by drinking a mug of Green beer or a pint of Guinness Stout, or two, or three. Hence, St. Patrick may have driven the pagans out of Ireland, but he saved the pagan holiday of Bacchanalia for us all.

In the Middle Ages, on St. Patrick's Day, the Celts in

Ireland dressed up all in green, even dressing as *Green Man*, a pagan nature spirit that comes to life this time of year. And, as is consistent with other Celtic pagan holidays, they had bonfires, music, singing, feasts, and did a good deal of drinking ale and spirits. And, during this time of the year, they really had something to celebrate.

Winter was over, the weather was getting warmer, food - especially vegetables and berries - would soon become more abundant, and firewood (often a scarce commodity) would become less needed. So, if you want to know how the ancient Celts celebrated the vernal equinox, you might just look at our modern St. Patrick's Day celebration.

By the way, the vernal equinox is celebrated with the color green because it is at this time of year in the northern latitudes that nature turns green again, and that is why we wear green on St. Patrick's Day. Then, on Easter, which might be over a month after the equinox, and again on May Day, we celebrate with bright colors because that is when the spring flowers are blooming.

As for leprechauns, they are merely the Irish version of the Norse myths of elves. Actually, every culture has their version of an elf. In England they're called fairies, in Scotland they're called *siths*, the Cornish have *pixies*, the French have the *fee*, the Italians have *imps*, in Greek *nymphs*, in Hawaiian *menehune*, and in Arabic they have the *djinn or djinni*, which is where we get the word *genie*. And, as we've seen over and over again, each different culture always makes up their own unique mythology for each holiday, with gods, goddesses, elves, or other supernatural creatures.

This time of year, many different cultures perceived that these magical creatures of nature were at work in the forests and glens. It was not uncommon for the English to talk of seeing fairies this time of year, or for the folks down in Cornwall to tell stories of pixies. But, among the ancient Irish, it was the elusive leprechauns that they told of. They spent their time making and mending shoes and hording gold. According to legend, if you manage to catch a leprechaun then he has to grant you three wishes.

PESACH & THE CHRISTIAN CELEBRATION OF EASTER

With the advent of Christianity, the Church in Rome created a new holiday, and unlike other Christian holidays that we've seen thus far, this one was strictly Christian in nature. This holiday was meant to celebrate the crucifixion and resurrection of Christ. As we mentioned in a previous chapter, it was the Venerable Bede who decided how to set the proper date for this holiday, and he even named the holiday. Ironically, Bede arrived at this date, in part, by observing the pagans of Briton.

The British pagans would celebrate the pagan goddess of fertility, Ēastre, on a lunisolar holiday associated with the spring equinox using the Julian Calendar. During the life of Bede, the Church fathers were struggling to figure out on what date they should celebrate the resurrection of Christ.

They knew that it should be on a Sunday after the crucifixion, which was the day before Passover. But, Passover is a lunisolar holiday on the Hebrew calendar. It was on a different date each year. And, the Hebrew calendar was completely different from the Julian calendar. Without any Hebrew scholars handy, there was often some confusion in knowing when Passover should be.

Without the date of Passover, they didn't know when the resurrection should be celebrated. Bede resolved it; he knew that that Passover was a lunisolar holiday, celebrated on a full moon after the spring equinox. He used the same system that the pagans of Briton used to set their lunisolar holidays. He simply picked the first Sunday, after the first full moon, after the spring equinox, using the Julian calendar. And, though we now use the Gregorian calendar, we still use the same process to set the date of Easter, to this very day.

What is odd about Bede and the English Church fathers is they not only used the pagan system for identifying this lunisolar spring holiday, but they also used the same time of day that the pagans had used for their fertility festival, at dawn. Again, we get the word East from the fact that Ēastre was the goddess of the Dawn. Well, that is not so strange; we saw the same thing occur with the Church fathers celebrating Christmas with a midnight mass, as the pagans had done. But, what is really odd, you might say blasphemous, is that they even named the holiday Ēostre or Ēastre, after the pagan goddess of fertility. Of course, this is where we get the name Easter.

So, this begs the question: why do we name the resurrection after a pagan goddess? Why not call it Resurrection Day? In Rome, they call it Pasqua, originally from the Hebrew Pesach, meaning Passover. But, in English, Bede and the English Church were okay with simply continuing to call it Ēastre, as it had always been called among the pagans. And, of course, the common folk celebrated Christian Easter as they had always celebrated pagan Easter, with flowers, painted eggs, bunnies, egg hunts, and other imagery of spring. I think this tells us how popular the pagan celebration of spring was in England at that time. The best they could do was to encourage people to at least think of Jesus when they were celebrating their traditional rites of spring.

Naturally, one of the highlights of this holiday, like Christmas and Passover, is a feast. And, in ancient Rome, as today, a roast pig was usually the centerpiece of the feast. To this day, millions of Americans celebrate Easter as people have for thousands of years with flowers, painted eggs, bunnies, and a feast of ham. It is ironic that what started out to be the most Christian of holidays, held on the very day of the resurrection of Jesus Christ, ended up being totally pagan, from its lunisolar date and how it is traditionally celebrated, even down to the pagan goddess that it's named after.

INDIA: THE HOLI FESTIVAL

There are similar celebrations all over the world, too numerous to mention. One that has gained popularity in recent years is the annual *Holi* Festival. This is a Hindu lunisolar holiday. It's very much like Easter but it is celebrated on the full moon before the spring equinox, as opposed to Passover and Easter, which is the first full moon after the equinox. The Holi Festival is a party to end all parties. It is a celebration of love, merry-making, and spring colors. People celebrate it with colorful spring flowers, wear brightly colored clothes, and even paint themselves in bright spring colors. It is a celebration of the victory of light over darkness and good over evil. Though originally Hindu in origin, it has spread to non-Hindu countries throughout Asia and even parts of Europe and North America.

CONCLUSION

I think it's clear, just as with Imbolc, that the spring equinox consists of several different holidays, on different dates, and corresponding to different religious traditions and histories. But there are a couple main themes that we see over and over. First, the theme running through all these holidays is fertility, life, birth, and re-birth. And, of course, all these spring equinox holidays correspond to dawn on the Wheel of Time, which is when we celebrate them. It is the birth of the year, symbolic of rebirth in the human life cycle, celebrated at dawn, the birth of a new day. This is sometimes celebrated on the birth of a new moon in some societies, and other times it's celebrated on a waxing or full moon, symbolic of abundance.

This is usually celebrated with symbols of fertility, such as eggs, bunnies, chicks, and flowers. Obviously, this is the time of year when all living things, especially in the northern hemisphere, seem to come back from the dead. Flowers bloom, grass grows, and the birds are singing again. The livestock have given birth and have their babies at their side. In the wild we see the same, with wolf pups and bear cubs. It seems the whole world comes back to life at this time of year.

In various cultures, such as the ancient Romans and among Christians, there is another theme we find. There are two holidays, back to back, one marking the death of a sun god and one marking his rebirth, like Good Friday and Easter Sunday. And, there is the worship of a Great Mother, either giving birth to all life or specifically giving re-birth to her mortally wounded lover and consort, such as Isis and Osiris, Ishtar and Marduk, or Cybele and Attis.

Finally, there is also another odd holiday tradition that seems to come, in part, from the traditional Roman pagan holiday, Bacchanalia, combined with a Celtic pagan celebration of spring, both of which involve a good deal of drinking and merry-making. Of course, the result is none other than the Christian holiday, St. Patrick's Day, a giant party to celebrate the arrival of spring, wear green, and drink massive quantities of beer.

2ND MIDPOINT

Point on the Solar Cycle:	Midpoint between Spring Equinox and Summer Solstice
Pagan Sabbath Name:	Beltaine
Approximate Solar Date:	May 1st
Dates of Lunisolar & Other Holidays:	April 30th through Mid May
Time of Day to Celebrate:	9 am or Mid Morning
Symbolic Meaning on the Life Cycle:	Puberty/ Young Adulthood/ Parenthood
Corresponding Modern Holidays:	May Day, Mother's Day, Children's Day

Beltaine, better known as May Day, is celebrated on May 1st, and it is the midpoint between the spring equinox and the summer solstice. To the ancient pagans, this was the start of summer. Of course the actual midpoint date changes from year to year, but for whatever reason almost everyone celebrates this holiday on May 1st. And, there does not appear to be many lunar holidays corresponding to this holiday. For the ancient Celts, it is one of the four fire festivals, and it signified the beginning of summer. For many in the northern hemisphere, it represents the start of the best weather of the year and the real start of the agricultural season.

In the human lifespan, if the spring equinox represents birth on the Wheel of Time and the summer solstice represents the peak of adulthood, then this is the midpoint between the two, and it represents puberty. Well, to be more precise, it represents that point halfway between birth and mature adulthood that we usually refer to as the teenage or young adult years. Keep in mind that the Wheel of Time and all these holidays are really about life and death, and all the holidays represent the key points along the cycle of life and death. On the Wheel of Time, Beltaine represents the point at which the child grows up and begins to reproduce and have children of their own. If you think about it, the real spirit of Beltaine often echoes the meaning of Imbolc and Valentine's Day.

Think of it this way, there are two points in each person's life that involve conception and fertility. The first is when we ourselves are conceived in our mother's womb. The second is when we marry and conceive children of our own. It is like two generations of the life cycle. If Imbolc is the conception of the year, then Beltaine is the mating season of the year, literally the time when birds and bees appear most active in nature, flowers bloom, and fruit is first formed.

But, it is interesting how we celebrate February and May so differently. We associate the first holiday with Love (Valentine's Day), but we associate the second holiday with parenthood (Mother's Day). And, this is echoed in what we see in nature as well. In February we see that the ewes are pregnant, but we don't yet see the offspring. We see the buds on the vine, but not the flower or the fruit. Later, in May, all the livestock have their babies suckling at their side, all the vines have flowered, and the fruit is forming. I think this mirrors the maturation process that occurs in life; when we're young, love and sex are pure romance, but as we get older we discover the resulting responsibilities of parenthood. But, to be clear, on the Wheel of Time, February (Valentine's Day) represents conception, Easter represents birth, and May (Mother's Day) represents parenthood.

MAY HOLIDAYS IN ANCIENT ROME

In Rome, they celebrated this time of year with the holiday known as *Floralia*, literally a celebration of Flora, the goddess of flowers. This especially refers to the flowering of fruit trees, which promises a bounty of delicious food in the coming summer and fall. They celebrated much as we do this time of year, with baskets of fresh-cut flowers. Also, there is an obvious connection between flowers and sexual reproduction. When we want to talk about sex in front of children we often refer to the *birds and bees*. What we are really referring to is pollination. The flower is synonymous with pollination and it is emblematic of the anatomy of sexual reproduction. The flower precedes the fruit, just as sex and pregnancy precedes the birth of a baby. All these nuances were probably present to one extent or another in the Roman festival of flowers, Floralia.

The Romans also celebrated with the *Ludi Florae,* or

the *Floralia Games*, which lasted for 6 days, from April 28th to May 3nd. The games were not just competitions but also included theatrical performances, acrobats, spectacles, and once they even included an elephant walking on a tightrope.

CELTIC RITES OF BELTAINE

At this time of year, the ancient Celts celebrated another one of their four fire festivals, which occur on the cross-quarter days. This festival, Beltaine, marked the beginning of summer. On the eve of Beltaine they would build bonfires and drink and feast and dance around the fire. They believed that the smoke would give the people good luck and fertility. Another Beltaine tradition is the coronation of the May Queen, who would preside over the festivities. But, what makes this holiday unique is that it celebrates the act of mating and copulation.

We know that one of the pagan traditions on this holiday was to have sex. In ancient times the May Queen would pick a May King for the festival, and their coupling would be emblematic of the holiday. The young folk would join them in having sex in the fields to bless their crops with fertility. There is a legend of one such tradition where young men and women would wear masks, to conceal their identity. They would then take an anonymous partner, and have sex with them in the fields. It was believed that if you had sex this night, the young woman would surely get pregnant.

Probably the best-known aspect of this holiday is the

Maypole, a giant pole, with brightly colored ribbons hanging from it. Children would traditionally grab the end of a ribbon and dance around the Maypole, wrapping the pole in ribbons as they do so. Many have suggested that the Maypole may represent an ancient sacred tree, also known as the *Tree of the World*. What most people may not know is that the Maypole is also a sexual symbol.

The Maypole represents the sexual anatomy of a flower. The pole itself represents the carpel, containing the style and the stigma of a flower. At the base of the carpel is the ovaries, the female reproductive cells of the plant. The ribbons represent the stamen, consisting of the anther and filament, the male reproductive cells of the plant. The intermingling of the two, such as wrapping the Maypole with colored ribbons, represents how flowers reproduce. So, when children dance around the Maypole, wrapping ribbons around it, they are reenacting the dance of bees pollinating flowers. As sweet and innocent as it may appear, it is really symbolic of pollination and sexual reproduction.

NORSE/GERMANIC WALPURGISNAUGHT

In German it is known as *Walpurgisnaught*, or in English *Walpurgis Night*. It is a feast to commemorate St. Walpurga, the St. Patrick of Germany, literally the person who first brought Christianity to the Germanic people. But this is overlaid on top of an older Norse holiday celebrating what is essentially a Norse pagan version of Beltaine. As such, it is also known as *Heksennaucht*, which literally means *Witches Night*. In the middle-ages it was believed that witches would hold a party and possibly an orgy on this night, on the highest mountain in the Harz Mountains. This holiday is still celebrated throughout northern Europe among the Norse cultural descendants.

The *Maibaum* (May Tree) or Maypole is also an integral part of these May Day celebrations as well. Usually, it is erected on April 30th, and they dance around it all night. But, many towns have permanent Maibaums. To this day you can see Maibaums prominently displayed in the town square of many villages in Southern Germany and Austria. Also, in traditional German cultures, this is a time of year that they make and drink *Maibock*, which is a particularly strong type of beer, also known as *helles bock*.

THE MYSTERY OF PENTECOST & SHAVUOT

There is one more ancient holiday at this time of year, but its connection to the Wheel of Time is a little mysterious. The Christians know this holiday as the Pentecost, which is based upon the Jewish lunisolar holiday: Shavuot. This holiday can fall anywhere from mid-May to early June. Remember that Easter is based on the date of Passover. Well, Shavuot is 50 days after Passover, and so the Pentecost is 50 days after Easter. The word *Pentecost* comes from Greek, and it literally means "50 Days".

According to Christians, we celebrate the Pentecost

because this is the day that the Holy Spirit descended onto the Disciples of Jesus. But, this day had already been celebrated for over a thousand years by the Jewish people as supposedly the day that God revealed the Torah to Moses.

Notice the relationship between the two. This marks the day that Moses received the first covenant with God, 50 days after deliverance from bondage. Now on the exact same day, over a thousand years later, the Disciples received the second covenant with God, 50 days after Jesus delivered us salvation upon the cross and was resurrected.

What most people in the West may not know is that Ramadan, a major holiday in the Islamic faith, celebrates the time when God gave the Qur'an to Mohammed. Sound Familiar? Remember Shavuot celebrates God giving the Torah to Moses. So Ramadan has a similar meaning. Then, the Christian Pentecost has a similar Christian meaning as these older holidays.

But, what is the connection to the Wheel of Time? Well, Shavuot is on the 6th day of Sivan, the 9th month on the Jewish calendar. The Jewish calendar is a lunisolar calendar, so the 6th day of the 9th month is always a waxing quarter moon, in the 9th moon of the year. And, Ramadan is also a lunisolar holiday; it is celebrated on a waxing crescent moon, in the 9th month of the Islamic calendar. Coincidence? So, it seems likely that Shavuot evolved from a regional pagan holy day in prehistory, just as other lunisolar holidays we've seen throughout history.

But, this still leaves us with a mystery. If this was an

ancient pagan holy day, what was the original meaning of this day in prehistory? And, does it relate to the Wheel of Time? Well, one way of thinking of this is that it may have been an early attempt to celebrate a cross-quarter day. Think of it this way. The solstices and equinoxes can be marked with solar observatories and solar markers, as we have shown. But the easiest way to find the mid-points between them is simply to count the days from one solar event to the next.

I may be just spit-balling, but consider this. From the spring equinox to the summer solstice is about 93 days. So, the mid-point is 46.5 days from the equinox. That is very close to the 50 days used to find the day of Shavuot. But, why would it be off by 3.5 days? Well, 3.5 days is exactly one half of one week. And there is a one-week difference between a full moon (Passover) and a waxing quarter moon (Shavuot). Perhaps, if they split the differnce, that could account for the discrepancy. As such, that would make Shavuot and Pentecost consistent with the other ancient May celebrations that we've seen, a lunisolar celebration of the midpoint between the equinox and the solstice. But, we may never know for sure.

Since Christians used the Roman solar calendar, all these lunisolar holidays were made meaningless anyway. In fact, the only way they could even find the 6th day of Sivan was to count 50 days from Easter. Then, at some point, the Islamic calendar became unhinged from the solar year completely. This left their holidays spinning wildly throughout the year. So, now Ramadan, is celebrated in January every 16 years.

A CELEBRATION OF REPRODUCTION

Nowadays, May Day is not such an important holiday in America, yet it continues to be a popular holiday in Europe, and some German-American communities in the United States. In America, we have Mother's Day on the second Sunday in May. Likewise, in much of Eastern Europe, Mother's Day, or Dzien Matki, is the second Sunday in May. In France, Mother's Day is the last Sunday in May. And, this is about the same time of year that most countries hold their versions of Father's Day, either in May or early June.

In Japan, May 5th is Children's Day or *Kodomo no Hi.* This ancient holiday (originally named *Tango no Sekku*) is a celebration of children and recognizes the contributions of mothers and fathers as well. It's interesting that they have this holiday at this time, as it is another type of celebration of fertility and reproduction. I would suggest the fact that so many different cultures all celebrate children, mothers, and fathers in the same season, in May or early June, is no coincidence. This is the season that represents sexual reproduction and parenthood on the Wheel of Time.

Honesty, I cannot stress this enough; our modern-day celebrations at this time of year (Mother's Day & Children's Day,) are closer to the true meaning of this season on the Wheel of Time than any other holidays at this time of year. Though giving flowers and dancing around the Maypole may have a symbolic reference to reproduction, Mother's Day and Children's Day are spot on. As I mentioned before, while Imbolc represents the conception of life, and the spring equinox represents birth, May represents parenthood.

OTHER MODERN MAY HOLIDAYS

Just as other holidays have taken on new meanings over the centuries, or have been replaced by newer holidays, so has May Day. For many people around the world, they know May Day as *International Worker's Day*, an international version of Labor Day. As such, there are worker's parades and festivities throughout the world on May Day, especially in socialist countries. It is a global celebration of worker's rights, freedom from tyranny, liberty, and democracy.

Last but not least, as a Southern California resident I would be remiss if I did not include Cinco de Mayo. This is a celebration of the Mexican Army's victory over the French forces, at the battle of Puebla, on May 5th 1862. Now, it has become more of a celebration of Hispanic culture in general. Everyone is an honorary Mexican for the day on Cinco de Mayo. Ironically, it is a bigger holiday in the United States than it is in Mexico. In Southern California and along the border, it is celebrated with a feast of Mexican food and a late night of drinking and mariachi music.

CONCLUSION

In conclusion, Beltaine, like other holidays, is celebrated in a variety of ways, but they all have something in common. It may be celebrated as an all-night bonfire and orgy, or you may dance around the Maypole, representing the sexual anatomy of a flower. And, Mother's Day may be celebrated as a sincere appreciation for mothers. But, they all represent a specific point in the annual cycle of nature and the human life cycle. This time of year is marked by flowers, birds and bees in nature.

In addition to the birds and bees, this is the conclusion to the calving season, the time when we see animals nursing their young. So, May Day starts the season that represents puberty and young adulthood, and that means that it also represents both sexual reproduction and parenthood on the Wheel of Time.

SUMMER SOLSTICE

Point on the Solar Cycle:	The Summer Solstice
Pagan Sabbath Name:	Litha
Approximate Solar Date:	June 21st
Dates of Lunisolar & Other Holidays:	Mid June to Early July
Time of Day to Celebrate:	12 Noon
Symbolic Meaning on the Life Cycle:	The Peak of Life/ Childbearing Years
Corresponding Modern Holidays:	Father's Day, St. John's Day, Independence Day

We now come full circle, to the place where we began, the summer solstice. We started this journey in Chapter 1 by looking at the archaeological sites that mark the solstices and equinoxes. One of the most famous of these was Stonehenge. And, if you will remember, it was at Stonehenge that they had such an elaborate and ritualized celebration of the solstices, especially the summer solstice. So, we know that this was once one of the most important holy days of the year.

We've also spent a great deal of time investigating the winter solstice, both how it was celebrated in antiquity, and how it has evolved over the last millennium. But, what happened to the summer solstice? This appears to be one of the 8 major holidays on the Wheel of Time that has lost some of its luster. It does not appear to be as important to us as the winter solstice and Christmas. Actually, we do still celebrate this holiday but not in the way you might think. First, let's look at the history of this holiday.

What does this holiday represent on the Wheel of Time? Well, if the winter solstice is the peak of winter and the season of death, then the summer solstice is the peak of summer and the season of life! It is the absolute apex of the life of the year, the peak of the growing season, midway between spring and harvest. And, on the human life cycle it represents the peak of life as well, the point where we are fully grown, and not yet starting to grow old.

It's hard to put an exact age on this point in the human life cycle, but I'd say it's roughly in the 30s. This is to the human life what summer is to the solar year. And, the midpoint of human life is about 35 years old. This exact age is somewhat debatable, but there is ample evidence to suggest that this is the approximate age in the human life cycle that correlates to Litha, the summer solstice, the peak of the year.[2] So, this is what we are symbolically celebrating on this holiday. This holiday represents the peak of life, the peak of the year, the peak of all things.

THE SOLSTICE IN ANCIENT TIMES

The ancient Egyptians celebrated the summer solstice on June 21st as the birthday of *Aten*, another sun god. Actually, it was Aten that was at center of the cult of Aten, the first monotheistic religion established by the Pharaoh *Akhenaten*, who was a sun worshipper. This probably sounds pretty familiar by now; it seems as if each of the major holidays involves the birth, rebirth, reincarnation, or resurrection of one solar deity or another. And, the summer solstice, the longest day of the year, seems a likely time to celebrate a sun god.

This is celebrated as another festival of lights, and the Ancient Egyptians had a ritualized lamp lighting ceremony, indoors and at night, so there is no darkness on this day, inside or out, day or night. Many celebrations involve bonfires or a festival of lights, but this was the peak of all festivals of light throughout the year, as it is the peak of the sun's light.

Ancient Rome had a different spin on this holiday. They celebrated Fortuna, the goddess of good fortune, on June 24th. Actually, she was more like the goddess of fate, and one could never know what she might bring, good fortune or bad. She had a giant wheel, literally *the Wheel of Fortune*. In fact, her name comes from the word *Vortumna*, which means *she who revolves the year*. So, there is a very clear reference to the movement of the Wheel of Time. And, just as we've seen with the winter solstice, the summer solstice was also seen as a turning point in the wheel of the year.

Fortuna would not only make the wheel spin around to another fall and winter, but she would also spin her wheel of fortune to see what would be the fate of this year, great fortune or disaster. The people would celebrate with typical items of the season (flowers, fruits and vegetables) and gather on boats decorated with flowers and sail down the Tiber river in a boat parade with singing and prayers to Fortuna, not unlike our own Rose Parade, but on water. This is similar to Floralia, which they celebrated on April 28th, but whereas Floralia celebrated the start of summer, Fortuna celebrated the peak of summer.

CHINA: DUANWU FESTIVAL

In China, for many centuries right up to the present day, they celebrate the Duanwu Festival, the Chinese summer solstice holiday. This is held on the fifth day of the fifth month of the Chinese lunisolar calendar, which starts in early February. So, like Chinese New Year, it falls on a different day each year. For example, in 2012 it fell on June 23rd and in 2015 it fell on June 20th. Interestingly, they also celebrate this holiday on boats, as the Romans did. In fact, it is also known as the Dragon Boat Festival. There is a feast with much eating and drinking of wine, but the highlight is when they take to their boats, decorated like dragons. Of course, at night there are spectacular fireworks, for which the Chinese are famous.

NORSE: SONNENWENDE FESTIVAL

The ancient Norse people thought about this holiday much like the Romans did. They celebrated *Sonnenwende,* which means the *Sun's Turning,* which again refers to the Wheel of Time and the turning of the wheel of the year. Keep in mind that Sunne was the Norse sun goddess, so this holiday is also very similar to the Egyptian celebration of Aten or the Roman celebration of the goddess Fortuna. And, like other cultures, they would also celebrate with great bonfires and many torches to create a spectacular night-time fire show.

Not unlike the May Queen tradition, on Sonnenwende they would select a Midsummer Bride, and she would select a Bridegroom, and they would spend the day living like a married couple. The entire holiday centers on the sun goddess Sunne. They would greet her at dawn and lay out in the sun in midday. Note that midday is the time of day that corresponds to the midsummer solstice.

ANCIENT CELTS: LITHA CELEBRATION

The Celts called the summer solstice *Litha*, and they would celebrate the sun god. Actually, they celebrated the horned god, in his incarnation as the sun. Druids may have referred to this as *Alban Heruin*, the opposite of Alban Arthuan, the winter solstice. Litha is a fire festival and they also celebrate not just with bonfires but also with torches of hay or straw. Most impressively, they also created burning sun wheels, which were giant wheels, coated in tar, lit on fire, and rolled down hills, throwing off a shower of sparks, to create a spectacular effect. This was their version of fireworks, and it was probably quite a show.

Each of the ancient pagan people had their own version of this holiday. In Ireland, they celebrated the solstice in honor of the fairy goddess Aine who was the goddess of summer. People would celebrate in much the same way, building incredibly huge bonfires, so high you would need a ladder to add wood to the fire. And, they would run through the fields and around the village with brightly lit torches. It was, again, basically a fireworks show.

The Welsh did about the same thing, but they worshiped the goddess Ceridwen, the dark moon goddess of fertility. Their celebration would include cauldrons, grains, and images of the moon, which are all symbolic of Ceridwen. And, of course, their celebrations included a lot of fires, bonfires, torches, and fire wheels.

THE MODERN SOLSTICE CELEBRATIONS

The Catholic Church in Rome, as with other pagan holidays, attempted to relabel this as a Christian holiday. So they called June 24th *St. John's Day*. Note, they used the same date as the Roman's Festival of Fortuna. But, of course, the church suggested that the day be spent in church at a mass for St. John or in quiet meditation and prayer. Nonetheless, throughout the Christian world, St. John's Eve, as it came to be known, continued to be a fire festival and a cause for celebration.

In Europe, even today, there are huge celebrations on St. John's eve. This is especially popular in Spain, Portugal, and Scandinavia, where it is an official holiday. They have massive feasts with music, drinking and much merry-making. And, as with the ancient Celtic celebrations of midsummer, there are fireworks, lots and lots of fireworks. They not only have the usual modern aerial fireworks show that we are used to but, like the ancient Celts, they have every type of fire event you can think of. There are, of course, huge bonfires but some places also have fire-eaters, fire twirlers, and even fire jumpers, were celebrants leap over a small bonfire.

In some places, such as San Pedro Manrique, in Spain, some brave souls also perform fire-walking. It is a tradition that they literally walk barefoot on a bed of hot coals on St. John's eve. In some places, such as Florence, Italy, they also celebrate St. John's day with games and a parade where participants dress in Renaissance attire and then, of course, they finish the day with fireworks at night.

And, of course, there are many other holidays around the world marking the summer solstice. Every culture has their own version. But, how is the summer solstice celebrated in modern America? Most people have never heard of either Litha or even St. John's Day. So, does that mean that we no longer have a midsummer festival? And if not, why not?

Why don't we mark the midsummer solstice with an official holiday? Why don't we spend the day in the park, have a parade with a big picnic or barbeque, play games, and later watch fireworks at night? Oh, ...of course! That is exactly what we do at midsummer, but we call it the Fourth of July. And, like so many lunisolar holidays, it occurs within 2 weeks of the summer solstice. Is this just a wacky coincidence? One might wonder, did the founding fathers plan all of this on purpose? They were, after all, mostly high-ranking Masons with some strange and ancient pagan traditions. Even today, St. John's day is a popular holiday among Masons. But, I'm not sure that this totally explains how we celebrate the Fourth of July.

I think that the traditions of the ancient holidays are so much a part of us that, even if we had no holiday in Summer, we'd make something up just as an excuse to spend the day in the sun, barbequing, and watching fireworks at night. It seems that we can't help but celebrate midsummer very much as our ancestors have for the last 10,000 years. If we had no Fourth of July, we might have ended up celebrating West Virginia Day on June 20th, or the Newfoundland Discovery Day on June 22nd, but one way or another we'd still celebrate midsummer the same as we have for thousands of years. After all, this is the very peak of the solar year and it symbolizes the very peak of life on the Wheel of Time. And, what could express the penultimate pinnacle of life better than a fireworks show? That's something that just screams:

"The apex! The peak of it all!"

This is true with other holidays as well. We celebrate Cinco de Mayo with a huge party reminiscent of Beltaine, yet there is no connection between these two holidays at all, except that they fall within a few days of each other. And, even if they never heard of Imbolc, most people celebrate Valentine's Day in very much the same pagan spirit that our ancestors celebrated St. Brigid's Day or Lupercalia. While some of this may be due to the persistence of ancient folk traditions being subtly passed down over the generations, I think there is more to it than that. This shows us that the Wheel of Time is not just a meme of our culture, or even of ancient cultures, but rather it is in our DNA, like circadian rhythms. It is simply the natural result of experiencing and celebrating the seasons of the year and the seasons of life, as we perceive them.

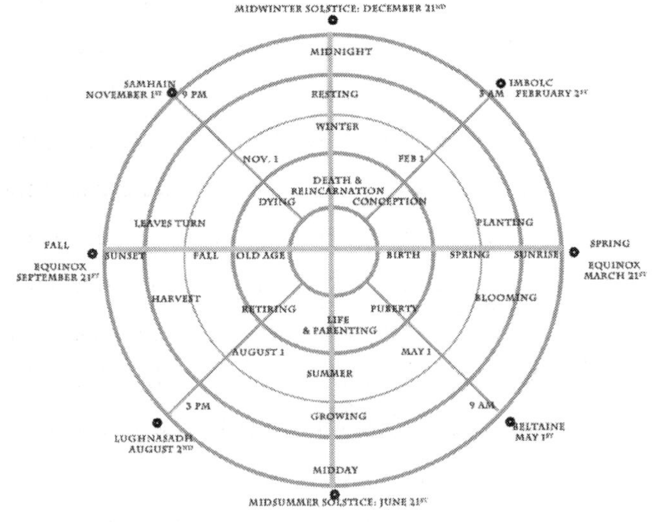

Figure 10

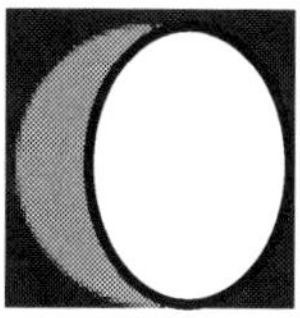

3RD MIDPOINT

Point on the Solar Cycle:	Midpoint between the Summer Solstice and the Autumn Equinox
Pagan Sabbath Name:	Lughnasadh, Lammas
Approximate Solar Date:	August 2nd
Dates of Lunisolar & Other Holidays:	Mostly August: From July to September
Time of Day to Celebrate:	3 pm or Mid Afternoon
Symbolic Meaning on the Life Cycle:	Mid Life
Corresponding Modern Holidays:	Assumption of the Blessed Virgin Mary, State and County Fairs

Lughnasadh is the midpoint between the summer solstice and the autumn equinox. And, to the ancients, this was the start of the autumn season. If you look at the Wheel of Time in Figure 10, you will see that this time of year represents the start of middle-age on the human life cycle. If the solstice was the peak of life, and the autumn equinox represents the twilight years of life, then this represents that point in life when you are just past your prime. It is the time of life that we call *middle-age*, not young, but not yet old. Likewise, by August 2nd you could say that the year is now middle-aged. It too is just past its prime.

Many may wonder why would anyone want to celebrate being middle-aged? But, if we look at the seasons in nature and in agriculture, we know why. This is the first big harvest of the year. And, the same is true in the human life cycle. This is when we begin to reap the rewards of all our years of hard labor.

At middle-age, you are more established. By this age, many people are no longer struggling to get by, and they can begin to reap the rewards of life. Their kids are grown or nearly grown, their careers have done the same, and hopefully their bank accounts as well. If it was their goal to make a mark in society or in their profession, they have hopefully begun to do so by now, certainly the successful ones have. At this time of life, we begin to reap the rewards of just what we have sown, for better or worse. And, in nature it is the same. In many pagan cultures this is a celebration of the first grain harvest or the feast of first fruits. Certainly, it is the peak of the vegetable and produce harvest.

Interestingly, this is another one of those holidays that, like Imbolc or Beltaine, most people would say they've never heard of and don't celebrate. But, unlike those other holidays, I can't honestly say that you ever *have* heard of this one. Unlike Groundhog Day or May Day, or even the Fourth of July, there really isn't a major or even minor holiday at this time of year. In fact, in modern American culture, there is a complete lack of holidays between the Fourth of July and Labor Day, in the first week of September.

Of course, this was one of the 8 major holidays on the pagan Wheel of Time and, as such, it was celebrated by many pagan cultures, such as the Egyptians, Romans, Norse, Druids, and now the Wiccans. So, why are there no modern holidays this time of year? How did Lughnasadh get lost in modern America, when it is still celebrated in Ireland and other Gaelic countries? Well, as I just mentioned, this is the start of harvest time, and that could be a factor in why we don't celebrate more.

In America the wheat harvest begins in August. For farmers, this is the busiest time of the year. In fact, it's the reason why we originally gave students the summer off, so they can help out on their families' farms. There are other reasons why we don't have holidays this time of year, but this is the most likely.[3] But, maybe, we do celebrate this time of year in our own way and we just aren't aware of the connection to Lughnasadh. To see if this is true, lets learn a little more about how our ancestors celebrated this holiday.

ANCIENT EGYPT: WAG FESTIVAL

In ancient Egypt, in about the second week of August, they would celebrate the Wag Festival. This is a funerary festival, not unlike the *Dia de los Muertos*, the *Day of the Dead* in Latin-American culture. This holiday in Egypt celebrated the death and rebirth of Wesir, another name for Osirus. Aside from its funerary affectations, this holiday appears to be the New Year festival for the ancient Egyptians. This is their first month of the year on the Egyptian calendar, called Thoth, and it signaled the beginning of the season of the flooding of the Nile.

Actually, the first day of the month of Thoth was the new year and two weeks later, on the 18th of Thoth, was the Wag Festival. This lasted for several days until the 20th of Thoth, which culminated the seasonal holiday with a day of drunkenness, not unlike the Roman Bacchanalia or our St. Patrick's Day. Ancient Egyptian papyrus documents reveal that they consumed a great deal of beer and wine on this holiday. If this does not sound like how we celebrate August, remember that their economy was based upon their unique climate and was tied to the flooding of the Nile, which occurred in early fall.[4]

ANCIENT ROME: NEMORALIA

In Rome, they celebrated *Nemoralia*. As with so many ancient holidays, this was originally a lunisolar holiday celebrated on the first full moon after Lughnasadh, the midpoint between the solstice and the autumn equinox. And, like other holidays, they later began celebrating it every year on the same day, the ides of August, on the 15th of the month. This was a festival of torches, to honor Diana, the goddess of nature, of the hunt, the moon, and childbirth. This was a holiday for women and slaves.

The women would start by washing their hair and dressing it with flowers. They would then form a procession, all wearing a wreath of flowers, and carrying torches, and walk from Rome to a sacred grove on the banks of Lake Nemi, known as Diana's mirror. There they would leave small written messages on ribbons, tied to the alter or to trees. The messages were prayers to the Goddess Diana.

THE ASSUMPTION OF THE BLESSED VIRGIN MARY

Of course, since Nemoralia was a pagan holiday the Catholic Church also saw fit to create a Christian counterpart, the *Assumption of the Blessed Virgin Mary*, on the same day, August 15th. This holiday commemorates Mother Mary's heavenly-birthday, literally the day she went to Heaven. It seems fitting that they replace a feast for a pagan goddess with a feast for Mary, the closest thing to a goddess that they have in Catholicism. Though not as well known in modern America, this is still a major feast day among Catholics around the world.

THE CELTIC FESTIVAL OF LUGHNASADH

In the British Isles, the celebration was not all that different. In ancient Celtic mythology, this fire festival was created by the sun god Lugh, hence its name *Lughnasadh*. It was one of their four main fire festivals, a cross-quarter day, and the start of the fall season. Just as in Egypt, this was also a funerary feast, and there was also an athletic competition and a large dance. And, just as in Rome, all this was in honor of a goddess, Tailtiu. She was Lugh's mother and an earth mother associated with the harvest, which feeds humanity.

Notice the theme of the nature goddess Diana and the earth-mother goddess Tailtiu. This is a time to give thanks to mother earth for her bounty. To understand this holiday, you again have to realize that this time of year is when they began harvesting wheat and barley, known simply as corn or barley-corn.

It makes sense that they pay tribute to Lugh, the sun god, in one of the warmest months, but why the recurring theme of death and funerary rituals? That seems odd. Well, this was the beginning of their harvest season and, as such, it commemorates the death of the corn to feed the people. It is also a time when they harvest their livestock by slaughtering them. So, in a very real sense, harvesting plants and animals means taking their life.

At this time of year, they would construct corn dollies, also known as corn mothers, out of bunches of wheat or barley. The corn dolly is a goddess figure, anywhere from a few inches high to a few feet high, and thought to embody the spirit of the grain (corn) and the earth goddess. This was a time to celebrate and pay homage to the earth mother for her blessings through the grain, which gives life to us and our animals.

LITHASBLOT & LAMMAS

The ancient Norse people of Northern Europe also celebrated August 2nd as a harvest festival. They called it *Lithasblot.* The tradition among the Norse people of England, the Anglo Saxons, was the same but they called it Lammas, which comes from *Loaf Mass.* They would ceremonially bake the first bread with the first harvested grains of the season and serve this loaf at a feast. This holiday was incorporated into the Catholic calendar as well, and a mass was probably held to bless the first loaf of the season, hence it was the Loaf Mass, or Lammas. And, in Wales they had a similar harvest festival that they called *Gwal Awst,* with very much the same traditions.

Many places, such as Ireland and parts of England, still do celebrate Lughnasadh or Lammas with corn dollies, bonfires, and dances. But, why don't we celebrate Lughnasadh in modern America? We've seen how this time of year is centered on celebrating agriculture, whether the flooding of the Nile or the first grain harvest in England. So, why don't we celebrate the harvest? Why don't farmers, ranchers, bakers, and others have a festival or a fair to show off what we've harvested in the growing season? And, we could have food, games, and dances as well. Well, it should seem obvious by now how we celebrate this time of year. Can you guess?

OUR MODERN LUGHNASADH

In much of the United States Lughnasadh is when we hold our annual agricultural fairs, better known as the State Fairs and County Fairs. Once you think of it, it makes perfect sense. For many of us, the State Fair is the highlight of the year. Talk about a feast! When else do you eat a barbequed pork chop on a stick, chocolate-covered deep-fried corndogs, deep-fried butter on a stick, and red-velvet funnel cakes, all in the same day? There are rodeos, live-stock auctions, produce competitions, pie-eating contests, dances with live music, and, of course, a carnival with rides and games. And, again we see a relationship between the stage of the human life cycle that we call middle-age and the mid-life of the year. They are both marked by a harvest of what we have sown and hopefully a celebration of our abundance.

Our State Fairs are an American version of Lughnasadh because they are, first and foremost, agricultural and harvest festivals. It is a chance for the farmers and ranchers to show off their work. It is also a time for all of us to show off our work, whether it's quilting, winemaking, fruit preserves, arts and crafts, or floral arrangements. Whatever people produce, it is shown off and celebrated at the annual State Fair. Additionally, there are also County Fairs and Regional Fairs. And, while it is true that there are State and County Fairs at other times of the year, many if not most celebrate their annual fairs sometime between the summer solstice and the fall equinox, the most common date being around mid-August, the time of Lughnasadh and Nemoralia.

Where I live, we hold our County Fair in mid-August, the same date as the ancient Roman Nemoralia and the Catholic celebration of the Assumption of Mary. Many states such as Iowa, Idaho, Kansas, Oklahoma, Oregon, Nebraska, Nevada, New York, North Carolina, South Carolina, Washington and many more, do the same thing, with fairs anywhere from late July through September, all centered around mid-August.

One has to ask: how did this happen? Was this by design? Is the State Fair actually a carry-over from ancient pagan traditions? There may be some element of history and tradition carrying over from centuries past but, as I said before, there is another issue at work. For ranchers today, just like our ancestors, this is the time of year is when their livestock is sold at auction. So, at this time of year, it makes sense to show off your livestock, and award a blue ribbon to the biggest bull or the most beautiful rooster. Kids in 4-H show off the livestock they have been raising all season, before the auction.

Because our economy and food supply is so tied to the earth and the seasons, we therefore perceive our seasons and create our annual holidays very much like our ancient ancestors did. So, it seems inevitable for us to hold our agricultural festivals at about the same time of year as our ancestors did. The only thing that's changed is that we've lost the deeper meaning and reverence associated with this celebration.

Again, the Wheel of Time is not so much a creation by people, but a reflection of the earth and her natural seasons, which is echoed in the seasons of life, including the human life cycle. Thus, the Wheel of Time is a natural phenomenon, as natural as summer itself. Though we may not think of it this way, when you go to your local County or State Fair you're participating in an annual festival that has existed for thousands of years, not unlike Christmas or Easter.

So, when you're at a State Fair, whether you're examining the prize bull or the blue ribbon cabbage, or kicking your heels up, drinking and dancing, it's comforting to know that you're actually celebrating Lughnasadh very much like your ancient ancestors did.

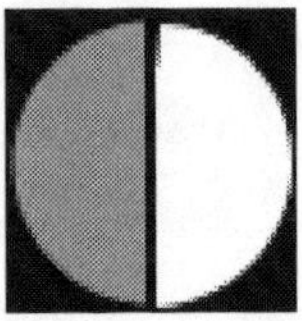

ATUMNAL EQUINOX

Point on the Solar Cycle:	The Autumn Equinox
Pagan Sabbath Name:	Mabon
Approximate Solar Date:	September 21st
Dates of Lunisolar & Other Holidays:	Mid September through October
Time of Day to Celebrate:	6 pm or Sunset
Symbolic Meaning on the Life Cycle:	Retirement/ Old Age
Corresponding Modern Holidays:	Rosh Hashanah, Yom Kippur, Oktoberfest, Harvest Festivals, & Thanksgiving

We just reviewed a type of harvest festival, Lughnasadh, which marks the first harvest of the year. But, September 21st, the autumn equinox, is the peak harvest time and the completion of the growing season. And, again, there are not many ritualized holidays in modern America corresponding to this important and ancient Sabbath. But, there are a couple, and we will discuss them. Before we get to the holidays, however, first let's look at the meaning of Mabon. What does it represent on the Wheel of Time?

Mabon, the autumn equinox, is the midpoint between the summer solstice and the winter solstice. It is the second time in the year when the length of the day and the length of the night are equal, hence the word *equinox*. But as you can see on the Wheel of Time, this means that the year is quite old and about to die. Literally, the leaves will soon start to turn color, wither, and fall to the ground. Nature is about to go dormant for the winter.

In the human life cycle this corresponds to old age or what we call *retirement*. Just as in the last section on Lughnasadh, this time of year corresponds to reaping all of the good things that we can harvest from life, both in agriculture and in the human life cycle as well. The growing season is over, the harvest is in, and now we can relax and rest. All of our hard work has been completed. In short, this time of year corresponds to the *golden years* of life.

The meaning of Mabon and the harvest season is completion, satisfaction, and the ability to sit back and enjoy all the fruits of your labor. The weather is starting to get cooler. It is not so comfortable to sit outside in the evening, just as getting older has its discomforts as well. But, the cupboards and cellar are packed full of canned preserves, the granaries are packed full of grain. If you have a large freezer, it's probably packed full of meat. If you make wine, your barrels are full. Likewise, in the human life cycle, if you are retired then your work is done, you may well have a big family with kids and grandkids, maybe even great-grandkids, and hopefully a fat pension and an RV.

This is the richest time of the year, and this was especially true for our ancestors. As I've said before, remember that they could not just go to a store and buy food. Whatever food they had amassed in the fall had to last them until spring and early summer, when they would start once again to harvest berries and vegetables. This was the one time of year that they could splurge a little. They were sitting on top of a mountain of food and drink, with little work left to do in the fields. This must have been a grand time of year for our ancient ancestors. And, there were some ritualized celebrations in antiquity.

ANCIENT MESOPOTAMIA: FESTIVAL OF AKITU

In ancient Mesopotamia, they would once again celebrate Akitu. I say once again because they celebrated this holiday twice a year, on each of the equinoxes. Originally, they appear to have had a 6-month year, so they had two years for every single solar year. And, this was their second New Year festival. The Babylonian god Marduk, a version of a previous Sumerian god Tammuz, was believed to be born in the spring, die in the summer heat, and be reborn in the fall, hence the two New Years. However, it appears that this was later reduced to just one New Year holiday in the spring to conform with the annual solar cycle.

Though they honored the resurrection of Marduk at the autumn equinox, they primarily honored the death of Tiamat, goddess of chaos and the sea. She was synonymous with the primordial chaos that existed before the world began. According to their mythology, Tiamat was Markuk's grandmother. But, Marduk defeated and killed Tiamat and it was her body that formed the earth and heavens. This was their creation myth. And, this myth was at the center of their autumn equinox celebration. What does this have to do with harvest or any other aspect of modern fall festivals? Probably nothing. They still observed the equinox but as we've seen over and over again, each culture created their own story to explain the meaning of the holiday.

CARPO, THE GODDESS OF AUTUMN

The Greeks and Romans celebrated this holiday more like we might today. In ancient Greece, they celebrated *Carpo*, goddess of Autumn. She was the daughter of Zeus and one of the three *Horae*, the goddesses of the seasons (they only had three seasons, spring, summer, and fall). Carpo was the goddess of the fruit harvest, which occurred this time of year. She was the goddess of ripening and withering, the dual aspects of the fall. And, presumably they celebrated with all the bounty of the season, including plenty of fresh fruit and new wine.

THE MERCATUS ROMANI

In the previous section we mentioned how in modern America most people don't consider mid-August a holiday as such; yet we do have a lot of festivals that time of year, but we just call them County Fairs. Well, this may not be such a modern concept after all; it looks like a similar phenomenon happened in Rome. In Ancient Rome, the fall equinox appears to have been celebrated by a *Mercatus*, meaning a market or fair. This was their big harvest festival, and it was called *Mercatus Romani*. And by the sound of it, it had a lot of similarities to our County Fairs.

It occurred immediately after the conclusion of the *Ludi Romani*, or *Roman Games*. The games included chariot races, gladiatorial battles, boxing, horsemanship competitions, and dancing. Like the Greeks, the winners received a wreath that was worn with great honor, kept and collected, like one might keep a trophy today.

ROSH HASHANAH & YOM KIPPUR

As we've mentioned previously, this time of year on the Jewish Calendar is known as *Rosh Hashanah* and, just like the ancient Babylonians, this is their New Year's celebration. Of course, being the start of a new year, it is celebrated on a new moon. They also use a lunisolar calendar where every new moon is the first day of a month. So, every year Rosh Hashanah falls on the first day of the month of Tishrei, and it marks the beginning of the High Holy Days. There is a dinner feast as well, called the feast of trumpets. It is a joyous holiday, but at this time of year the focus is on taking stock of your life and your sins throughout the year. Then on the 10th day of the month of Tishrei, they celebrate Yom Kippur, the day that marks the end of the High Holy Days. This is a day of fasting and atonement, which should be spent in solemn prayer.

ASIA: THE CHUNG CH'UI FESTIVAL

In China, Vietnam, and various places throughout Asia, they celebrate a mid-Autumn Festival called *Chung Ch'ui*. This is very much like our own Thanksgiving. It is during this festival when they express gratitude for all our bounty and blessings of the past year. This harvest festival celebrated on the 15th day of the eighth month in the Chinese Han calendar. Note that their calendar is a true lunisolar calendar, so the 15th of the month is always on a full moon. This holiday is celebrated on what we call the harvest moon, the full moon closest to the autumn equinox. In fact, in Asia the holiday is also known as the *Harvest Moon Festival,* or just the *Moon Festival.*

I think it is interesting here to note that the ancient Taoists celebrated the autumn equinox by honoring the *Shen* (spirits) of the west and autumn. Notice that we get the word East from Easter, celebrated at sunrise on the spring equinox, and here we see the autumn equinox associated with the west, the direction of the setting sun. This is exactly what we see on the Wheel of Time. The end of the life of the year corresponds to sunset, the end of the day, and also to the final years in the human life cycle.

MABON & MEA'N FO'MHAIR

To the ancient Celts, they called this holiday Mabon, and it was also a harvest festival. To the Druids, this was the holiday known as Mea'n Fo'mhair, and it was in honor of Green Man, the god of the forest, as this was the fruit harvest. Both celebrated with gifts of cider, fruits, and herbs. And this was also one of the traditional days for getting married. This is another fall festival of thanksgiving for the gifts of nature and a good harvest. And, of course, it was at this time of year that the Druids performed sacrifices, using their wicker man, a giant wooden cage made of woven branches, in which they burned criminals alive. While such sacrifices no longer exist, there are still many such wicker man burnings performed each year, to this day, to commemorate the autumn equinox.

HALEG MONATH & WINTER FINDING

Among the ancient Norse, Anglo-Saxons, and Germanic peoples, the month of September was known as Haleg Monath, or Holy Month. And they had a celebration that lasted all the way from the equinox on September 21st to the Samahain on November 1st. It was a huge celebration known as *Winter Finding*. Like the Druids, this was known as the second harvest or the fruit harvest. If Lughnasadh was the beginning of the harvest season, then this was the end of the harvest.

For them too this was a time of thanksgiving, when people celebrated their bounty and abundance with gratitude to the goddess Freyja. The god Odin was also thanked for his blessings at this time of year. They celebrated with new beer, made with the recent grain harvest, by now fully fermented and ready to drink. They also celebrated with a feast of meats, sausages, and breads, accompanied by piles of fresh fruit. This was one of the biggest parties of the year. And, for them too it was a traditional time to get married.

THE AUTUMN EQUINOX IN MODERN TIMES

One famous marriage that occurred this time of year actually sparked a new holiday, which is a version of Winter Finding and one that we are still celebrating to this day, even in America. In 1810, the Bavarian crown prince, Ludwig the First, married the princess Therese of Saxe-Hildburghausen. It was a very big wedding, and to celebrate they held a huge party that lasted for 5 days in the capital of Bavaria, Munich. There was an enormous amount of food, sausages, fruits, breads, and massive amounts of beer. There was also music, dancing, and even a grand horse race.

The party was so popular that it became an annual event. The wedding was originally on October 12th, but this annual celebration became synonymous with their fall Winter Finding celebration, so the date was moved back to coincide with the autumn equinox, approximately September 21st. The original party lasted 5 days, but it has now been extended to two weeks of celebration. Of course, many German-Americans and others still celebrate this holiday to this day with music, bratwurst and beer. We know it as *Oktoberfest*, the German harvest and beer festival, and in some places it's just known as *Brats and Beer*.

Of course, not unlike ancient Rome, most of us simply celebrate this time of year at a local Fall, Harvest Festival. It seems that communities all over America and in Europe put on their own Harvest Festival at various times from mid-September through October. Many of these sell either local produce or arts and crafts, or a combination of both. Many of these festivals run all the way up to Halloween. And, like Winter Finding, there is some overlap between harvest festivals and pumpkin patches, selling pumpkins in a month-long run up to Halloween. Some festivals occur later than others, some in November.

Oktoberfest and harvest festivals, like the State Fair in the last section on Lughnasadh, captures the true spirit of the holiday, even if the specific connection to the equinox has been lost. But, we have not lost the concept of the Harvest Moon, which is the full moon closest to the autumn equinox. The Harvest Moon is still widely mentioned in local newspapers, on local TV news, and among friends and family.

There is something special about that moon. I think it's because of all the associations that it has with the ancient pagan holiday, whether we are conscious of it or not. The sight of it rising in the early evening (the time of day that corresponds to this holiday) evokes deep feelings to many people.

Finally, I have to include the greatest American harvest festival, our feast of thanksgiving, simply known as *Thanksgiving*. You may think it odd that I include a holiday in late November in the section on the autumn equinox, which is in September. But, just like Winter Finding, many of the Harvest Festivals do occur late in the fall.

THANKSGIVING

In many respects our Thanksgiving is really a traditional celebration of the Harvest, complete with the horn of plenty, images of fall leaves and all. In fact, one of the Latin names for the fall equinox is Cornucopia, which for us is representative of Thanksgiving. So, why is it stuck in the wrong month?

Our American Thanksgiving was actually based on an English holiday created by the Puritans during the Reformation. It was the pilgrims, the first American colonists, who brought this holiday with them from England. During the Reformation, the Puritans rejected all of the Catholic holidays that had their roots in paganism, including Christmas and Easter. Instead, the Puritans sought to replace all of the pagan-inspired Sabbaths with two simple types of holidays: Days of Fasting and Days of Thanksgiving.

Well, in 1621, after the Puritan colonists of Plymouth Massachusetts had a particularly satisfying harvest, they decided to celebrate with a Day of Thanksgiving. The practice became a tradition and was repeated by their descendants for many generations to come. Finally, George Washington made it an official holiday of the new republic, starting on Thursday, November 26th, 1789, and it was celebrated every year afterward on the fourth Thursday of November.

So, you see, the Puritans actually would have gone out of their way to avoid the autumn equinox as a date for their harvest feast, as that would be too much like a pagan celebration. That is why this particular holiday is not anywhere near any of the 8 major holidays of the year. Nonetheless, they somehow managed to include many aspects of a traditional pagan harvest-feast anyway. It seems that sometimes there is just no escaping the Wheel of Time.

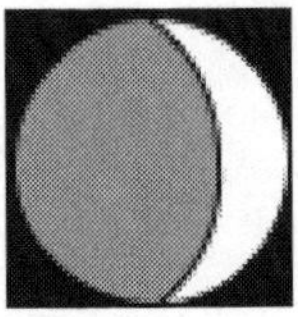

4TH MIDPOINT

Point on the Solar Cycle:	The Midpoint between the Fall Equinox and the Winter Solstice
Pagan Sabbath Name:	Samhain
Approximate Solar Date:	November 1st
Dates of Lunisolar & Other Holidays:	3 days: October 31st - November 2nd
Time of Day to Celebrate:	9 pm or all Evening
Symbolic Meaning on the Life Cycle:	Death/ Dying
Corresponding Modern Holidays:	Halloween, All Saints' Day, All Soul's Day, Dia de los Muertos, Day of the Dead

Well, we finally come to our last of the 8 major Sabbaths on the Wheel of Time, Samhain. This is the mid point between the autumn equinox and the winter solstice. And, this point on the Wheel of Time represents the moment of death, as it is the start of the winter, the season of death. It is considered the death of the year as almost all of nature appears to die at this time of year in the northern hemisphere. And, the further north you go, the more dead it appears.

Of course, we in America celebrate the eve of this holiday more than the day itself, and I will explain why later. But, suffice it to say that, like Beltaine, which is traditionally celebrated on the eve of May Day, and Christmas, which many celebrate on Christmas eve, we celebrate this holiday on the evening of October 31st. Yes, we all know this holiday very well, and we call it Halloween.

Why celebrate death? Well, quite simply it is because death is an important part of the cycle of life. If we can't accept and embrace death, then we are not fully embracing our life-cycle, which according to our pagan ancestors was sacred. If life is sacred, then the life-cycle is sacred, and that means that death too is a sacred event. In many parts of the world and even in the Catholic Church, this day is a solemn event in which we pay our respects to all those who have passed-on in the last year.

But, there is also some cause to celebrate because our pagan ancestors believed in reincarnation. So, the end of one cycle is just the beginning of another cycle. In death, we slough off our old, decaying, painful body, and replace it with a young, supple, new body. So, this is not a sad event, but a wonderful and miraculous part of the entire, perpetual life-cycle. Now let's look at some of the ways this holiday has been celebrated.

EGYPT: FESTIVAL OF HATHOR

In ancient Egypt, this was another celebration of some of their solar deities. In this case there were three solar deities involved. On about October 31st (actually the 15th of Koiak on the Egyptian Calendar), they would hold the Feast of Sekhmet and Bast. These were two sun goddesses, daughters of Ra and Hathor. Both were depicted as felines and both were goddesses of dance and love. So, it appears that this was a more joyous feast, in honor of the daughters of Hathor, welcoming the coming of Hathor.

Then, two days later, on about November 2nd, they celebrated the Festival of Hathor. She was the mother-goddess of love, joy, and dance, not unlike Aphrodite or Venus. More importantly, it was Hathor who was considered the *Mistress of the West*, welcoming the dead into the next life. As such, we can infer that this was a somewhat more solemn occasion and combined both funerary and harvest rituals. The *West* is symbolic of death in that it represents the setting sun, the death of the day. The cult of Hathor was one of the oldest in Egypt and has its roots in the predynastic period, 5,000-8,000 years ago.

ROME: LUDI VICTOIAE SULLANAE

The Romans did not appear to have any ritualized funerary holiday, but they did hold a week-long series of Roman games from October 26th through November 1st, called the *Ludi Victoiae Sullanae*, or *The Victory Games of Sulla*. This may have no connection to this time of the year, but according to Cicero and others at the time, it was a major event, perhaps, like our Olympics, Superbowl or the World Series.

NORSE: VETRNÆTR

Among the Norse peoples of northern Europe, this time of year was known as *Vetrnætr* or *Winternights*, a Norse winter festival. The name *Vetrnætr* is Old Norse and is made up of two words: *vetr,* meaning winter, and *nætr*, meaning nights. It is said that Winternights is one of the three most important festivals to the Norse people. It is a festival that marks the start of the winter, and it is the Norse New Year's festival. At this time, a *blót* (sacrifice) to the Norse gods is performed as a thanksgiving for a good year and a good harvest. Prayers were also made at this time to survive the harsh winter ahead.

CELTIC: SAMHAIN

Among the Celtic peoples, this was known as Samhain, pronounced Sah-win, and marked the real and symbolic death of the year. This was one of the four major fire festivals of the year, also known as cross-quarter days, the four midpoints between the equinoxes and solstices. Each fire festival marked the beginning of a season. This marked the beginning of the season of winter, which on the Wheel of Time, was the season of death.

We know that the Celts had other festivals to honor their dead, but this Sabbath was the Sabbath of death. It meant that the people would soon enter a period where they were surrounded by death on a daily basis. Dead trees, dead grass, dead vegetables, hardly any plant life at all, except evergreens, which did not provide much in the way of nourishment.

For nearly half the year, they were forced to survive on meat and milk, and possibly bread if they had saved enough grain. So, this date marked the death of the year, and symbolically it represented the moment of death in the life cycle. As such, everything about death was celebrated at this holiday.

We can only infer from later customs how the ancients may have celebrated this holiday. But it appears to have lasted for 3 days, starting on the night of October 31st. Remember that to the Celts the day started on the night before. So, this was the eve of the first day of the season of death. Then, it appears that they celebrated for the next two days.

Based on later rituals, such as Halloween and Day of the Dead, the first night may have been more of a bonfire party, when the barrier between this world and the next was at its thinnest, and ghosts were capable of crossing over. The next couple days would be more solemn, paying respects to those who had died in the previous year and laying wreaths, food, drink, or other offerings on their graves or funerary mounds.

THE EVOLUTION OF SAMHAIN & HALLOWEEN

Naturally, as we've seen with all 8 of the major pagan Sabbaths, Samhain was incorporated into the Catholic Church, pretty much lock, stock, and barrel. At first, the Church had another day set aside to commemorate the dead martyrs, and that was in May. But, as with other holidays, it appears that they felt the need to create a holiday to compete with Samhain, or at least relabel it as a Christian holiday.

This was probably meant to ease the conversion to Christianity and to reduce the pagan influence. So, in the eighth century, Pope Gregory III created two Christian holidays on November 1st and 2nd called All Saints' Day to honor the martyrs and All Souls' Day to honor all who have died.

Back in England, this was probably celebrated just as Samhain had been for centuries. The word *saint* is Latin in origin. The term in English for saint is *hallow*, stemming from the Old English *halgod* or *halig*, which is where we also get the word *holy*. So, in England, All Saints' Day became *All Hallows' Day*. The 3-day festival was referred to as Allhallowtide, Hallowtide, or Hallowmas. And, All Hallows' Eve became known as *Hallow'een,* which, of course, we still celebrate to this day.

It's hard to say exactly how a solemn pagan Sabbath became a wacky costume party for kids, but we know that in olden times people would leave offerings of food, drink, and sweets for the dead. They did this to avoid being haunted, as this time of year was when the veil between life and death was thin, and ghosts could crossover. According to legend, at some point kids and teens would dress-up as ghosts and steal the offerings, especially the sweets.

They might have also threatened superstitious people that if they didn't provide an offering of sweets for the dead they'd be sorry, for they would probably be haunted and the ghosts would play *tricks* on them that night. Eventually, this practice evolved to the point where the children would simply throw a sheet over their head, moan, grown, and yell "trick or treat", and good-natured people would pretend to be scared and give them candy.

Many might think that this is a mockery of the original All Hallows' Eve celebration. But, if you think of it, it's actually a pretty good way to celebrate Samhain. We have our children dress up as ghosts and roam the neighborhood, going door to door seeking offerings for the dead, and then we pretend that they are real ghosts, we act afraid and give our symbolic offerings to the dead. It's perfect. It's a fun, family-friendly way to pay homage to a holiday that commemorates the dead, and to symbolically make offerings to the dead.

The only problem is that, in the last few decades, the focus has shifted from just skeletons and ghosts to Superman, the Hulk, Darth Vader, giant lobsters, aliens, or just about any costume you can imagine. I once even saw a man dressed as a large, over-stuffed chair, and when he sat down he really became a chair, quite comfortable too, I might add.

Clearly, this does not embody the spirit of Samhain. This is one holiday that I wish people really would remember the reason for the season. It's really about death and honoring he dead, and that can include skeletons, ghosts, or even devils and angels, but not lobsters, aliens, and super-heroes, unless they happen to be dead.

While we, in North America, primarily just celebrate Halloween, people throughout the world, predominantly in Catholic countries, continue to celebrate All Saints' Day and All Souls' Day. People traditionally visit the gravesites of their loved ones and lay wreaths and flowers on the graves. In some parts of the world they may also have a picnic at the cemetery, to spend time with the deceased, remember the dead, and to better include them in the living family.

DIA DE LOS MUERTOS

There was one other society that had elaborate funerary rituals in early antiquity, and that was the pre-Columbian cultures in Latin America. In the ancient Aztec culture, this holiday was to honor *Mictecacihuatl* or *Lady of the Dead*, the Aztec goddess of the underworld, and her consort *Mictlantecuhtil*. This appears to have been a very important holiday, in which they would remember and pay respects to the dead. It dates as far back as 3000 years ago and perhaps earlier. It appears, however, to have originally been celebrated in the 9th month on the Aztec Calendar, which corresponds to August on our calendar.

After their conversion to Christianity, this Aztec holiday was still celebrated but it was moved to November 1st and 2nd and combined with All Saints' Day and All Souls' Day.

Among Spanish-speaking people, this celebration is generally referred to as *Día de los Muertos* or *Day of the Dead.*

The tradition of dressing up like skeletons and the traditional imagery of skulls and death are probably closer to the original celebration of Samhain than our modern Halloween. And, like the original All Hallowtide, it lasts from the night of October 31st through November 2nd. Millions of people still celebrate this version of Samhain every year, in both North and South America.

SUMMARY: FROM EIGHT POINTS, MANY DATES

This concludes a roundup of all eight major pagan Sabbaths of the Year, which corresponds to the eight points on the pagan Wheel of Time. In looking at all these holidays as a group, I think there are a couple of important patterns that stand out.

First, I'm sure you will notice that the actual dates of the different holidays very wildly, and yet are usually within a week or two of the eight points of the Wheel of Time. I hope it's obvious why this is. There are really three things going on here. First, there are the eight points on the Wheel of Time corresponding to the phases of the solar year. And, they account for many of our holidays, such as Candlemas, May Day, and Halloween.

Then, there are also the lunisolar holidays, each of which is related to one of the eight points on the solar year. For instance, a holiday may be on the first full moon after the equinox or the new moon closest to Imbolc. On a lunisolar calendar, the days of the month, literally the days of the lunar cycle, are also the phases of the moon. So, the first of the month is always a new moon, the 15th would always be a full moon, and so on. You see this most clearly with Egyptian, Hebrew, and Chinese holidays. Modern examples of this are Chinese New Year, Easter, Passover, and Rosh Hashanah.

Often times we see that cultures observed both the solar and the lunisolar date, side by side, such as the spring equinox and Easter in our culture. We observe the date of the equinox as the official start of spring, but we celebrate Easter on the full moon after the equinox. I think this was even more common in ancient times.

They observed the point on the solar calendar, such as the equinox but then they celebrated it on the appropriate phase of the moon closest to that date, like we do on Easter. Also, some holidays are always before the solar event and others are always after the solar event. So, the Hindu *Holi* festival is always on the full moon before the spring equinox, but Easter is always the full moon after the spring equinox. This adds even more variability.

Finally, over the course of history, people took lunisolar holidays and plotted them on solar calendars. This gets tricky. Again, the new moon on a lunisolar calendar is always on the first day of the month, and the full moon is always on the 15th day of the month. So, if a lunisolar holiday fell on a full moon, it was always on the 15th.

Then when they switched over to a solar calendar, as the Romans did, the 15th of the month no longer had any connection to the lunar cycle. So it just appeared to be an arbitrary date, but it was actually a vestigial lunisolar holiday.

For instance, the ancient Roman holiday, Nemoralia, was originally celebrated on the first full moon after the midpoint of Lughnasadh, literally on the ides of August, or August 15th, on a lunisolar calendar. But, by the time that the Church created the Feast of the Assumption, which replaced Nemoralia, the Romans were only using the solar Julian calendar. So, it was simply August 15th, regardless of the phase of the moon. And, this date is separate from Lughnasadh, the solar midpoint of August 2nd. So, the date of the Assumption (August 15th) could easily be seen as just an arbitrary date, separtate from Lughnasadh, if you did not know the full history of this holiday.

To make it more complicated, there appears to be many exceptions to the rule, such as St. Patrick's Day which is on March 17th, several days before the equinox, Allhallowtide which lasts 3 days from October 31st through the 2nd of November, and St. Valentine's Day on February 14th, replacing Lupercalia, which was actually February 13th - 15th. And, then there's the Roman holiday, Sol Invictus, also known as Christmas, which is a winter solstice holiday that is celebrated 3 days after the solstice. Some of these, like Christmas, we can explain, and some we just have no idea.

Finally, to make it even more complicated, sometimes they picked a date related to a certain day of the week, such as Mother's Day on the second Sunday in May, or Easter, which is actually the first Sunday after the full moon, after the equinox.

MANY STORIES, ONE MEANING

Yes, the dates of the 8 holiday festivals do vary wildly throughout the year, but that is nothing compared to the stories each culture has created for their holidays. Each different culture or religion at each point in history has come up with their own rationalization for what they are celebrating and why. Each have their own gods or saints, and each have their own stories associated with said gods and saints.

We saw that, to the ancient Romans, December 25th was associated with the sun-god, Sol Invictus, to the Egyptians it was the birth of Horus, but to the ancient Norse people it marked the flight of Odin, and to Christians it marked the birth of Jesus and was later also linked to Saint Nicholas, and now Santa Claus.

This variability is so seemingly scattered and random that it nullifies the face validity of any holiday in any culture. Basically, it appears that no one has any idea why they celebrate the holidays that they do in the way they do. But, as we've seen, a deeper examination actually reveals the opposite. There definitely are certain themes that have persisted right up into the present.

I hope that, if nothing else, you have seen how there are really only eight themes that explain all the holidays of the year. These correspond to the eight points on the Wheel of Time, each containing a specific meaning. And, all the holidays of the year are grouped around the eight points. They are merely different manifestations of eight basic concepts. Each of the eight sets of holidays have their own theme related to the time of day, the time of the year, the phase of the annual agricultural cycle, and the corresponding phase of the human life cycle. It's right there if you look for it, yet to the untrained eye it is often completely missed.

Ask someone what Chinese New Year, Groundhog Day, and Valentine's Day all have in common, and most people can only say that they are all about the same time of year. Other than that, they would have no idea. And, what does St. Patrick's Day have in common with Easter? Or, how about May Day and Mother's Day or Christmas and our New Year's Eve? What is the connection there? People can only say they are about the same time of year but otherwise they see no connection at all between these various groups of holidays.

Of course, as we have seen, each of these seemingly different holidays, closely grouped at a certain time of year, are absolutely and definitely related to each other. And, they are not just related to each other, but stemming from a singular attempt to understand and celebrate time, the seasons, and life itself.

There is absolutely nothing even remotely arbitrary about celebrating Christmas on the 25th of December, and it has absolutely nothing to do with Jesus either. All these different holidays look random, but they are really nothing of the sort. Take Christmas for instance; each different culture and religion are all celebrating exactly the same thing: the return of the sun. It's just that they've become garbled over thousands of years by hundreds of different cultures and religions, overlaying their own mythology and beliefs on top of a singular ancient holy day.

So, the reincarnation of the sun became the rebirth of the sun god, which morphed into the birth of some other sun god, and finally the birth of the son of god. The same can be said for each of the eight points of the Wheel of Time and all the multitude of holidays they have spawned.

And, New Year's day, one week after Christmas, is literally the birth a new solar year, very much related to the ancient idea of the rebirth of the sun. Our ancestors merely decided to start the new calendar year on the first day of the next calendar month (January), instead of on December 25th. And, this was very sensible. Can you image how confusing it would be if December 25th 2020 was one day after December 24th 2019?

While there appears to be hundreds of different holidays, all with different histories, different meanings, and different stories and religions associated with them, I hope it's clear now that that is really just an illusion. There are only eight points on the Wheel of Time, which gave rise to thousands of holidays. And, now you know the rest of the story.

PART III:

CONCLUSION: THE ANCIENT FUTURE OF SPIRITUALITY

CHAPTER 12

THE RIDDLE SOLVED: OUR SPIRITUAL ROOTS REVEALED

For most people, our current holidays are whatever you've been told they are. If you are a neo-pagan or Wiccan you might celebrate the spring equinox with a feast in honor the Goddess of Fertility, but if you are a Christian then you may believe the reason for the season is really the resurrection of Christ. And, if you are Jewish, you are probably quite sure that Passover had something to do with Moses leading the Hebrews out of bondage in Egypt.

No one is really right and no one is wrong. You can and should commemorate the holiday to whatever is most important to you. What we've seen so far in this book is not so much that there is a right way or a wrong way to celebrate any particular holiday; far from it. Rather, we have simply constructed an instrument, the Wheel of Time, which helps us to gain clarity on why, when, and how we celebrate our holidays the way we do. This is especially important when our traditions seem arbitrary or don't seem to fit the narrative given to us through our religious teachings.

The Wheel of Time is a simple, efficient tool that explains why we celebrate Christmas at midnight, Easter at sunrise, Halloween in the evening, and Rosh Hashanah at sunset.

It explains why we celebrate Passover on a full moon, and why the Jewish and Chinese both celebrate the New Year on a new moon, even though they are at different times of the year. It explains why our day starts at midnight, yet the Jewish day starts at sunset. It explains why we celebrate Christmas with evergreens, Easter with rabbits, and Halloween with skeletons.

It explains why native Americans made petroglyphs to mark the equinoxes and solstices with a spiral design. And, it explains why people all over the world for much of the last 10,000 years appear to have been obsessed with marking the phases of the solar year.

The Wheel of Time illuminates an immensely rich and detailed system of how people in the ancient world perceived the cycles of time and of life. And, it explains how we came to practice our current religious holidays the way we do. For some reason, this is a topic that has remained especially obscure and clouded with misinformation. But, now you know the rest of the story.

In short, the Wheel of Time is like any other law of nature; it is true and valid even if the people using it are completely unware of what they are doing or why they are doing it. Almost no one in our society thinks of the Wheel of Time when they practice their traditional holidays. In fact, I dare say, no one even knows of the Wheel of Time in its full complexity. Nonetheless, they still follow it with faithful devotion.

This is a valuable tool for archaeologists and anthropologists. As I've shown over and over, if you have a few bits of information about a society's beliefs and practices, you can extrapolate from that and make many specific predictions about their culture, their holidays, and ceremonial practices, using only the Wheel of Time. For instance, knowing just that Rosh Hashanah is on a new moon, based on the Wheel of Time, I would predict that Passover would be on a full moon, and indeed it is.

This helps us to better understand what people did and why they did it, even when only fragments of information are known. If you can plot a few bits of information from a particular ancient civilization on the Wheel of Time, the Wheel may tell you many other bits of information that were previously missing or incomplete.

NEOLITHIC VS. NEO-PAGAN

There has long been a debate regarding Neolithic pagan vs. neo-pagan traditions. Modern day neo-pagans proudly say that their traditions date back to the time before Christ. Skeptical scholars, on the other hand, are quick to say that neo-paganism is a fairly recent invention and probably has little or nothing to do with the actual pagan practices of prehistory. Hopefully, if I've done nothing else in this book, I have at least resolved this debate once and for all.

Clearly, the English Christians of the middle-ages did not invent the traditions of Yule, Ēostre, or May Day, nor were they created by the Pope in Rome. Many of these holiday customs were obviously carried over from traditions that predated Christianity. So, the resurrection of paganism, what we call neo-paganism, did not have to reinvent very much at all. They just had to scrape off the veneer of Christianity. All the vestigial elements of paganism were already there, lurking in the corners of our modern holidays.

Another issue debated by scholars is whether the ancients observed all eight points of the Wheel of Time. I mentioned earlier in the book that I saw a line from a scholar that read: *Many historical pagan traditions celebrated various equinoxes, solstices, and cross-quarter days. But, none were known to have held all eight days above all other annual sacred times.*[1] We can now see that this statement is not only factually incorrect, it is plainly obtuse. What other *sacred times* were there? As we have shown, all the ancient holy days, which later became our modern holidays, can be linked to these eight points of the solar year.

In fact, all four cross-quarter days are listed as the start of the four seasons in the Tochmarc Emire, in the Ulster Cycle, set in the 1st century, and recorded from oral tradition between the 8th and 9th Centuries.[2] And, these cross-quarter days could only be determined by observing the solstices and equinoxes. There is no other way. This proves that the ancient Celts regularly identified and marked all eight points of the solar year and celebrated four of them with fire festivals.

We have also shown that the cross-quarter fire festivals, celebrated by the Celts, were documented by Roman historians at least two thousand years ago. And, the Celts were not alone. The Roman scholar Marcus Terentius Varro also conceptualized the year in eight parts as defined by the solstices, equinoxes, and the four midpoints between them, then adjusted them only slightly to fit key turning points in the annual agricultural calendar.[3]

To be fair to skeptical academics, there is a good deal of research presented in this book that is relatively recent. For instance, there was the research done at Stonehenge, which revealed insights into the true purpose and meaning of the monument. This is information that was simply not known 20 years ago. If you went to college over 20 years ago, or studied under a professor who had not kept up with current research, you may have been taught outdated or incomplete information about Stonehenge, and about both paganism and neo-paganism as well.

Hopefully, in this book I have shown the two major sources that shaped most of our modern Christian holidays, and they are the southern pagan traditions of Babylon, Egypt, and Rome, and the northern pagan traditions of the Celts and Norse. The southern pagan traditions were codified, for better or worse, by the Catholic Church in Rome. Taken largely from Roman traditions, the Church specified the dates of the holidays, the time of day to observe each holiday, and the major themes of the holidays.

Christians in England and elsewhere took their directives from Rome. And, the northern pagan traditions were added by the people themselves, who never really stopped celebrating their traditional pagan holidays. So, the Catholic Church facilitated the continuation of pagan traditions by enshrining these holidays as an integral part of Christianity.

As Rome tried to facilitate the conversion to Christianity, they unknowingly gave Christians permission to continue their pagan traditions. Actually, it may not be so unknowing. The whole idea of blending Christian and pagan traditions was a very Roman approach to conquering new lands. In pre-Christian Rome, they never sought to make people stop worshipping their gods or practicing their festivals. Rather, they sought to incorporate new peoples and customs into the unified tapestry that was the Roman Empire.

The Romans would show the locals that the Norse god Odin and the Roman god Mercury were basically the same god; they just had different names for him. The same is true for the Norse goddess Frig and the Roman goddess Venus, as well as the Norse god Thor and the Roman equivalent, Jupiter. And, if there was a festival to celebrate a Roman god, they allowed the local people throughout the Roman Empire to celebrate the holiday with their own local traditions and gods as well.

So, the Holy Roman Empire, that we call the Catholic Church, was really just continuing the same Roman imperial practices that the Caesars had done for centuries. When Rome conquered a new territory, they didn't prefer to slaughter the locals and obliterate their culture. Rather, they first tried to work with the locals, to absorb and assimilate the people into the greater empire. This was an integral component of the *Pax Romana*.[4]

The Popes in Rome did precisely the same thing when converting people to Christianity. They sought to absorb and assimilate new lands and nations into the Holy Roman Empire, while allowing the local people to keep much of their customs and traditions. Just as Caesar had taught the Norsemen that their god Odin was really the same as Mercury, the Pope wished to show the Saxons that the Easter holiday, celebrating the resurrection of nature, was also a celebration of the resurrection of Christ. And, of course, this approach worked, and eventually the entire former Roman Empire was converted to Christianity.

THE REASON FOR THE SEASON

It seems clear now that all of our modern or Christian holidays are nothing of the sort. They reveal a much older framework of annual holidays corresponding to specific meanings for each holiday and often even specific times of the day for each celebration. This is not really new information. I notice that, just about every holiday, you can find news stories, Facebook posts, or even advertising reminding us that the holiday in question actually predates Christianity and was celebrated by the ancients for many thousands of years. This is especially true for the biggies: Christmas, Easter, and Halloween.

And yet, there is still some controversy about this topic. The former Fox News personality, Bill O'Reilly, used to go on a rant every December that there was a *War on Christmas,* waged by non-Christian, politically correct, culturally-inclusive liberals. And, every year, I still hear people encouraging us to remember the real *reason for the season*, meaning the birth of Christ. Yet, as we've seen throughout this book, Christmas is just the current name for this holiday. Whether you are Christian or not is irrelevant. It does not change the fact that our so-called Christian holidays were almost completely cut and pasted from pre-existing pagan holidays.

Please know that I do not denigrate a person for being a Christian. I think it is wonderful that devout Christians celebrate the concept of resurrection in their celebration of Easter and celebrate the promise of salvation in their celebration of Christmas. I would just like people to acknowledge that the Christian faith is only one way to celebrate these holidays; people all over the world have celebrated these holidays for many thousands of years, each with their own mythology, gods, traditions, and customs.

The Christians did not invent Easter or Christmas, rather they overlaid their own theological beliefs onto existing annual holidays, which were originally created to celebrate the Wheel of Time with all of its deep and nuanced symbolism. Each season is imbued with an organic meaning, such as salvation or resurrection, each of which also represents a phase of life in both nature and in the human life-cycle, which was sacred to the ancients.

I hope it is clear now that the ancient pagans were, first and foremost, worshipping life and nature. They saw sacredness in all living things. Life was sacred, death was sacred, Earth was sacred, indeed Nature itself, often personified as a goddess or god, was sacred. So, naturally, they celebrated each changing of the season with reverence and awe, and solemn ceremonies, just as we do with baptisms for newborn babies and funerals for the dead.

After all, why do we observe birth and death with such reverence? Aren't these basic aspects of nature and the human life cycle? Yes. And don't we have reverence and awe for these occurrences? Of course we do. This is the root of human spirituality. When we observe a person's birth or death with humility, reverence, and awe, we are tapping into the very impetus for the creation of religion. And, the Wheel of Time is a way to celebrate these aspects of life and nature every year, regardless of whether you have a birth or death in the family that year. With the Wheel of Time, we celebrate the concept of birth and death and everything in between as being sacred.

In addition to observing each aspect of nature and the life cycle, the ancients saw connections between all cycles in nature, birth, death, the sun, moon, stars, and that of plants, animals, and the entire human life cycle. That is why many, if not most, cultures have ceremonies for marriage and puberty, as well as birth and death. Think of it this way; all these milestones are actually points on the Wheel of Time, and echoed by the seasons of the year. This is what is meant by the term Earth-based spirituality.

Earth-based spirituality means observing nature and the life cycle as sacred, and celebrating each phase with reverence and awe. It is clear now that they saw a correlation between the daily solar cycle, the lunar cycle, the annual solar cycle, and the living cycles of nature, especially the agricultural cycle and human life-cycle. All of these were sacred and interrelated. This system of interrelated cycles is what we call the Wheel of Time. It now appears that this concept was the skeletal framework for all Earth-based spiritual practices that we call paganism, and eventually for all of our modern holidays as well.

HOLIDAYS' FUNCTION IN EARLY SOCIETIES

The ancient holidays and rituals also served very practical functions in society. Long ago, before the Romans imposed their own order on the rural people of Europe, the people marked their agricultural duties by the annual phases of the sun. Beltaine was when the livestock were driven into higher pastures for grazing, then at Samhain they brought them back to stable them before the winter. Each holiday marked a specific action that needed to be taken in agriculture, such as planting, growing, harvesting, and pruning. The holidays ritualized all these actions with solemn observances that reminded people of the sacredness of their actions and the miracle of life and nature.

These holidays reminded the people that Mother Nature feeds us, nurtures us, takes care of us, and therefore we should honor her as well. Have you ever seen time lapse photography of plants growing? It is truly a miracle that gigantic trees literally just sprout out of the ground from a tiny seed. And, some of our best foods literally grow on trees. Or, think of the chickens that give us fresh eggs every day. Nowadays, most of us take it all for granted, but it's really amazing if you think about it. And, these ancient holidays gave people an opportunity to honor and celebrate these miracles and to remind them of their spiritual significance throughout the year.

The ancient holidays also marked all the firsts and lasts of the year. Lammas marked the first bread from the wheat harvest. Mabon marked the first fruit harvest. And, the ancient Winter Finding festival, what we today call Oktoberfest, welcomed the changing season with the first beer of the grain harvest, after being fully fermented and ready to drink. The ancients celebrated the summer sun, the fall leaves, the return of the sun in midwinter, and the glorious resurrection of life in spring. They didn't just worship nature; they celebrated the miracle of life itself.

These holidays created structure for early human societies. They gave purpose and meaning to each and every month of the year. So, prehistory pagan cultures were not just disorganized tribes of people wandering around looking for food. There was very specific work to be done at each time of the year, and very specific and even spiritual meanings connected to the work they did.

Each phase of the year was marked with highly ritualized ceremonies. This carried over into the work they did during each season. They didn't just worship their gods and goddesses one day a week, they lived their spirituality 24/7. It was woven into every aspect of their life and work. One might even say that the development of the Wheel of Time was the foundation of society and religion as we know it.

SUSTAINABILITY & EARTH-BASED SPIRITUALITY

Our pre-history ancestors managed to create a culture that thrived for many thousands of years. How? They did this by anchoring their traditions, customs, beliefs, ceremonies, and holidays to Nature and her stable, continual, and unending cycles. This guarantees a sustainable culture. Other fads and fashions may come and go. As we've seen, myths and stories of the gods come and go. But, the winter is always the winter, with only minor fluctuations. And, the spring is always spring. Sprouts come up in spring, and each autumn the leaves always turn and fall. Always.

Likewise, each generation of people are conceived, born, grow up, then grow old and die, pretty much as we have always done. Though each generation seems to think that they invented love, fun, freedom, disenchantment with society, and profound sorrow, their elders know better. And the young see this and learn from their wise elders.

But when a culture worships the new inventions of society more than nature, then newness is valued over tradition. Over a hundred years ago, wise elders might have appeared to be ignorant to their children and grandchildren, because they didn't understand all the miracles of the Industrial Revolution. And, if the elders were fools about these things, perhaps they knew nothing of love, freedom, or sorrow either. Why preserve any of their old traditions? After all, times are different now, right?

When we lose our time-honored ancient traditions, society breaks down, collapses, and unravels. The result is a lack of cultural sustainability, social upheaval, disintegration of social values, and even a breakdown of the family structure. And, isn't that exactly what we've seen since the Industrial Revolution? So, an earth-based spiritual practice can be the foundation of a more sustainable culture, because it does not change with each passing fad, as it is anchored in the cycles and seasons of the Earth and Nature.

This connection between Earth-based spirituality and sustainability is fascinating to me. Several years ago, I completed and published an original translation of the ancient text, the *Tao Te Ching*, by Lao Tzu, and in it I found a very similar concept.[5] The Tao Te Ching was written approximately 2500 years ago, but my research suggested that it was probably an anthology of old, treasured poems or songs. So, it might have been hundreds, even thousands of years older than previously thought. Lao Tzu may have simply written down old sayings that were previously passed down through oral tradition or inscribed on bones and other artifacts. This could move back the date of the earliest verses to the late Neolithic age, predating Lao Tzu by a thousand years.

This is important because it means that the Tao Te Ching may be the oldest text in the world to describe a late Neolithic pagan belief system. To read Lao Tzu is like looking into the mind of a pagan shaman from prehistory. So, what does Lao Tzu say? Interestingly, in modern terms we'd say that it's a lot about Earth-based spirituality and sustainability, and about the importance of the cycles of nature.

He taught about the virtues of the *Tao*, which translates to the *Way*. By Tao, he meant something like the Way of truth, the Way of Heaven and Earth, the Way of Nature, or the Way of the Universe. He talks about observing the cycles of nature and learning from it. He said that the Tao existed before the first Dynasty, which means before human society; I think he means the Tao is the wisdom learned from studying nature. He wrote that the Tao created the world and everything in it, including humanity. But, he does not personify the Tao as a god or goddess. If he personifies it at all, the Tao is simply referred to as our *Mother*. The Mother of Creation.

Lao Tzu also writes a great deal about striving to be eternal and not dying out. This is often misinterpreted to mean that we can live forever or have a very long life, but he specifically states the opposite meaning in one passage. He urges us to accept death as a natural part of the life cycle.[6] Death, he says, is part of the Tao. Rather, he was urging us to create a society that would not die out by anchoring it in the Earth and Nature. Thus, he reasoned that if we can anchor our society in these ancient and unchanging cycles, then our society would be unending. Nowadays, we would say *sustainable*.[7]

In Lao Tzu's writing, we have a clear literary narrative of what we see in so many Neolithic archaeological sites from around the world, a philosophy of learning about and learning from the cycles of nature, the sun, moon, earth and heavens. This helps to explain the philosophical rationale for creating and following the Wheel of Time in the first place. They were trying to learn and understand the cycles of nature. That, in turn, helps explain pagan practices celebrating the eight major pagan Sabbaths of the year. This was a ritualized expression of their knowledge of and reverence for the cycles of nature and the universe.

> *I observe their cycle…Is called the cycle of destiny…The cycle of destiny is our eternal nature. To know our eternal nature is enlightenment. To not know our eternal nature is disastrous.*[8]
>
> -Lao Tzu

Basing their major holy days on the seasons and phases of the solar and lunar cycles reinforced a sustainable lifestyle, generation after generation, for many millennia. It also helped to impart wisdom upon the young. They were taught to learn about life by observing the phases and cycles of nature or what Lao Tzu simply called *the cycle of destiny*. Reverence and celebration of the seasons reinforced this as well. Being wise and well-schooled in the cycles of nature was a vital aspect of creating a sustainable future. And, this is almost exactly what Lao Tzu wrote over 2500 years ago.

SUMMARY: THE POWER & PERSISTENCE OF PAGAN PRACTICES

One thing is clear from our study of the holidays; the

pagan traditions of prehistory have endured into the modern age. People all over the world continue these traditions to this very day, though they may not know it. Today, as I write this, it is St. Patrick's Day. How many people observe this holiday? Millions? Hundreds of millions? Yet, how many know that this is actually an ancient pagan celebration known as Bacchanalia to the Romans, celebrating the rites of spring and heralding the coming of the vernal equinox? This, more than anything else, is a testament to the sustainability of Earth-based spirituality. In fact, if there were no St. Patrick's Day, would people in the northern latitudes still go outside on the first nice day of spring and maybe celebrate with a cold beer? Of course they would.

In the last chapter, I have pointed out over and over again that we don't even need historical continuity to preserve our holidays because the urge to celebrate our holidays is in our DNA. Literally, it is part of being a human on earth. Just as you don't need to teach a child to catch snowflakes on their tongue, or to dive into a pile of fall leaves, or to collect wildflowers in the spring, our celebration of the seasons is a natural and organic occurrence. If we had no Christmas, we would do something to celebrate midwinter, and it would probably be a lot like what we call *Christmas*.

So, what does it say about pagan traditions that they are so persistent as to survive the rise and fall of Zoroastrianism, the rise and fall of the cult of Isis, the rise and fall of Rome, and the rise and current deline of Christianity? It suggests that pagan Earth-based spirituality may be the most sustainable spiritual practice in the world because it cuts to the very heart of what spirituality is: a simple reverence for the miracle of existence, the preciousness of mortal life, and the immortality of the soul.

These simple seasonal holidays have endured for many millennia, despite changing cultures and religions. We've seen how the solstice has always been the solstice as it went from being a celebration of the birth of Marduk to the birth of Horus, to the birth of Mithras, to the birth of Christ. After 5,000 years, even the decorations didn't change all that much. It appears that our current organized religions are really just window dressing on top of the underlying structure of the Wheel of Time, which is as organic and natural as any other observation of nature.

The Wheel of Time is the product of thousands of years of accumulated wisdom, stemming from a spiritual reverence for nature by our ancestors. It is their gift to us and our birthright. The question is: Are we wise enough to use it?

CHAPTER 13

THE RISE OF ATHEIST SPIRITUALITY

As I mentioned in the preface of this book, one of the factors that prompted me to write this book was a current movement among millennials toward what you might call *atheist spirituality*.[1] This is a recognition that there is, in fact, a spiritual dimension to humanity, even among people who do not believe in any god or religion. Clearly, no religion has quite captured the ultimate truth, since all of their theologies are different and often incompatible with each other. Yet, that does not nullify millions of people's experiences that can only be described as *spiritual*.

I read a recent interview with the actor Jason Segel, from the TV show *How I Met Your Mother*.[2] He had made a movie for Netflix called *The Discovery*, about a scientist discovering proof of an afterlife. His background is both Jewish and Christian. And, his remarks on religion and spirituality were a great example of what we mean when we talk about this growing movement of atheist spirituality. He is critical of anyone who is too assured of their point of view. He says that, "*you're supposed to surrender to the mystery of it all, and the second you try to name it, you've really missed the beauty of it in a lot of ways*".

He went on to say that having religion or a specific idea about God actually leads us away from our spirituality. Segel says, "*I think if you get too caught up in what God does and doesn't want you to eat, you're sort of missing the point, you know?*" He refers to novelist David Foster Wallace's speech *This is Water.* In it, Wallace gave the following parable:

> *"There are these two young fish swimming along, and they happen to meet an older fish swimming the other way, who nods at them and says, 'Morning, boys. How's the water?' And the two young fish swim on for a bit, and then eventually one of them looks over at the other and goes, 'What the hell is water?'"*

People thinking about spirituality is like the fish thinking about water. Segal goes on to say, "*One of the things that's hard about spirituality is you want to look outside for it, but you're right in the middle of it, so it's very hard to see. You're in it right now*".

Like most of us with similar views, Segel can only glean bits and pieces of insight from what he's seen and read. He says that he's read Joseph Campbell and Carl Jung, and he points to a convergence of religion and science. Modern scientists are talking about a *Multiverse*, suggesting that there are different dimensions to the Universe. Of course, many religions from around the world have been saying the same thing for a long time, albeit using different language. What if the afterlife is just another dimension of the Multiverse?

My favorite part of the Segel interview is when he says

that he thinks that, in a venn diagram of spirituality, all beliefs tend to overlap when it comes to selflessness and kindness. That's something that people of almost all spiritual beliefs agree on. Of course, this begs the question: What is spirituality? Is it a behavior? Is it just being a good person? How is that different from ethics?

DEFINING SPIRITUALITY

At this point, I feel it necessary to, once again, define what I mean by the term spiritual. I say, *once again*, because the term has already been defined; it is in the dictionary if you want to look it up. Anyone writing on this topic is usually asked to define the term *spiritual* at some point, such as Sam Harris, author of the recent book *Waking Up: A Guide to Spirituality Without Religion.*[3] When Sam Harris was interviewed on Bill Maher's show, *Real Time,* one of the first things that Bill asked him about was the term spirituality. *I don't know what that means, and neither do you, because,... what does that mean, spirituality?* Bill asked.[4] And, I think a lot of people wonder the same thing, and that's even true for so-called religious experts.

Years ago, I heard a radio talk-show on religion called *Religion on the Line*, hosted by the nationally syndicated radio host, Dennis Prager. The host and guests on the show were discussing two distinctly different topics, *spirituality* and *religion*, but they were discussing them as though the two were interchangeable. Finally, a caller phoned in to say, what

I'm sure many of the listeners were thinking, that spirituality is completely independent of organized religion. Spirituality is an experience that people feel and religion is, at its best, an attempt to understand and explain that experience. I agreed with the caller and was certain that the host, Mr. Prager, would as well.

Surprisingly, Mr. Prager, scoffed at this idea. He asserted that without organized religion there could be no spirituality. It appears that he really had no concept of a non-religious spiritual experience. For him, spirituality appeared to be merely a byproduct or epiphenomenon of organized religion. And, without religion, the term was utterly meaningless. So, for Mr. Maher, Mr. Prager, and all those baffled by the term, let me try to define what I mean by *spiritual.*

According to the Oxford English Dictionary, the first definition of the term is that which is pertaining to the *human spirit*, as opposed to material or physical things.[5] The second definition is relating to religion or religious beliefs. And, I would have to agree with that order. The primary definition of *spiritual* refers to an experience or phenomenon that is quite simply not of this world, that is related to our consciousness, the supernatural, or something non-corporeal. Only secondarily does it have any connection to religion. There are many examples of spiritual experiences. I myself have had numerous experiences that I can only describe as spiritual, and I know I'm not alone.

At the funeral of Nancy Reagan, her daughter, Patti Davis, said that after President Reagan passed away, her mother would hear her late husband's footsteps coming down the hall at night when she was in bed. Then, Mrs. Reagan would actually see the late President Ronald Reagan come in and sit down on her bed. She reported that this was very comforting to the late First Lady.

Was this a religious experience? Maybe. But, what if this happens to someone who is not religious at all? In that case, this can only be described as a secular spiritual experience. It is either that or a hallucination. But, I don't think anyone would suggest that Patti Davis or Nancy Reagan were psychotic. In absence of any psychotic disorder, when these experiences are reported by someone of sound mind, we can only describe this kind of experience as something *spiritual.*

Now, it is not the purpose of this book to convince you of any theological or mystical beliefs. I am merely trying to define and explain the concept of *spirituality*, in the clearest way possible. So, according to the dictionary and many philosophers around the world, spirituality is not really a belief so much as it is an experience or phenomenon. And, it is an experience that many, if not most, people have had in their life.

One of the best-selling memoirs in recent years was *Proof of Heaven*, about a person's near-death-experience, while lying in a coma. [6] I think the book's popularity speaks volumes about this topic. Millions of people have had a *near-death experience* (NDE), or an *out-of-body- experience* (OBE). And many more have had some other spiritual experience either in a lucid dream, a vision, or through some other remarkable event. The rest of us have probably known someone who have had at least one such experience.

These appear to be natural phenomena that happen to both religious and non-religious people alike. As a psychologist, I have had hundreds of clients who have had similar experiences. I've also had many clients who have claimed to have seen or heard a loved-one who has passed away, as Nancy Reagan did. These experiences did not appear to be hallucinations brought on by a psychotic disorder, but rather a phenomenon experienced by perfectly normal, otherwise sane people.

The reason why I go to such depth to define spiritual experiences, in all their mystical details, is to convey a simple yet profound idea; that there is a spiritual dimension to human life, which is as real as any other aspect of humanity. Just as we acknowledge other aspects of being human, such as loneliness, daydreaming or orgasms, a spiritual experience is also a common phenomenon of consciousness.

Having a spiritual experience such as those described above is no more or less a part of being human than it is to experience premonitions or déjà vu. We can't always scientifically explain such phenomena. We can only theorize how they occur. But, we can't deny that they exist.

SPIRITUALITY AS AN ORGANIC PHENOMENON

My apologies to Bill Maher and Dennis Prager, mentioned earlier. I don't know if either of them have ever had a spiritual experience, or an NDE or OBE for that matter. But, if they did they may have chalked it up to some other cause. If Bill Maher had such an experience, he might have attributed it to something that he had smoked. If Mr. Prager had a similar experience he may have attributed it to his deep religious beliefs.

Regardless of how we rationalize such experiences, it seems clear that these experiences happen to people who are not religious, not psychotic, and not using drugs. In short, it is just part of being human. Spirituality is a basic dimension of humanity, and quite possibly a very real but separate dimension of the Universe. As such, it is an organic phenomenon.

One explanation of our spirit is that it is like an energy field. We know that there are gravitational fields, and there are electro-magnetic fields, so why not consciousness fields? If consciousness is a quantifiable energy, then perhaps it can exist as an energy field. I didn't come up with this idea myself; there have been many scientists in the past who proposed this.

The first person to speculate on this concept was a scientist and philosopher by the name of Oliver Reiser, back in the 1920s and 30s.[7] His book on *Cosmic Humanism* became a cult classic back in the 60s, with an audience who had had psychedelic experiences and were hungry for answers. By the way, the name of Reiser's theory, Cosmic Humanism, was actually coined by his colleague, Albert Einstein.

I don't know if consciousness can be quantified as an

energy field or not, but the general idea makes sense. And, I know that there is currently university research being conducted on this topic. If consciousness is like an energy field, it would certainly explain a lot. And, if consciousness is independent of brain functioning, then it might be very much like what we call *the soul.* As such, it might validate and explain why we have these experiences that we can only describe as *spiritual.*

This suggests that spirituality is some kind of organic phenomena, naturally occurring in human beings. Also, it seems that as we connect with nature and the Earth, we connect with this spiritual dimension on a deeper level. And, this isn't just coming from some minority group of fringe philosophers. These are popular trends in America that have been progressing for many years.

ATHEIST SPIRITUAL MOVEMENT

Currently, religion is on the decline in America, Europe, and elsewhere around the world. Yet, at the same time, a type of non-religious spirituality is more popular than ever. Beginning with the *New Age* movement back in the 1960s and 70s, there has been a steady rise in people being spiritual, but not specifically religious. In fact, *Atheist, Wiccan*, and *None* are among the fastest growing religious categories in recent surveys.[8] And, Wicca is just a popular form of neo-paganism.

This clearly indicates that people are rejecting traditional religion, but not necessarily rejecting spirituality. In fact, it seems that there is a hunger for something that is spiritual but non-religious. How else could you explain the growing popularity of yoga or mindfulness meditation? It seems there are now yoga studios in every city across America. And, as I will explain, a similar trend is occurring in many professions as well.

For many years, homeopathy, which is not based on traditional science, has been an important component of alternative medicine. Homeopathy, according to many scientists, is really just superstition.[9] The basic principle of homeopathy is that an herb or extract is so totally diluted that the only thing that remains is the *vibration* of the herb. Proponents claim that this essence of the herb has healing powers. Modern science, however, has never validated the existence of any such vibration or invisible essence.

But, if it has no scientific validity, then why is it so popular now? I've even heard of medical doctors using homeopathy. And this growing movement of open-mindedness exists in other professions as well. I know for a fact that similar trends are occurring in the field of psychology and even in agriculture.

In the last 10 years, the field of psychology has seen the rapid growth of *Mindfulness Meditation* and *Mindfulness-Based Stress Reduction* (MBSR), and its applications for everything from major depression to PTSD.[10] Back in the 1980s, I remember seeing a psychological research study completed at a major university, which studied the effectiveness of both eastern meditation and secular forms of meditation such as relaxation training, as compared to a control group of no meditation. The study proved that both eastern and secular forms of meditation were beneficial compared to the control group. You would think that that would be proof of the effectiveness of meditation. Not so.

The scientific community was so biased against meditation at that time that the success of secular meditation in this clinical study was seen as merely a placebo effect, and nothing more. Now, 30 years later, the entire field has embraced secular meditation as a basic component of effective psychotherapy. Many in the field believe that it is something we should all be doing on a regular basis, like exercising or flossing.

Even in the vineyards of California and elsewhere, the hot new topic in organic agriculture is *Biodynamic Farming*, which is so pagan that it might even make a Wiccan blush. If you don't know, in Biodynamic Farming there are a number of different preparations that you use to make your crops grow well.[11] The preparations can be quite involved and often seem like a form of Voodoo.

One biodynamic preparation involves killing a cow on your property, cutting off the horn and filling it with the dung of a lactating cow. This preparation is mixed with crushed quartz crystal and buried in the vineyard in spring, near the spring equinox, but only on certain days that are auspicious for such activities. You have to consult a biodynamic calendar to determine the best day to bury the horn. Then, six months later, you dig up the horn on the harvest moon, mix with spring water, and spray your crops with it to help them survive the winter and come back strong in the next spring.

There is another preparation, which requires a native stag's bladder. It can't be a stag from another vineyard, it has to be from your own vineyard. You might think that this sounds pretty crazy, but if you go to wineries and wine tasting rooms across California, you will find that this is a popular trend, and many wineries proudly claim that they are a Certified Biodynamic winery.

What is happening? Has the entire Western Civilization gone native? Most of these trends have no basis in modern science. Yet all of them are embraced as valid alternatives to traditional science and are clearly appealing to many professionals nowadays.

I think it's obvious what is going on here. People are clearly disillusioned with the current scientific zeitgeist and are looking for alternatives. Many people feel that there is something lacking in the epistemology of modern science, and find traditional religions empty and hollow. They are looking for something deeper and more meaningful, than science or religion.

I think what we are searching for is the wisdom of our ancestors. We may be wrong, perhaps our ancestors knew no more than we do, but there is the perception that they were a little more grounded and lived a little closer to the natural world. As such, they had a wisdom that was a little deeper than that of today. Just as Lao Tzu said of the ancient Taoists, they studied the cycles of nature and, in the process, learned the Tao, the *Way* of life and the Universe.[12]

I can summarize the last 20,000 years of spirituality like this. First, before there were gods, there was some form of pre-theist nature worship. The sun, moon, stars, and seasons were studied and revered with awe and wonder. Then, men created gods and goddesses to better relate to the forces of nature. They were originally personifications of nature, like the goddess of wind, the goddess of fertility, and the god of thunder, and so on.

Later, theologians created many specific doctrines about the nature of the gods and our relationship to them. Religions became more specific in detail and more rigidly practiced. As societies grew more complex, religions also grew more complex. They grew and evolved and then eventually they splintered into a thousand competing sects.

Then, in the modern world, our religions have appeared to collapse like a house of cards. People have been abandoning traditional religions for decades. After all, when hundreds of different religions each say that they, and they alone, are the one true religion, it makes a mockery of the whole endeavor.

And, science is no help; it doesn't acknowledge the existence of spirituality at all. So, now we have come full circle, just as it all began, tens of thousands of years ago. Many are going back to the idea of finding a basic spiritual dimension to our everyday lives, without the need of gods or religion. They are trying to see the sacredness of nature and sense the miracle of life all around us.

Currently, there is a growing spirituality movement. As Marianne Williamson, author of the New Age classic, *A Course in Miracles*, once said, "*Quantum physics, spiritual understanding, and a more holistic perspective in general have come together to produce a serious challenge to the old-paradigm.*" She went on to say that "*People know that there's more going on in this life than just what the physical eyes can see.*"[13]

Just in the last few years there have been numerous books published on the topic of atheistic spirituality. I mentioned Sam Harris' book, *Waking Up: A Guide to Spirituality Without Religion*, but there are many others. There is R. Budd's *Spirituality for Atheists*, Mark Gura's *Atheist Meditation, Atheist Spirituality,* and Andre Comte-Sponville's *The Little Book of Atheist Spirituality.*[14]

At the same time, there has been a corresponding interest in paganism, such as in Anthony T. Kronman's book *Confessions of a Born-Again Pagan.*[15] Sometimes atheism and paganism are combined into some type of atheistic nature worship. There have been many other such books and articles to come out in recent years, and they all cite the need for some form of spirituality based on nature or human consciousness, in the absence of traditional religion.

Unfortunately, one thing is clear in all the above books; obviously, it is very challenging for atheists to grapple with the topic of spirituality. It's like the analogy of the fish contemplating water, that I had mentioned before. As a group, these authors appear to be groping in the dark when trying to understand the nature of spirituality.

One writer titled his chapters with each of the different aspects of spirituality as he sees it, such as *Spirituality is Passion, Spirituality is Joy, Spirituality is Rational*, and so on. I don't mean to disparage his work, but I almost expected to see a chapter titled *Spirituality is A Ham Sandwich*. It appears that no one thus far has a clear and concise idea of spirituality that resonates with both atheists and believers alike. That is why so many authors, including myself, have had to define the term. It is probably one of the most misunderstood concepts in modern society.

THE WHEEL OF TIME AS A CONCEPTUAL FRAMEWORK

In addition to understanding our past, perhaps the most important feature of the Wheel of Time is really a framework for creating our future. What we are lacking at this point in history is a strong conceptual framework for creating a form of spirituality without the need of a god or religion. And, I think the Wheel of Time serves that purpose. When I say a form of spirituality, I am talking about something that both touches us deeply and corresponds to a set of outward traditions and customs, which reflects and supports our innate spirituality.

This would be a spiritual practice that contains both beliefs about what is sacred and holidays to celebrate those beliefs. And, it can even be organized, in the sense that we can get together at a park or a building, and share a holiday festival with others. After all, what office doesn't have an office Christmas party, and it's usually not very religious.

In fact, about the only thing that atheist spirituality doesn't need is a god or goddess. And, even that is ok, so long as we are clear that it is only a personification of an ideal, like Lady Liberty or Mother Nature. Where can we find a conceptual framework for spirituality that combines all these aspects? I would argue that a minimalist, earth-based spirituality, based on the Wheel of Time is a good place to start.

I suggest a minimalist approach because I think the one thing that we've seen, over and over again, is that it's the details that divide us. And, what we need now more than ever is something that will unite us, not divide us. You can get 100 people of different religions that all believe in God. That's easy. But, what is the name of this god or his chosen prophet? That's when disagreements begin.

Let's just take those who believe in Jesus, and then ask specific questions about texts that they read, how they interpret specific scriptures in the bible, how they practice their religion, or how they celebrate their holidays, and there are even more disagreements. The more specific you get, the more divided people become. When talking about spirituality, to say *the devil is in the details* is an understatement.

I think this has to do with the nature of truth itself. I always think of the metaphor of the three blind men trying to identify an elephant. The one man held the trunk and said, "it must be a type of large snake." The man next to the leg felt it and said "no, it must be a tree trunk." The man on the side of the elephant said that he was feeling a leather-covered wall. Individually, they were all correct, but each only had a piece of the puzzle; none had the big picture.

When religious groups attempt to nail down their perspective of spirituality, they are automatically deviating from the big picture of spirituality. Just as any specific part of an elephant is less accurate than looking at the whole thing.

Perhaps it's just as Jason Segel said, "*you're supposed to surrender to the mystery of it all.*" If you read the Tao Te Ching, by Lao Tzu, he is extremely vague about the Tao. He basically says that you just cannot put it into words. Most of the 91 passages are attempts to describe the indescribable. In one passage he says of the Tao, that it is "*always disappearing, it is elusive, its core being a pattern.*" He then cryptically says, "*It is evident in the origin of all things".*

That's interesting but it doesn't help us to see the Tao any more clearly. Then, as if he hears our skepticism, Lao Tzu goes on to say, *"How do I know of the of the origin of all things? This is it!"* [16] He is essentially saying that, like a fish looking at water, we are so immersed in the Tao that we are completely lacking in perspective, and so we can't even see it. What is the Tao? How do I know of the origin of all things? This is it! Right here and now.

Perhaps a better analogy is like a wisp of smoke; you can easily see it all around but you cannot nail it down, or put it in a box. And, that is the challenge of understanding, and discussing human spirituality.

It is interesting that Lao Tzu says the Tao, at its core, is a pattern. I'll never forget talking to Buckminster Fuller shortly before his death. Someone had asked him: what was the meaning of life? I thought he'd say something like: "how the hell should I know?" But, he responded quite seriously and poetically. He said, and I paraphrase, that a person's life is like a song, eternal and unique. It is a pattern, and though we are all made up of the same atoms and molecules, the differences in the patterns make each one of us completely unique, and our individual vibrations, like a song, continue across the universe, forever.

Many think that, when Lao Tzu talked of the Tao, he was partly referring to a pattern seen in learning how things grow, as he refers to this in so many different verses. He refers to one pattern in particular, which we know as the *watercourse way* or the *path of least resistance*. It is seen in the pattern of rivers cutting through the Earth, which is the same as the shape of our veins or the branches in trees. They are all the same, an unmistakable pattern of squiggly lines, but no two are exactly alike. And, that is just one pattern in nature. How do you know of these patterns? You see them in nature by studying the life cycle of rivers, plants, animals and people. The same patterns are everywhere in nature, even in the rivers of Jupiter's moon, Europa.

I believe that some form of Earth-based spirituality, which is based upon the Wheel of Time and otherwise very minimalist as to specific tenets, is a belief system that we can all share because we already do. As we've shown in this book, when you strip away the layers of history, theology, and mythology, we all celebrate the same holidays, at about the same time of year; we just tell ourselves different stories about the history and meaning of these holidays.

And, best of all, the Wheel of Time can be a powerful and enduring framework for celebrating our spirituality in the absence of any traditional religion. It offers a whole host of specific spiritual practices for you and your family that are not based on any religion, yet acknowledge the sacredness of life and the cycles of nature.

The Wheel of Time offers a unifying spiritual oneness because it incorporates all religions, all people and all living things on Earth. If someone wanted to create a world religion, this would be it. And it appears that that's just what it was thousands of years ago, prior to recorded history. As we've seen in the earlier chapters, there are very similar archeological ruins that were used to mark the points on the wheel of the year, and they are found on almost every continent on Earth.

It appears that all these different cultures observed very similar meanings for each of the different phases of the solar and lunar cycles. They further conceived of these repeating cycles in time and life as being like a wheel and often represented them as a spiral or a mandala. It is these solar and lunar phases, combined with what they symbolized on the life cycle, conceived as an ever-turning wheel, that created the Wheel of Time. Using this system, ancient paganism was a world religion that endured for thousands of years.

The Wheel of Time merges spirituality with science.

Science geeks may or may not go to a church but, even if they do, that is not their most devout form of worship. You find them staying up all night witnessing a meteor shower, or wearing a welding mask to witness a rare solar eclipse or a transit of Mercury. They pull out magnifying glasses to examine the first buds and spores of spring. They are endlessly fascinated with distant galaxies, tiny bugs, and mass migrations.

In short, those who love science are really worshiping and revering nature, and that is what the Wheel of Time helps us to do. We can still celebrate all of our modern holidays as we always have because, as we have shown, all our holidays are really just celebrations of nature. Except, now that you understand the original meaning of the holidays, you can appreciate them even more because now they are imbued with our love and reverence for nature and life itself.

We see that there is really no conflict between the worship of nature through science and the worship of nature through paganism. Now, there is finally a spiritual practice for atheists and nature-loving science-geeks. What this means is that, at last, you don't have to give up *reason* in order to find something sacred in the world.

SUMMARY: A FOUNDATION FOR PEACE

One final thought. At a time in history when we are again having bloody wars over religion, such as terrorism in the middle east, could Earth-based spirituality be a possible solution? In a millennium filled with as many bloody holy wars as we've had on this planet, what we desperately need is something to unite people of all faiths. The one common denominator shared by almost all religions is the Wheel of Time. It is the one thing that links us and binds us together. It offers the best hope of creating a platform for a future spirituality that we can all share.

I have not intensively studied Islam or their religious holidays. As such, I have not focused on their holidays for this book. But I do know that Ramadan begins on a crescent moon, it lasts one complete lunar cycle, and it originally took place in the hottest month of the year. In fact, I believe Ramadan means something like *the hot month.* Of course, like Christianity, they have their own beliefs about why they celebrate their holidays, and what their holidays are meant to commemorate.

But, the correlation of any holiday with both lunar and solar cycles tells me that that holiday, like all other holidays, is at least somewhat related to the Wheel of Time, which predated all religions. Earth-based spirituality reminds us of our connection to each other as fellow humans on the planet Earth. Perhaps the Wheel of Time could be the basis for a new Pax Romana, a foundation upon which people of all faiths could celebrate our differences, while still feeling interconnected to each other through the Wheel of Time.

I know it might sound crazy but perhaps we can build bridges with other faiths by illuminating the underlying connections between us. You may celebrate Christmas, or Hanukkah, or Yule, or Alban Arthuan, or Kuleda, or Dongzhi, or Pongal, or Soyal, but we know that all these holidays stem from the same underlying observance of the winter solstice. And, the solstice, unlike religious beliefs, is a very real, scientific phenomenon, and is a basic part of life on earth. And, what it symbolizes in the life-cycle is just as real and universal.

Though each religion has a different story of what they celebrate and why, the underlying theme of the holiday is essentially the same. With the winter solstice, the message is the same in all religions: the promise of salvation and the promise of a new spring, however you may define that. It is also a holiday celebrating the turning of the Wheel of Time. Of course, how could it not be universal? As we've seen, all the different religious holidays, at each time of the year, all stem from the same pagan root-holidays in prehistory.

Earth-based spirituality can be a uniting principle that includes and binds all religions together. So, you can keep your specific religious beliefs, and still acknowledge a deeper connection with people of other religions. Just think what might happen if the people of the world could see that all religions stem from a common root.

This would not create a religion or a particular sect of religion, but would build a network of bridges between all religions and all of humanity. There may be many different denominations of Christianity, such as Baptist, Lutheran, Methodist, etc. Nonetheless, they are all Christians. Perhaps, we could create an underlying, Earth-based, spiritual platform that people of all faiths can acknowledge.

The above sentiment might seem like a pipe dream. But, just remember that Christianity was once an outlawed religion, and that Christians were persecuted, hunted down, and killed by the Roman Empire for literally hundreds of years. In spite of that, eventually Christianity became the official religion of Rome. So, who knows what the world might be like in a couple hundred of years when global climate change reshapes the shorelines of the world, as well as our societies' beliefs, and attitudes? Perhaps a new form of Earth-based spirituality could unite people of all faiths around the world after all.

Perhaps the realities of global climate change will be a wake-up call to people of all faiths. Just as the Judeo-Christian and Muslim religions have been so prominent the last millennium, perhaps Earth-based spirituality will grow to be a worldwide movement in the next millennium. Then people all over the world, of all faiths, can share a common reverence for life and for our planet, as embodied by the Wheel of Time. This wouldn't end all human strife, but it would certainly be a start.

And that's a cheerful thought.

EPILOGUE:

THE ILLUMINATION OF CHRISTIANS

There's one thing about my research into the history of Christian and pagan holidays that perplexes and amuses me. There are some fundamentalist Christians nowadays that acknowledge that our Christian holidays originally stemmed from pagan holidays. I have heard them speak and have read their literature. I have researched many of them for this book. I actually found this form of Christianity quite refreshing. Each time, I found myself agreeing completely with everything they had to say. And, I am astonished that here is a fundamentalist Christian openly declaring that perhaps Jesus is not the reason for the season of Christmas.

Such people usually go on to explain that the Christian holidays are really identical to pagan holidays, celebrated thousands of years before the life of Jesus. They say that virtually everything people associate with our Christian holidays actually originated in far more ancient pagan beliefs and practices.

The whole time, I am in total agreement with them. Then, at some point, they all do the same thing; they take a sudden sharp turn in their thinking, and it surprises me every time.

At some point in their discussion, article, book or sermon, the person in question almost always says something to the effect of:

Now that we know that everything we hold dear about our Christian traditions and holidays are really far more ancient and meaningful than we had ever imagined, we should STOP celebrating them. And, if there is any deeply spiritual, pre-Christian symbolism that lies at the very heart of our Christian holidays and traditions, then we should AVOID it at all costs.

This makes no sense to me at all. It's actually quite comical. It reminds me of the old George Burns act, with his wife Gracie Allen. At the end of his show, he'd say *"Say goodnight, Gracie."* And she'd say *"Goodnight Gracie!"* In other words, she got the information right, but she misunderstood the meaning. And that's what I think many of these well-meaning Christians may be doing.

Of course, I understand where they are coming from. Their intention is to be faithful to their Christian beliefs and not to mistakenly practice any pagan rituals or traditions. But, I don't think that they fully grasp what they have learned about the history of their own religion.

What we have shown in this book is that the very essence of Christian beliefs, including the virgin birth, Jesus being the son of god, the miracles, the resurrection after 3 days, and the promise of salvation, were all borrowed from previous pagan beliefs. It was only the specifics of the story, such as the name *Jesus*, where he lived, and the time in which he lived, that was truly unique. It is the same story with a different protagonist. And, isn't it the moral of the story more important than the name of the protagonist?

Consider the following analogy. Let's say that I'm the proud owner of a Lexus. And, I really love my Lexus. Then, one day, suppose someone told me that my beautiful new Lexus was actually made by Toyota. Would I suddenly hate it now that I know it's a Toyota? Would I drive it straight to the dealership, and trade it in on a Chevy?

Millions of Christians are really celebrating ancient pagan holidays, thinking that they are celebrating Christian holidays. And, they dearly love their holidays. But, when confronted with the truth, and once they realize the real history of Christianity, you'd think they might become more interested in the history of their religion, or in paganism, or both. Most people probably do, but there is a minority of Christians who become even less open-minded.

I have only met one person who actually changed his religion after he learned the true history of Christianity while studying to become a Pastor. And, he became a Messianic Jew. Go figure.

Once you understand the real history and meaning of Christmas, how, why, and when we celebrate it the way we do, then it's obvious; the real *reason for the season* of Christmas is the winter solstice. After all, the solstice and the rebirth of the sun god was the very reason that the holiday existed in the first place, thousands of years before the birth of Jesus.

But, there is a deeper, even more spiritual meaning: the promise of new life in the middle of the season of death. The evergreen tree, holly, and mistletoe, which stay green all winter, symbolizes that there is still life even after death. The turning of the sun again towards spring reminds us of the promise of reincarnation and rebirth, or at least an afterlife. This is the deeper, more spiritual meaning that predated Christianity, and, whether we realize it or not, I think it is an underlying factor in how and why we celebrate Christmas to this day.

I don't think that the early Church leaders were mistaken when they combined these pagan traditions with Christianity. The existing pagan traditions were imbued with deep meaning, which is not inconsistent with the teachings of Jesus. The two complimented each other. The meaning and symbolism were already there. And, Jesus humanized it, and made it more relatable.

Unfortunately, some conservative Christians hold fast to the story of the Bible, but reject many of the spiritual traditions of Christianity, like the symbolism of the evergreens at Christmas, or eggs at Easter. They reject everything except the orthodox theology of the Apostle Paul in the Bible, even though it bears little resemblance to the actual teachings of Jesus, as quoted in the same Bible.[1, 2]

For now, I will continue to encourage devout Christians who have learned about the pagan origin of their holidays to continue celebrating Christmas, Easter, Halloween, and all the rest. I encourage them to invest in these holidays the very spirit, heart, and soul of their spiritual beliefs.

I say this to help people redeem their holidays but, more importantly, to reaffirm and strengthen their spiritual faith, which I believe is of great value. Because, while many people nowadays are discovering that they can practice their spirituality in the absence of religion, unfortunately some continue to practice their religion in the absence of spirituality.

APPENDIX:

A CATACLYSMIC START TO THE BRONZE AGE

The following is an edited excerpt from a previous book *The Einstein Connection: Ancient Myths & Scientific Theories of an Approaching Global Cataclysm,* by D. W. Kreger.

Any historian or archaeologist will tell you that recorded history began roughly 5,000 years ago, at just about the start of the Mayan Long Count in 3,114 BCE. There are two odd features of this. First, civilization seems to have broken out everywhere at once. Fairly advanced civilizations appeared in Egypt, Mesopotamia, Mesoamerica, South America, China, the Mediterranean, Great Britain, and the Indus Valley in India, all about the same time.

There were also massive building projects all around the globe at that time as well, such as Newgrange in Ireland, Stonehenge in England, Skara Brae in Scotland, Hagar Qim in Malta, the White Temple and Anu Ziggurat in Uruk, Shahr-i-Sokhta in Persia, Mohenjo-daro in the Indus Valley, and the Great Pyramids of Egypt, and all of them date from roughly the same period. And civilizations with rich traditions of science, literature, mythology, art and architecture were popping up everywhere. The Sumerian civilization, the Yang Shao civilization of China, and the first dynasty of Egypt, and the beginning of the Olmec culture, all date to about the 3rd Millennium BCE.

Secondly, as already mentioned, they were all fairly advanced compared with the civilizations that followed. That seems strange. We all know that cultures are supposed to progress and develop over time, not begin more advanced then digress, and become less advanced over time. Similar to the Harappan civilization, the oldest structures in Egypt, the Great Pyramids, are the most advanced in the history of Egypt.

And of course many of these structures such as Stonehenge, Newgrange, or Hagar Qim are marvels of engineering that were not surpassed for thousands of years. One could argue that the architecture of the Egyptian Pyramids has never been surpassed. In every case, these building projects occurred in about the same time period and what came later was always less advanced.

We see this same pattern with the stone masonry in Central and South America. Many believe that the massive and advanced stone work of Machu Piccu, Sacsahuaman, and the giant Olmec carvings are older than archaeologists think, and may well date to the second or third millennium BCE. The Olmecs, who predate the Maya and Aztecs, were the ones responsible for creating the brilliant Maya calendar system, and also created some huge, very skillful, anatomically correct human sculptures. When you compare the massive stonework mentioned above to that of the Maya or Aztecs, which followed, the earlier civilizations appear to be more advanced technologically and artistically.

The same is true in Mesopotamia. The Assyrian King Aššurbāniapl collected ancient clay tablets from far and wide, forming a library in Nineveh in the 7th century BCE. He apparently collected tablets of ancient knowledge including literature and astronomical information that were possibly thousands of years old at the time. Yet, the culture that he lived in was not believed to be as sophisticated or erudite as the works that he sought to preserve.

It appears that with each new millennium in the Mesopotamian region, the culture became gradually less sophisticated and less knowledgeable. Eventually Nineveh was sacked and burned by the Babylonians, and the region descended even further from its former glory. From Sumer to the Assyrian culture, to the chaos that followed, each generation appears to have lost some of the knowledge and culture of their ancestors. How is that possible? That's not how society is supposed to progress.

THE TURNING POINT

Something happened in the 3rd Millennium BCE, but what? One possible scenario that fits the archaeological data might go something like this. A great and advanced global civilization was all but wiped out by some global catastrophe, possibly the great flood that is often mentioned in ancient mythology. The survivors might have migrated and created a new civilization, which started out as very advanced, then gradually they forgot the advanced knowledge and technology of their ancestors. When did this occur? Well, there is no record of any advanced civilization anywhere much prior to about 3,100 BCE. And what cultures did exist, such as the Varna and Çatalhöyük cultures disappeared at right about this same time period. This was the start of what we call the Bronze Age. Prior to this date, it is believed that humanity was coming out of the Stone Age.

In Egypt, Sumer, Crete, Shahr-i-Sokhta, Mohenjo-daro, and elsewhere, the Bronze Age broke out at about the same time all over the world. The Bronze Age of China soon followed, but as I documented in my previous book, *The Secret Tao*, in many respects the early Bronze Age dynasties of China were more barbaric and less sophisticated than their supposedly stone age ancestors, the Yang Shao people of 3,100 BCE.

So roughly 5,100 years ago advanced civilizations appeared all over the world at once. And, at about the same time, they all started to gradually de-evolve, losing wisdom, and losing ancient knowledge. They lost the building techniques that we see in the Egyptian Pyramids or Stonehenge. They lost the knowledge of the electrical devices found in Akrotiri and Bagdad, and the knowledge of how to prepare maps with proper longitude and latitude, as demonstrated by Charles Hapgood.

They seem to have eventually lost knowledge of advanced city planning seen in the Harrapan cities of the Indus Valley (3000 BCE), knowledge of the precession of the equinoxes, knowledge of the earth orbiting the Sun, knowledge of binary star systems, and much, much more. Some things, such as warfare, greed, and classist societies increased, but it seems that the noblest aspects of humanity, especially scientific knowledge, were gradually becoming lost, only to be rediscovered thousands of years later.

CATACLYSM OF 3,100 BCE

So what happened about 5100 years ago? Well, according to many geologists it may indeed have been a time of global geo-thermal instability and increased seismic and volcanic activity. Additionally, some spectacular, if not particularly sudden, flooding occurred. In addition to the possible Harappan cities found in the bay of Khambhat, the history of Mesopotamia also may lie under the sea, and might have occurred about the same time.

Jeffery Rose, a research fellow at the Institute of Archaeology and Antiquity, at the University of Birmingham has been doing some very interesting underwater archaeology in the Persian Gulf. In a recent article he cites the fact that the Persian Gulf was a lush green fertile plain, about the size of Great Britain, prior to the melting of the last ice age. He calls this land the Arabo-Persian Gulf Oasis, as it was between the deserts of Arabia and Persia.

The Arabo-Persian Gulf Oasis was a lush flood-plain at the bottom of a confluence of four major rivers, two of which are the famous Tigris and Euphrates rivers. If you know your Bible then you might recognized this description. This *oasis* may well have contained the site of the mythical Garden of Eden. And, just as in the bible, the people there were progressively driven out, and eventually their land was completely flooded, as in the epic of Gilgamesh and the story of Noah.

After the ice age ended and the ice began to melt, this large basin of land began to fill with water. Slowly over thousands of years, somewhere between 6,000 BC and 4,000 BC, according to Rose, the area became the sea that we now know as the Persian Gulf. This explains the sudden appearance of cultures all around the Persian Gulf, dating to just before 3,100 BC, including Mesopotamia, ancient Iran, and the Indus valley.

Recent archaeological digs in Iran, just north of the Persian Gulf have confirmed that a number of fairly advanced and sizeable cities were established at about the same time, 3,200 BCE; these include Shahr-i-Sokhta, Shahdad, Jiroft, and Tepe Yahya. Note that these cities were about halfway between the contemporary civilizations of Sumer in the west and Mohenjo-daro in the east, and were located just north of what was the Arabo-Persian Gulf Oasis.

Such flooding may also explain migration into parts of what is now Arabia, Egypt and Yemen. And of course all of these cultures appear fully formed, with little history of progressive development, because they had probably been developing for 10,000 years in the now flooded Persian Gulf Oasis. All traces of their early attempts of civilization, like their Harappan neighbors, might now be completely lost to the sea.

MESOAMERICA PRIOR TO 3,100 BCE

We know that sea levels rose all over the world at this time. Though we have less clear evidence in other parts of the world, there is no doubt that other early civilizations emerged about the same time in the Americas, India, and China. The great Olmec civilization, beginning with the "Pre-Olmec" culture, began at least 4,500 years ago, within a few hundred years of the beginning of the Long Count, 3,114 BC, a calendar system which was actually created by the Olmecs. As mentioned before, the Olmec culture appears very advanced. But where did the Olmecs come from? Again, the oldest artifacts of the Olmecs may also be underwater.

There are vast areas off the coast of the Gulf of Mexico that have not been fully explored. It is estimated that both the Yucatan peninsula and the state of Florida had a land-mass that was more than twice the size of today, and there was a strip of dry land nearly as wide as Florida that extended all the way around the Gulf, which is now submerged. Though no Pre-Olmec sites have been found in these areas yet, there are thousands of square miles to cover, and no systematic effort has yet been attempted.

Some archaeological sites have reportedly been found in shallow water off the coast of Cuba, under the Yucatan Channel, and underwater in Belize. And of course there is the now famous Bimini road in the Bahamas, off the coast of Florida. This may just be a strange rock formation, but appears to be a series of square blocks laid down, in a straight row, three abreast like a road, about a half a mile long.

Archaeological finds from prior to the third millennium BCE have turned up, but not where you'd normally expect to find them. In the last decade underwater archaeological sites have been discovered in the Yucatan Peninsula in cenotes, which are caves that are now filled with water, but were once dry thousands of years ago. Reportedly a whole host of artifacts have been found in the cenotes, which indicate evidence of human habitation going back 10,000 years or more.

Some people report finding roads, walls and other stone structures as well in these cenotes. This corresponds very well to the accounts of the Xibalba (underworld) in the Popol Vuh. In this way we can validate that there was indeed a time, prior to the recorded history of the Maya, in which the people of Mesoamerica lived in a now flooded underworld.

In South America, there are the ruins of Tiahuanaco a vast pre-Incan city with a population of more than 40,000 people. The city appears to have been occupied for a very long time, up until about 1,000 years ago. While most artifacts at Tiahuanaco are more recent, 2,000 years old or less, there is one artifact that has caused quite a stir. In one unexplored area near the ruins, a local worker in the 1950's found the Fuenta Magna, a bowl with what appears to be Sumerian cuneiform writing on it, it has been dated to 3,100 – 3,500 BCE. Of course, skeptics claim it is a fake. Later, however, archaeologists found yet another artifact in the same area, a sculpture more consistent with the look of other sculpture at Tiahuanaco, and it too has cuneiform writing on it.

We may never know when Tiahuanaco was actually founded because we cannot date the rocks using carbon dating techniques, we can only date when the rock itself was formed in the Earth, not when it was carved. But if it was founded around 3,100 BC, as the date of the Fuenta Magna suggests, then it certainly fits with other fairly advanced civilizations springing up all over the world at the same time. And it even suggests a possible connection with the flooded ancient people of the Arabian-Persian Gulf Oasis, the Sumerians.

GLOBAL FLOODING

In Asia, there are vast areas off the coast of China in the Yellow Sea near the mouth of the Yellow River valley, which were once dry land and are now submerged beneath the sea. This area extends from China all the way out to Korea and the southern coast of Japan. This region is another area where some think that they have found a giant underwater stone structure. It is here that they have discovered the *Yonaguni* monument. Though, it is still unclear if it is human-made or merely a natural stone monument that was used by humans, but there is no doubt that this monument was on dry land, thousands of years in the past.

The flooding is not in dispute. It is a geological fact that there was global flooding at the end of the last ice age, finally concluding around 5000 to 6000 years ago, resulting in our present shorelines. The question is whether this explains the many flood myths found from around the world, and also explains the beginning of the current Mayan Long Count as being a little over 5000 years ago.

This would indeed have been seen as a new epoch of humanity as hundreds of thousands of people, possibly more, were forced to migrate to higher and drier land just prior to about 3,100 BC. This certainly seems to validate the Gilgamesh/Noah narrative that is so ubiquitous in myths from around the world. It also validates the great flood reported in both the Maya and Aztec mythologies.

-The above appendix was an edited excerpt from a previous book: *The Einstein Connection* by D. W. Kreger.

SUMMARY

The above excerpt may help to contextualize our research on the Wheel of Time. It suggests, just as the Vedic Scriptures claim, there was an advanced ancient civilization that existed before recorded history. That civilization was then destroyed through some type of cataclysm, possibly due to global flooding. It also suggests that ancient advanced civilizations in different parts of the world may have been in contact with each other, shared ideas, information, and even cultural beliefs. For instance, we know that the ancient Mayan Calendar is almost identical to the ancient Egyptian Calendar. Both are quite intricate, very advanced, and otherwise unique, but how could this occur, unless they had some contact with each other?

As we've seen in this book, people all over the earth built massive monuments, often for the express purpose of marking certain days of the year or phases of the sun. The connections between all these different monuments from around the world are a bit uncanny. I have tried to explain it away to some extent, saying that it's just an artifact of being a human on the planet Earth. I said that it's inevitable that people on opposite sides of the planet might have similar ideas and beliefs, especially regarding a common phenomenon, like the seasons. But, maybe it's more than just that.

If there was a global civilization that existed in what we call the Neolithic Age (10,000 to 4,500 BCE), then that would certainly explain a lot of the coincidences presented in this book. Maybe it wasn't just a coincidence that civilizations all over the world celebrated the same 8 major holidays, all imbued with very much the same cultural and spiritual meaning. Then they each deviated from each other in the millennia that followed. If this is true, then the Wheel of Time might well have been a universally known system of thought in an ancient global civilization. And, that's ...pretty cool.

REFERENCES & NOTES

CHAPTER 1: UNDERSTANDING NEOLITHIC PEOPLES & THEIR PAGAN BELIEFS

1. This is an excerpt from a previous book by D.W. Kreger, *The Secret Tao: Uncovering the hidden history and meaning of Lao Tzu* (Windham Everitt, 2011), 8-10.

2. Andrew Curry, 'The Neolithic Toolkit', *Archaeology Magazine,* (Nov/Dec. 2014).

3. According to the *Oxford English Dictionary*, Third Edition (2005).

CHAPTER 2: ARCHAEOLOGICAL EVIDENCE OF THE BRITISH ISLES

1. Roff Smith, 'World's Oldest Calendar Discovered in U. K.' (July 16, 2013), www.*National Geographic.com.*

2. To build your own solar observatory in your backyard, see the *About Stonehenge* website, and under the Education menu, see Build Your Own Stonehenge, accessed at www.aboutstonehenge.info.

3. A great survey of the area, including a CD Rom with photos and GIS computer generated images is found in Sally Exon, et al., Stonehenge Landscapes: Journeys Through Real and Imagined Worlds (Archaeopress, 2000).

4. Mike Parker Pearson & The Stonehenge Riverside Project, *Stonehenge – A New Understanding: Solving the Mysteries of the Greatest Stone Age Monument* (The Experiment LLC, 2013).

5. C. Gaffney, et al., 'The Stonehenge Hidden Landscapes Project', *Archaeological Prospection* 19:2 (April/June 2012),147-155.

6. Mike Parker Pearson, *Stonehenge – A New Understanding.*

7. Giulio Magli, *Mysteries and Discoveries of Archaeoastronomy* (Copernicus Books, 2009), 274.

8. Mike Parker Pearson, *Stonehenge – A New Understanding.*

9. See NOVA, episode: 'Secretes of Stonehenge' on PBS (2010).

10. Julius Caesar, *The Gallic War,* (Oxford University Press, *2008), 127.*

11. Kreger, *The Secret Tao,* 157

12. Ibid

13. C. Gaffney, et al., 'The Stonehenge Hidden Landscapes Project', 147-155.

14. For more information, see Muiris O'Sullivan, *Dumha na nGiall: Tara, The Mound of the Hostages* (Wordwell Books, 2005).

15. For more information on Mound of the Hostages, see www.Knoweth.com, under Tara, see Mound of Hostages.

16. Michael Dames, *Silbury Treasure: The Great Goddess Rediscovered* (Thames & Hudson Ltd, 1978); and Dames, *Silbury: Resolving the Enigma* (The History Press Ltd, 2010). Also see Dames *The Avebury Cycle* (Thames & Hudson Ltd., 1996) for his interpretation of the annual fertility cycle corresponding to the agricultural year.

17. Eric A. Powell, 'White Horse of the Sun', *Archaeology* 70:5 (2017), 9-10.

18. Hugh Williams, *Gildas the Wise: The Ruin of Britan, Fragments from Lost Letters, The Penitential, Together with the Lorica of Gildas* (Bedford Press, 1899). Also see John Allen Giles (1847) original translation in a new kindle edition, David Long (Ed) *The Fall of Roman Britan,* (Amazon Digital Services, Inc., 2016).

19. Eleanor Hull translation, 'The Wooing of Emer', *The Cuchullin Saga in Irish Literature* (David Nutt in the Strand, 1898), 55.

20. Fairfax Harrison translation, *Roman Farm Management – The Treaties of Cato and Varro* (Qontro Classic Books, 2010), 99.

CHAPTER 3:
STRIKING GOLD IN PREHISTORY EUROPE

1. Howard Crowhurst, *Carnac, The Alignments: When Art and Science were one* (Plouharnel: Epistemea, 2010).

2. Alexander Thom, 'The Carnac Alignments' *Journal for the History of Astronomy*', 3: (1972) 11–26. And see other articles by Thom: 'The Astronomical Significance of the Large Carnac Menhirs', 'The Uses and Alignments at Le Menec, Carnac', and 'The Kerlescan Cromlechs', all in *Journal for the History of Astronomy.*

3. Ulrich Boser, 'Solar Circle', *Archaeology* 59:4, (July/August 2006), http://ar-

chive.archaeology.org/0607/abstracts/henge.html.

4. The two sites are only 0.02 degrees of latitude apart. Stonehenge is at latitude: 51.17°North, and Gosseck Circle is at latitude 51.19°North.

5. Nora Chadwick, *The Celts* (Penguin Books, 1970), 28-33. Also see *The Mystery of the Four Golden Hats of the Bronze Age*, posted February 1, 2015, www.ancient-origins.net.

6. See *Bede: On the Nature of Things and on Times* (Liverpool University Press, 2010).

7. Sol Adoni, *Lost Ancient Civilizations: Gobekli Tepe - Dwarka - Bosnian Pyramids - Gornaya Shoria - Arkaim - Mount Lalakon* (Adoni Publishing, 2014)

CHAPTER 4: ANCIENT MONUMENTS FROM AROUND THE WORLD

1. D. H. Trump, *Malta Prehistory and Temples* (Midsea Books, Ltd., 2002).

2. Ibid.

3. Giore Cenev, *Ancient Secrets of Kokino Observatory*, (CreateSpace, 2012).

4. Paris Herouni, *Armenians and Old Armenia, Archaeoastronomy, Linguistics, Oldest History* (Tigran Metz Publishing House, 2004) .

5. For more on this topic see Erich von Däniken, *Chariots of the Gods: Unsolved Mysteries of the Past* (Berkley Publishing Group, 1970), or any of his newer books on ancient astronauts.

6. Peter Tompkin, *Secrets of the Great Pyramid* (Harper Collins, 1978), and Charles Piazzi Smyth, *Great Pyramid: Its Secrets and Mysteries Revealed* (Bell Publishing, 1994).

7. Zajo Hawass, *The Mysteries of Abu Simbel: Ramesses II and the Temples of the Rising Sun* (American University in Cairo Press, 2001).

8. B. M. Lynch, and L. H. Robbins, 'Namoratunga: The First Archeoastronomical Evidence in Sub-Shaharan Africa', *Science* 19: 4343 (May 1978), 766-768.

9. Giulio Magli, *Mysteries and Discoveries of Archaeoastronomy.*

10. Ibid, 250-251.

11. Bill McCann, *The Emperors of China in a Nutshell, Volume 1: From the Yellow Emperor to the Xia Dynasty* (CreateSpace, 2015).

12. He Nu and Wu Jiabi, *Astronomical Date of the 'Observatory' at Taosi Site* (Institute of Archaeology, Chinese Academy of Social Sciences, 2005), accessed at www.kaogu.cn/en/Forum/2013/1025/29941.html

13. Ibid.

14. R. J. Wenke, *Patterns in Prehistory: Mankind's First Three Million Years* (Oxford University Press, 1980).

15. Jai Maharaj 'First Astro Observatory of Harappan Civilization Found in Kutchh', *Hinduism Today* (February 27, 2012).

16. Dearborn, Schreiber, and White, 'Inimachay: A December Solstice Observatory at Machu Piccu, Peru', *American Antiquity* 52:2 (1987), 356-352.

17. Ibid, 356.

18. Ivan Ghessi and Clive Ruggles, 'Chankillo: A 2300 Year Old Solar Observatory in Coastal Peru', *Science* 315:5816 (March 2, 2007), 1239-1243.

19. D. W. Kreger, *2012 and the Mayan Prophecy of Doom* (Windham Everitt, 2012)

20. Anthony Aveni, *Skywatchers* (University of Texas Press, 1980).

21. Anthony Aveni 'The Caracol Tower at Chichen Itza: An Ancient Astronomical Observatory?' *Science* 181:4192 (1975), 977-985. Also see William Stockton, 'Ancient Astronomy Points to New Views of Mayan Life' *New York Times,* Science Section, (March 25, 1986).

22. James Aimers and Prudence Rice, 'Astronomy, Ritual, and the Interpretation of May E-Group Architechtural Assemblages', *Ancient Mesoamerica* 17:01 (2006), 79-96.

23. Takeshi Inomata, et al., 'Early Ceremonial Constructions at Ceibal, Guatemala, and the Origins of Lowland Maya Civilization', *Science* 340:6131 (2013) 467-471.

24. Özgür Baris Etli, *The Secret of Göbekli Tepe: Cosmic Equinox and Sacred Marriage,* Unpublished paper (Ege University, Turkey, 2015).

CHAPTER 5: EXCAVATING ANCIENT OBSERVATORIES OF NORTH AMERICA

1. From David S. Whitley, *A Guide to Rock Art Sites* (Mountain Press Publishing Co., 1996), 31-32.

2. D. W. Kreger, 'Pathological Skepticism', *Atlantis Rising Magazine* 105: (May/June 2014) 40, 67-68.

3. D. W. Kreger, *Documenting Evidence of a Native American Astronomical Marker*, Poster presentation at the Annual Meeting of the Archaeological Institute of America, Chicago (January 2-5, 2014).

4. See 'Bighorn Medicine Wheel' (Stanford Solar Center, 2008), accessed at www.solar-center.stanford.edu/AO/bighorn.html.

5. Ray Williamson, *Living the Sky: The Cosmos of the American Indian*, (University of Oklahoma Press, 1987).

6. John Niehardt, *Black Elk Speaks: Being the Life Story of a Holy Man of the Oglala Sioux* (University of Nebraska Press, 1988).

7. Whitley, *A Guide to Rock Art Sites*, 32.

8. Claudia Mink, *Cahokia: City of the Sun: Prehistoric Urban Center in the American Bottom,* 3rd Edition, (Cahokia Mounds Museum Society, 1992).

9. Giulio Magli, *Mysteries and Discoveries of Archaeoastronomy,* 120-124.

10. Ibid, 122-123.

11. Ibid, 139-140.

12. Ibid, 140.

13. Ibid, 138.

14. See Kreger, *The Secret Tao.*

15. For this and other amazing discoveries, see Ray Urbaniak, *Anasazi of SW Utah: The Dance of Light & Shadow* (Natural Frequency/Sanctuary House Press, 2006).

16. Kreger *The Secret Tao,* 86-91, 205, 302.

17. Kreger, *Documenting Evidence of a Native American Astronomical Marker.*

18. Ibid.

19. Ibid.

20. Eric A. Powell, 'Reading the White Shaman Mural', *Archaeology* 70:6, (2017), 32-39.

CHAPTER 6: HOW TO SOLVE AN ARCHAEOLOGICAL PUZZLE

1. Michael Wood, *In Search of the Trojan War* (University of California Press, 1998).

2. Marija Gimbutas, *The Civilization of the Goddess: The World of Old Europe* (Harper Collins, 1992).

3. Hull, 'The Wooing of Emer', *The Cuchullin Saga in Irish Literature*, 55.

4. Harrison, *Roman Farm Management – The Treaties of Cato and Varro*, 99.

CHAPTER 7: EVIDENCE OF ACHAEO-ASTRONOMY & CYCLIC MOTIFS

1. See Swami Sri Yukteswar Giri, *The Holy Science* (Self-Realization Fellowhip, 1990).

2. Ibid, p. 7

3. George Forbes, *History of Astronomy* (CreateSpace, 2014).

4. Ibid.

5. D. W. Kreger, *The Einstein Connection* (Windham Everitt Publishing, 2014), 110-118, 192-202.

6. Carl Jung, *Man and His Symbols* (Doubleday, 1968), 225.

7. Thomas McEvilley, *The Shape of Ancient Thought: Comparative Studies in Greek and Indian Philosophies* (Allworth Press, 2002).

8. Michael Baigent, *Astrology in Ancient Mesopotamia: The Science of Omens and the Knowledge of the Heavens* (Bear & Company, 2015).

9. James Hastings (Ed), *The Encyclopedia of Religion and Ethics* (Bloomsbury T&T Clark, 2000).

10. For more information, see D. W. Kreger, *2012 & The Mayan Prophecy of Doom* (Windham Everitt Publishing, 2012), 26-42.

11. Ibid, 28.

12. Ibid.

13. Ibid.

14. Khristaan Villela & Mary Miller (Eds), *Mexican Calendar Stone* (Getty Research Institute, 2010).

CHAPTERS 8 & 9 (COMBINED): HOW OUR HOLY DAYS EVOLVED, AMONG THE ENGLISH

CHAPTER 8:

1. Caesar, *The Gallic War.*

2. Helena Norberg-Hodge, *Ancient Futures: Learning from Ladakh* (Sierra Club Books, 1991).

3. Caesar, *The Gallic War,* 127.

4. Ibid, p. 128.

5. C. H. Oldfather, *Diodorus Siculus: Library of History, Loeb Classical Library* (Harvard University Press, 1935).

6. Caesar, *The Gallic War,* 128.

7. H. Rackham, *Pliny: Natural History, Volume IV, Books 12-16, Loeb Classical Library, No. 370* (Harvard University Press, 1945).

8. Garrett S. Olmsted, '*A* Definitive Reconstructed Text of the Coligny Calendar', *Journal of Indo-European Studies,* Monograph 39 (2001).

9. Thomas Kinsella, *The Tain: Translated From the Irish Epic Tain Bo Cuailnge* (Oxford University Press, 1981).

10. John Matthews, *Taliesin: The Last Celtic Shaman* (Inner Traditions, 2002).

11. T. H. White, *The Sword and the Stone*, third edition (Philomel Books/Penguin Books, 1993).

12. Matthews, *Taliesin: The Last Celtic Shaman.*

13. Hull, 'The Wooing of Emer', in *The Cuchullin Saga in Irish Literature,* 55.

14. Hugh Williams, *Gildas the Wise.*

15. Rebecca Fraser, *The Story of Britain: From the Romans to the Present: A Narrative History* (W. W. Norton & Company, 2005).

CHAPTER 9:

16. Ibid.

17. Bede, *The Ecclesiastical History of the English People* (Tiger of the Stripe, 2007).

18. Faith Wallis, translation, *Bede: The Reckoning of Time* (Liverpool University Press, 1999).

19. Ibid.

20. Nathan Bushwick, *Understading the Jewish Calendar* (Moznaim Publishing Corp, 1989). And, for more information about the history and meaning of the Jewish holidays see Micahel Strassfeld, *The Jewish Holidays: A Guide and Commentary* (Quill/HarperCollins Publishers, 1985).

21. Ibid.

22. Nennius, *History of the Britons* (Kessinger Publishing, 2004)

23. Ibid.

24. J. Williams (Ed.), *Annals Cambriae* (Nabu Press, 2013)

25. See *The Vulgate Version of the Arthurian Romances v. 1-7* (University of California Libraries, 1908).

26. Sir Thomas Malory, *Le Morte D'Arthur: The Winchester Manuscritpt*, (Oxford University Press, 1998).

27. Washington Irving, *The Legend of Sleepy Hollow and Other Stories From the Sketch Book* (Signet Classics, 2006); and Mary Shelly, *Frankenstein* (Barnes & Noble Classics, 2003).

28. Lord Byron, *Lord Byron: The Major Works* (Oxford University Press, 2008).

29. Ibid, and see Lord Byron, 'Fragment of a Novel' in *Mazeppa* (John Murry, 1819).

30. Bram Stoker, *Dracula* (Barnes & Noble Classics, 2003).

31. Charles Dickens, *Stories for Christmas by Charles Dickens* (Platinum Press, 2003).

32. Ibid.

33. Walter Scott, *Ivanhoe* (Penguin Books, 2000).

34. Jacob & Wilhelm Grimm, *The Collected Works of Brothers Grimm: The Complete Works* (PergamonMedia/Kindle Edition, 2015)

35. Clement Clarke Moore, *Twas the Night Before Christmas* (Golden Books/Random House, 1973).

36. L. Frank Baum, *The Wonderful Wizard of Oz* (Geo. M. Hill Co., 1900); and L. Frank Baum, *The Life and Adventures of Santa Claus* (Bowen Merrill, 1902).

CHAPTER 10: THE WINTER SOLSTICE: A GLOBAL SURVEY

1. Earl W. Count, *4000 Years of Christmas: A Gift from the Ages* (Seastone/Ulysses Press, 1997) and Anna Franklin, *Yule* (Lear Books, 2010), www.learbooks.co.uk.

2. Plutarch, *Plutarch: Complete Works* (Delphi Classics, 2013); and also see Geraldine Pinch, *Egyptian Mythology: A Guide to the Gods, Goddesses, and Traditions of Ancient Egypt* (Oxford University Press, 2004).

3. Steven Hijmans, 'Sol Invictus, the Winter Solstice, and the Origins of Christmas', *Mouseion* Series III: 3 (2003), 377-398.

4. Linda Raedisch, *The Old Magic of Christmas: Yuletide Traditions for the Darkest Days of the Year* (Llewellyn Publications, 2013).

5. Ronald Hutton, *The Pagan Religions of the Ancient British Isles: Their Nature and Legacy* (Wiley-Blackwell, 1993); and Pauline Campanelli *Ancient Ways: Reclaiming Pagan Traditions* (Llewellyn Publications, 2001).

6. For a great, short synopsis, see Cyrus Adler, *Hanukkah: A Short Story* (Amazon Digital Services, 2012).

7. For an interesting collection of celebrations from around the world, see Carolyn McVickar Edwards, *The Return of the Light: Twelve Tales from Around the World for the Winter Solstice* (Marlowe & Company, 2000).

8. 'Dongzhi Festival' at *www.chinaholidays.com/culture/winter-solstice-festival.html.*

9. 'What is Pongal' at *www.pongalfestival.org/what-is-pongal.html*

10. 'Soyal Ceremony: Hopi Kachinas Dance at Winter Solstice' at *www.wilderutopia.com/traditions/soyal-ceremony-hopi-kachinas-dance-at-winter-solstice.*

11. 'Witches and Witchtrials in England, the Channel Islands, Ireland and Scot-

land', at *www.personal.utulsa.edu/%7Emarc-carlson/witchtrial/eis.html*

12. See 'Christmas Abolished: Why did Cromwell abolish Christmas?' at *www.olivercromwell.org/faqs4.htm*

CHAPTER 11: THE EIGHT SABBATHS OF THE WHEEL: A GLOBAL SURVEY

1. Many sources were used for this chapter. Several sources with much information are: Trevor Barnes *The Kingfisher Book of Religions; Festivals, Ceremonies, and Beliefs from Around the World* (Kingfisher, 1999); J. Gordon Melton *Religious Celebrations: An Encyclopedia of Holidays, Festivals, Solemn Obervances, and Spiritual Commemorations* (ABC-CLIO, LLC. 2011); Pauline and Dan Campanelli, *Ancient Ways: Reclaiming Pagan Traditions* (Llewellyn Publications, 1998); H. H. Scullard, *Festivals and Ceremonies of the Roman Republic* (Cornell University, Press, 1981); Pan Historia, 'A Festival Calendar of the Ancient Egyptians' at http://panhistoria.com/-www/VirtualTemple/calendar1.html; Richard A. Parker, *The Calendars of Ancient Egypt: Studies in Ancient Oriental Civilization No.26,* (University of Chicago Press, 1950); and, of course, *The Encyclopedia Britannica, 15th edition* (Encyclopedia Britannica, 2003) and at *http://www.britannica.com.*

2. This brings up an interesting question: when is the peak of human life? When is that point in life that correlates with summer solstice? People have varying opinions about this, it depends on how you define *peak*. Though it may seem arbitrary, there is actually some evidence to use the human age of 35 as a correlate to the summer solstice on the Wheel of Time, the peak of the year. First, 35 is close to the midpoint of the average life-span. This is also the peak of the child-rearing years. And, this is usually the peak for the careers of sports figures, before beginning to deline or retire.

Finally, if we look at famous historic figures, this is often the peak of their careers and accomplishments. This is not usually the climax of their careers, which correlates to the Autumn of the year, and may occur when a person is in their 50s, or 60s; but, it's the midpoint of thier rise to success. John F. Kennedy was elected to Congress at the age of 30 and became a U.S. Senator at the age of 36, and president at 43. Likewise, Margret Thatcher became a member of Parliment at 33, Undersecretary at the Ministry of Pensions at 36, and Education Secretary at 45, eventually becoming Prime Minister.

The same is true in science. Madam Curie became the first female faculty member at the prestigious ENS graduate school in Paris at the age of 33, won the Nobel Prize at 36, and won her second Nobel Prize at 44. Albert Einstein wrote his first paper on relativity at the age of 28, wrote his landmark book on *The General Theory of Relativity* at 37, and won the Nobel Prize at 43. This is true for almost all fields. Francis Ford Coppola won his first Oscar for Patton, at the age of 32, and would go on to win Oscars for *The Godfather* at 34, *The Godfather Part II* at 36, and had 3 Oscar nominations and won multiple awards for *Apocalypse Now*, at 40.

3. There is another reason why we may not have a more ritualized holiday in place of Lughnasadh, August 1st through the 15th. In the modern world, August is the biggest month for summer vacations. In a recent survey, well over a third of respondents say they'll take their annual vacation in August (https://aytm.com/blog/daily-survey-results/vacations-surve). People like to take their vacations in August, especially early and mid-August, right when Lughnasadh would normally be celebrated. This is not conducive to ritual celebrations. And the wealthy have been doing this for centuries, effectively erasing the holiday from high society, leaving us only with State Fairs.

4. See the section titled *The Ancient Hebrews & The Wheel of Time* in Chapter 7. In that section it is pointed out that, because of their very different climate and annual seasons in the Middle East, their New Year celebration is in the fall, and the peak of their year is in the spring. Clearly the Egyptians had a similar notion of the year, modified by the annual flooding of the Nile, which was the basis of their agricultural economy.

CHAPTER 12: THE RIDDLE SOLVED: OUR SPIRITUAL ROOTS REVEALED

1. See the Wikipedia.org entry: 'Wheel of the Year', under the 'Origins' section, first paragraph, last accessed May 11, 2017, and presumably still on the website.

2. Hull, 'The Wooing of Emer', in *The Cuchullin Saga in Irish Literature,* 55.

3. Harrison, *Roman Farm Management – The Treaties of Cato and Varro,* 99.

4. Ali Parchami, *Hegemonic Peace and Empire: The Pax Romana, Britannica and Americana* (Routledge, 2014).

5. Kreger, *The Secret Tao.*

6. Ibid, 157, 231; clearly Lao Tzu is saying that we need to accept death, yet still preserve the sustainability of our people.

7. Ibid, 47-71.

8. Ibid, 157.

CHAPTER 13: THE RISE OF ATHEIST SPIRITUALITY

1. Sam Harris, *Waking Up: A guide to Spirituality Without Religion* (Simon & Schuster, 2014).

2. See Interview by Kyle McGovern (March 31, 2017), accessed on www.Vice.com.

3. Ibid, p. 6.

4. See Bill Maher, *Real Time* on HBO (October 24, 2015), accessed on YouTube at https://www.youtube.com/watch?v=rb6AQShZSiE.

5. See the *Compact Oxford English Dictionary of Current English: Third Edition, Revised* (Oxford University Press, 2008).

6. Eben Alexander, *Proof of Heaven: A Neurosurgeon's Journey into the Afterlife* (Simon & Schuster, 2012).

7. For a concise overview of the work of Oliver Reiser, see D. W. Kreger, *The Einstein Connection* (Windham Everitt Publishing, 2014), 119-133, 202-213.

8. There is a conglomeration of support for this, yet no definitive polling. And, every year, there's new research, with slightly different results. The following are just a few articles I've seen on this topic: Peter Foster, 'Is America losing faith? Atheism on the rise but still in the shadows', *The Telegraph* (February 8th, 2014); and Michael Snyder, 'The Fastest Growing Religion in America is Witchcraft' *The Truth* (October 30th, 2013) at http://thetruthwines.com; and Howard Bess, 'None is the fastest growing religious affiliation, but not cause for worry', *Alaska Dispatch News* (March 19, 2012), where he cites a Pew research poll.

9. See posting 'Evidence is clear that homeopathy is not an effective treatment', on the *Australian Medical Association* website, (April 18, 2010) https://ama.com.au/media/evidence-clear-homeopathy-not-effective-treatment.

10.For a good book on mindfulness meitation, see John Kabat Zinn, *Wherever You Go, There You Are; Mindfulness Meditation in Everyday Life* (Hyperion, 2005).

11. See Britt and Per Karlsson, *Biodynamic, Organic and Natural Winemaking: Sustainable Viticulture and Viniculture* (Floris Books, 2014).

12. Kreger, *The Secret Tao*, 157.

13. From Katy Koontz, 'Do You Believe in Miracles?', *Parade Magazine* (March 13, 2016), 11.

14. Harris, *Waking Up: A guide to Spirituality Without Religion*; also R. Budd, *Spirituality for Atheists* (Amazon Digital Services, 2014); Mark Gura, *Atheist Meditation, Atheist Spirituality* (InnerAction Press, 2015); and Andre Comte-Sponville, *The Little Book of Atheist Spirituality* (Penguin Books, 2008).

15. Anthony T. Kronman, *Confessions of a Born Again Pagan* (Yale University Press, 2016).

16. Kreger, *The Secret Tao*, 167.

EPILOGUE: THE ILLUMINATION OF CHRISTIANS

1. Reverend Britt Minshall, *The Jesus Book: Who He Really Was: What He Really Said – A Most Unreligious Book About a Most Unreligious Man* (The Renaissance Institute Press, 2012). This is a wonderful book, which deconstructs the Bible point by point, revealing the original teachings of Jesus and how that differs from the teachings of Paul and orthodox Christian theology.

2. An excellent historical exploration of the life and theological work of the Apostle Paul can be found in Hyam Maccoby, *The Mythmaker: Paul and the Invention of Christianity* (Harper San Francisco/Harper Collins Publishers, 1986).

SELECTED BIBLIOGRAPHY

Aveni, A., *Skywatchers: A Revised and Updated Version of Skywatchers of Ancient Mexico*. Austin: University of Texas Press, 2001.

Baigent, M. *Astrology in Ancient Mesopotamia: The Science of Omens and the Knowledge of the Heavens.* Rochester: Bear & Company, 2015.

Barnes, T. *The Kingfisher Book of Religions: Festivals, Ceremonies, and Beliefs from Around the World.* New York: Kingfisher Publications, 1999.

Burchfield, R. *The English Language*. London: The Folio Society, 2006.

Bushwick, N. *Understanding the Jewish Calendar*. Brooklyn, NY: Moznaim Publishing Corp., 1989.

Caesar, J. *The Gallic War*. Oxford World Classics. New York: Oxford University Press, 1996.

Campanelli, P. *Ancient Ways: Reclaiming Pagan Traditions*. St. Paul: Llewellyn Publications, 1998.

Chadwick, N. *The Celts*. New York: Penguin Books, 1971.

Count, E. W. *4000 Years of Christmas: A Gift from the Ages*. Berkeley, CA: Ulysses Press, 1997.

Crowhurst, H. *Carnac, The Alignments: When Art and Science Were One.* Plouharnel: Epistemea, 2012.

Cruttenden, W. *Lost Star: Of Myth and Time*. Pittsburgh: St. Lynn's Press, 2006.

Curran, B. *An Encyclopedia of Celtic Mythology*. Chicago, Il: Contemporary Books, 2000.

Dames, M. *Silbury Treasure: The Great Goddess Rediscovered.* London: Thames & Hudson Ltd, 1978.

Dickens, C. *Stories for Christmas by Charles Dickens*. New York: Platinum Press, Inc., 2003.

Drury, N. *Merlin's Book of Magick and Enchantment.* New York: Metro Books, 1996.

Exon, S., Gaffney, V., Woodward, A., & Yorson, R. *Stonehenge Landscapes: Journeys Through Real-and-Imagined Worlds.* Oxford: Archaeopress, 2000.

Fletcher, J. *The Egyptian Book of Living and Dying.* New York: Chartwell Books, Inc., 2012.

Harris, S. *Waking Up: A Guide to Spirituality Without Religion.* New York: Simon & Schuster, 2014.

Herouni, P. *Armenians and Old Armenia, Archaeoastronomy, Linguistics, Oldest History.* Yerevan Armenia: Tigran Metz Publishing House, 2004.

Hull, E. (Ed.) 'The Wooing of Emer', in *The Cuchullin Saga in Irish Literature.* London: David Nutt in the Strand, 1898.

Jung, C. *The Red Book: Liber Novus.* New York: W. W. Norton *& Co.,* 2009.

Kendal, C. B. (Trans.) *Bede: On the Nature of Things and on Times.* Liverpool: Liverpool University Press, 2010.

Kreger, D. W. *The Secret Tao: Uncovering the hidden history and meaning of Lao Tzu.* Palmdale, CA: Windham Everitt Publishing, 2011.

Kreger, D. W. *2012 and the Mayan Prophecy of Doom.* Palmdale, CA: Windham Everitt Publishing, 2012.

Kreger, D. W. *The Einstein Connection.* Palmdale, CA: Windham Everitt Publishing, 2014.

Kreisberg, G. (Ed.) *Lost Knowledge of the Ancients: A Graham Hancock Reader.* Rochester, VT: Bear & Company, 2010.

Kronman, A. T. *Confessions of a Born-Again Pagan.* New Haven: Yale University Press, 2016.

Maccoby, H. *The Mythmaker: Paul and the Invention of Christianity.* New York: Harper Collins Publishers, Inc., 1986.

Magli, G. *Mysteries and Discoveries of Archaeoastronomy: From Giza to Easter Island,* New York: Copernicus Books, 2009.

Malory, T., *Le Morte D'Arthur.* New York: Barnes & Noble, 2015.

Matthews, J. *Taliesin: The Last Celtic Shaman*, Rochester: Inner Traditions, 2002.

McVickar, C. *The Return of the Light: Twelve Tales from Around the World for the Winter Solstice.* New York: Marlowe & Company, 2000.

Minshall, B. *The Jesus Book: Who He Really Was: What He Really Said – A Most Unreligious Book About a Most Unreligious Man.* Baltimore: The Renaissance Institute Press, 2012.

O'Sullivan, M. *Dumha na nGiall: Tara, The Mound of the Hostages.* Dublin: Wordwell Books, 2005.

Pearson, M. P. & The Stonehenge Riverside Project. *Stonehenge – A New Understanding: Solving the Mysteries of the Greatest Stone Age Monument.* New York: The Experiment, 2013.

Raedisch, L. *The Old Magic of Christmas: Yuletide Traditions for the Darkest Days of the Year*. Woodbury, MN: Llewellyn Publications, 2013.

Reiser, O. L. *Cosmic Humanism: A Theory of the Eight-Dimensional Cosmos Based On Integrative Principles From Science, Religion, and Art.* Cambridge: Schenkman Publishing, Co., 1966.

Schwaller de Lubicz, R. A. *Sacred Science: The King of Pharaonic Theocracy.* Rochester, VT: Inner Traditions International, 1982.

Scullard, H. H. *Festivals and Ceremonies of the Roman Republic.* Ithaca: Cornell University Press, 1981.

Sjöö, M. and Mor, B. *The Great Cosmic Mother: Rediscovering the Religion of the Earth*. San Francisco, CA: Harper San Francisco, A division of Harper Collins Publishers, 1987.

Spence, L. *Druids: Their Origins and History.* New York: Barnes & Noble, 1995.

Stewart, R. J. *Celtic Gods, Celtic Goddesses*. London: Blandford 1990.

Time-Life Books (Eds.) *What Life Was Like in the Age of Chivalry: Medieval Europe, AD 800-1500.* Richmond: Time-Life Books, 1997.

Urbaniak, R. *Anasazi of SW Utah: The Dance of Light & Shadow*, Hurricane, UT: Natural Frequency / Sanctuary House Press, 2006.

Williamson, R. *Living the Sky: The Cosmos of the American Indian*. Norman: University of Oklahoma Press, 1987.

Woolf, A. *A Short History of the World: The Story of Mankind from Prehistory to the Modern Day*. New York: Metro Books, 2008.

Yukteswar, Swami S. *The Holy Science*. (1894) Los Angeles: Self-Realization Fellowship, 1990.

INDEX

ABOUT THE AUTHOR:

D. W. Kreger

Dr. Kreger is a psychologist, an expert on the occult, and a researcher in the fields of psychology, archaeology, and ancient mysticism. He holds a Ph.D. in clinical psychology, completed his post-doctoral training in neuropsychology, and is a Diplomate of the International Academy of Behavioral Medicine, Counseling, and Psychotherapy.

In addition to his psychological research, he has investigated archaeological sites in 17 countries around the world. His work has been presented at major academic conferences, and appeared in both research journals and popular media. He has published several books, including *The Tao of Yoda,* and *The Secret Tao.* His last book *LEWD: The Secret Hitory of English Dirty Words* was a finalist for the Eric Hoffer Book Award.

Currently, he is a consulting clinical psychologist in private practice. He lives with his family on a small vineyard, north of Los Angeles, CA.

Made in United States
Orlando, FL
29 June 2024

48422890R00264